A Burned Land

A Burned Land

The Trans-Mississippi in the Civil War

ROBERT R. LAVEN

McFarland & Company, Inc., Publishers
Jefferson, North Carolina

LIBRARY OF CONGRESS CATALOGUING-IN-PUBLICATION DATA

Names: Laven, Robert R., author.
Title: A Burned Land : the Trans-Mississippi in the Civil War / Robert R. Laven.
Description: Jefferson, North Carolina : McFarland & Company, Inc., 2019. | Includes bibliographical references and index.
Identifiers: LCCN 2018057304 | ISBN 9781476675589 (softcover : acid free paper) ∞
Subjects: LCSH: Missouri—History—Civil War, 1861–1865. | Kansas—History—Civil War, 1861–1865.
Classification: LCC E470.4 .L38 2019 | DDC 973.709778—dc23
LC record available at https://lccn.loc.gov/2018057304

BRITISH LIBRARY CATALOGUING DATA ARE AVAILABLE

ISBN (print) 978-1-4766-7558-9
ISBN (ebook) 978-1-4766-3416-6

© 2019 Robert R. Laven. All rights reserved

No part of this book may be reproduced or transmitted in any form or by any means, electronic or mechanical, including photocopying or recording, or by any information storage and retrieval system, without permission in writing from the publisher.

Front cover artwork: "Martial Law," artist George Caleb Bingham, 1868; "Battle of Big Blue," artist Samuel J. Reader, 1895 (© 2019 PicturesNow)

Printed in the United States of America

McFarland & Company, Inc., Publishers
  Box 611, Jefferson, North Carolina 28640
  www.mcfarlandpub.com

Table of Contents

Acknowledgments — vii
Preface — 1
Prelude — 3

1. "Our Once Happy Land" — 17
2. Union Militia — 29
3. Confederates — 41
4. Months of Discontent — 54
5. Arcadia Valley Confluence — 62
6. Objective: St. Louis — 82
7. Retribution — 96
8. Trial at Westport — 109
9. Blue Grass Ridges — 126
10. A Newtonia Gallop — 137
11. Afterword — 143

Epilogue — 149
Appendix I: Supreme Court Dred Scott Decision — 151
Appendix II: The Palmyra Massacre — 157
Appendix III: Removal Order for Persons on Missouri Border — 158
Appendix IV: Special Order for Shooting Six Confederate Prisoners — 160
Appendix V: Battle of Fort Davidson/Pilot Knob — 161

Appendix VI: Vitt's Mill, Union, Missouri — 164
Appendix VII: Battle of Westport and Byram's Ford — 168
Appendix VIII: Missouri State Guard and Confederate Troops — 174
Chapter Notes — 177
Bibliography — 181
Index — 183

Acknowledgments

In appreciation of all those who have aided in this endeavor, I will always be grateful. In particular I would like to recognize the staff at the Missouri Civil War Museum at Jefferson Barracks for their interest and encouragement, and their continuing efforts to rescue Civil War artifacts and monuments in the face of opposition. The research libraries and staff of the Missouri History Museum Library, Fort Davidson (Pilot Knob State Historic Site), Lexington Battlefield State Historic Site Library and Wilson's Creek National Battlefield and Research Library were most helpful. I must single out Fort Davidson and their staff for going out of their way to locate and copy the Report of William Cabell on Price's Expedition written after the war. This helped fill in some gaps in the record and added insight to the Expedition.

The Missouri State Historic Archives and The Missouri History Museum Library provided extensive collections for perusal and interest. I must also point out the local interest and help from people like Pastor Brown of St. John's Lutheran Church near Beaufort, Missouri. Here, at the Church Cemetery, he pointed out the mass grave of the soldiers killed in the Major Wilson incident along with his knowledge of those who were killed. Many people like this were helpful and are in themselves a part of that history which affected so many. From the cotton fields of the Missouri Bootheel through the St. Francis Mountains of the Ozark Region we traveled across the Missouri River, which dissects the center of the state. We traveled to the soybean and corn-covered borders of Iowa and Kansas to cover the length and breadth of the Trans-Mississippi conflict. Let this help be your guide.

Preface

My antecedents came to Franklin County, Missouri, in 1879. Arriving after the American Civil War and the conflict in Missouri, they purchased land near the town of St. Clair from a firm called Highland M and M Co., which owned large sections of land in and around St. Clair. It is possible that they may have bought land that had once been in the hands of the pro-South Massey family before some of them gave up their holdings and left the country for Brazil. The Massey's had been large land owners and developers, including an iron foundry. The end of the war saw many families leave Missouri and State Officials encouraged settlement from other areas of the country. My descendants, on my mother's side, arrived from Central Pennsylvania and remained in the area until the 1930s. My first arrival in the area was at Fort Leonard Wood as a young basic training recruit in the Army. I did not return until the end of the century and then again returned as an analyst with the Department of Defense.

I was aware of Missouri's role in the American Civil War, but had only a limited knowledge of the conflict there. My primary interest at the time was concentrated on the conflict in Maryland and Virginia, studying the exploits of Robert E. Lee and the contest with the many generals of the Army of the Potomac. This would eventually change as I rode past Lyon Park on Arsenal Street and entered into the old Arsenal Complex adjacent to that park. It was here, as I observed the old obelisk monument to General Lyon, that I realized I was too quick to dismiss the Missouri area as an unimportant part of the better known seat of conflict in the East. Slowly, in an unconscious way, I began to take note of areas within St. Louis and in the surrounding countryside. I learned much at the old Arsenal in St. Louis. The Arsenal itself has an interesting history. It began in the early 1800s when the French Long Lots of Chenie and Rutgers, which extended from the Mississippi River to Carondelet Avenue, were purchased and developed as a base of supply for the U.S. Military.

Many of the players in this drama had their roots in St. Louis or were living in the area at the start of the war. Ulysses S. Grant's wife was from a plantation called White Haven just south of the city and William T. Sherman worked in the city itself. Slowly but surely I began to realize the importance of the actions that took place in the Trans-Mississippi as I traveled and observed the locations of the many encounters that occurred all over the region. I was struck by how vast the area of conflict covered; it even reached the border with Iowa. In fact, as I crossed over from Iowa to Missouri, driving along the Great River Road, the difference was instantly apparent; here some of the old homes that once comprised farms and small plantations could be readily identified by the failing condition of the structures due to those places having been abandoned.

The fact that we live in a time where information is at our fingertips does not mean that that information is accurate by any means. For the historian or researcher, one thing never changes: full understanding of events comes well after it has occurred. The rush for instant gratification on electronic devices has in many cases simply dumbed down our understanding of events, including historical events. Unfortunately for society our history now comes from those who have not the training or education to actually inform or enlighten those thirsty for the truth. Journalists and Politicians are not Historians and we should not recognize them as such; in other words, take them with a healthy dose of salt.

We are at a crossroads in the study of History; it's time for true historians to add to Historiography. In some way, I hope my humble attempt to put the war in the Trans-Mississippi into perspective adds to and helps the individual in the understanding of the confrontation and gives light to the fact that Americans fought over ideas relevant to their time that we take for granted today. This is a key for understanding history; hindsight is always 20/20 vision.

The process in the study of History is to recognize bias and the constant effort to overcome it. It is therefore in this light that it is necessary to take a look at how some previous Historians broke ground in the writing of history, or Historiography. One of the greatest History writers was Thomas Carlyle, who researched his subjects from within and portrayed those subjects and events using first person. This type of writing is a very difficult thing to do, bringing alive those people and events as if they were speaking in the present. Documentaries and films try to do this, but it ultimately falls short and tends to work on emotion instead of the facts. Others, like Theodore Mommsen and E. A. Freeman, believed that a society and civilization could not be copied but must evolve and that one should be aware of unverified or unedited manuscripts. In other words, do the research for this to bring to life those events that have occurred well after those events took place.

Prelude

The long shadow of war had already begun to cover the areas of Missouri, Arkansas and Kansas well before the outbreak of conflict in 1861. With the acquisition of the land controlled by France, commonly known as Louisiana, in 1803, the newly formed United States had doubled its size. With that Louisiana Purchase the U.S. Government also inherited the French practice of allowing slavery in that territory. The federal government did nothing to stem slavery in the territory of Louisiana where it existed under French Law; on the contrary, slavery was allowed to extend to the area of Missouri and along the Missouri River. By the time of the Louisiana Purchase, under Thomas Jefferson, slavery had already been established in what was Missouri Territory of the Louisiana Purchase.

By 1820 the area of upper Louisiana, modern-day Missouri, had been increasingly settled by Southern immigrants, many from Virginia, Kentucky and Tennessee. The political situation of the time made it critical that there be a balance as to how many slave and non-slave states would be represented in Congress. With Alexander McNair as territorial Governor, the prominently Southern residence of Missouri Territory petitioned the Federal Government for admission to the Union. "When the Missouri territorial assembly petitioned Congress for admission to the Union in 1818, the U.S. comprised 22 states: 11 slave, 11 free. Until that time, the legislators had consciously alternated between admitting slave and Free states to preserve the balance of power among sectional interests. But some 2,000 to 3,000 slaves were then living in Missouri territory. To receive Missouri with a constitution permitting slavery would have upset the balance in favor of the South in the Senate, though not in the House."[1]

What then was to be done to allow states to enter the Union on the other side of the Mississippi in the Missouri Territory? The solution would become known as the Missouri Compromise of 1820. The people of Maine, a part of the State of Massachusetts, believed that they were not well represented in the State House in Boston and chose to separate in 1819. Being a non-slave entity, the U.S. Congress could now see an avenue for both Maine and Missouri to enter the Union. The Missouri Compromise of 1820 would hold up for another thirty years until the Kansas-Nebraska Act of 1850 again tested the sectional balance in regards to the slavery issue. A passage of the Missouri Comprise specifically states that slavery would from then on be restricted to below 36" 30' Latitude, making it inevitable that confrontation would once again rear its ugly head, this time between opposing forces in Kansas and Missouri.

The results of the Louisiana Purchase were two-fold: the doubling of the size of the United States and the sectional conflict over the admittance of states promoting southern plantation-style agriculture or northern free-state small farms. The Missouri Compromise only temporarily solved the issue. In the 1850s, territories north and west of the Missouri Compromise were admitted as states and conflict soon arose over what influence other states, like Missouri, would hold over them. In 1854, the U.S. Congress enacted the Kansas-Nebraska Act, allowing Kansas to enter the Union and the settlers there to decide whether it was a slave or non-slave state. This did not sit well with certain elements inside those two border states and disagreements soon led to outright violence.

If the Louisiana Purchase was the spark and the Missouri Compromise was the fuse, the Dred Scott Case was the accelerant for the start of the American Civil War. Dred Scott was a small and slight man of African descent who was a slave living in Missouri. In the 1830s he traveled with a Dr. Emerson to Rock Island, Illinois, in what was later to be the state of Minnesota, at the U.S. Military post of Fort Snelling. Those areas, according to the Missouri Compromise, were outside its bounds and therefore Scott could claim his freedom according to a suit brought on his behalf to a federal circuit court in 1857. In the new Court House of St. Louis, in the west wing adjoining the rotunda, the court session concluded that Scott was in fact a slave and therefore had no claim to citizenship. The case was appealed on writ of error to the U.S. Supreme Court.

Ironically the U.S. Supreme Court was very pro–States Rights at this time, upholding many of the policies put forth during subsequent Presidential Administrations. The case was brought before the Taney Court, Roger Taney being the Chief Justice at that time, and upheld the lower court ruling, citing:

> The question before us is, whether the class of persons described in the plea in abatement compose a portion of this people, and are constituent members of this sovereignty? We thinks they are not.... So in this case. As Scott was a slave when taken into the State of Illinois by his owner, and was there held as such, and brought back in that character, his status, as free or slave, depended on the laws of Missouri, and not Illinois

> ... it is the judgment of this court ... that the plaintiff in error is not a citizen of Missouri, in the sense in which that word is used in the Constitution; and that the Circuit Court of the United States, for that reason had no jurisdiction in the case.[2]

The decision was more than enough incentive for galvanizing abolitionists.

With the rise of the Abolitionist Movement came a militancy that arose against those who made their living according to a plantation culture and the political influence many of those had in the U.S. Government. This militancy was directed primarily from New England by leaders like William Lloyd Garrison and the press there. Fanning base emotion, this Abolitionist Movement reached people like John Brown and others living in Kansas, who found that they may have been chosen by God to suppress slavery no matter where it was found. Brown, acting on his own, eventually killed a number of people at Potawatomie and pro-South Missouri border ruffians put to the torch the town of Lawrence, Kansas, which would feel the effects of the American Civil War for years to come.

From the time of the Kansas-Nebraska Act to the firing on Fort Sumter, the border of Missouri and Kansas continued in intermittent warfare right up to succession. It can be fairly said the Kansas and Missouri conflict was the spark that sent the U.S. into Civil War. The violence on the border expressed itself in many ways. One of the worst events occurred almost exactly on the border on May 19, 1858, when pro-Slavery Missourians seized eleven Kansas free-stater citizens near the town of Trading Post. They marched them near the Marais des Cygnes and then executed a number of them, some escaping in the chaos of the moment. Outraged at the action, free-stater John Brown of the Potawatomie Massacre moved into the area and constructed a makeshift Fort. The murderous episode lent its force to the defeat of the pro-slavery Lecompton Constitution in Kansas. The lines were drawn and the animosities continued.

By mid-1861 Missouri was preparing for war. Governor Claiborne Fox Jackson responded to President Lincoln's call to support the U.S. Government by asking the legislature to secede from the Union and taking action against the City of St. Louis and the Federal Arsenal there. Although there were a large number of pro-Southern residents in the city, it was under the firm control of federal government personnel such as Frank Blair and, more importantly, General Nathanial Lyon. The abstract idea of States Rights and the peculiar institution were headed for a collision and Fort Sumter—notwithstanding the catalyst was in Missouri.

Lyon acted when he became aware of Confederate intentions as they established a camp outside the city at a place called Lindell Grove in May 1861. Lyon described it this way: "Their extraordinary and unscrupulous conduct, and their evident design, and of the governor of this State, to take a position of hostility to the United States, are matters of extensive detail and of abounding evidence. Having appealed to the South for assistance, every appearance indicated a rapid accumulation of men and means for seizing Government property and overturning its authority."[3] Seizing the moment, Lyon moved on the installation. "I proceeded yesterday with a large body of troops, supported by artillery, to the camp above referred to, and which is situated in the western part of the city, at what is known as Lindell's Grove, between Olive street and Laclede avenue, and arrived at 3:15 o'clock p. m., and demanded of General Frost, the commander, a surrender of his entire command."[4] With the threat to St. Louis and the Arsenal averted, Lyon moved west to confront another enemy force.

Tall, thin with red wiry hair and a fiery temper, Nathanial Lyon was an ardent abolitionist and believed he had been selected by the heavens to end the Confederate scourge. Once the Camp Jackson affair was settled, Lyon moved his Union forces in the direction of Boonville along the Missouri River in "Little Dixie," skirmished with John Marmaduke, and drove his force out of the area. Lyon then continued on toward Jefferson City, forcing out the Confederate Government of Governor Claiborne Fox Jackson and sending it southwest toward Springfield. Determined to end any Southern forces still threatening Union sovereignty in Missouri, Lyon was aware of Confederate forces, under former Governor Sterling Price, possibly preparing for action down near the border with Arkansas. There were many pro–South towns and communities in that area and Lyon believed he could end the constant border conflict by pacifying the area.

In the late 1850s the federal government contracted for a road to be built between Jefferson Barracks, on the Mississippi River, and Fort Smith, Arkansas, passing through Springfield, Missouri. Called the Wire Road or Telegraph Road, it was utilized by the Butterfield Stage line and was the main artery for moving any kind of force around the area. It was a venue of commerce with towns and hamlets along the way including small farms like the Ray Farm near Wilson's Creek, where water and rest could be procured. It was on this road that the forces of Sterling Price and Nathanial Lyon would converge on each other in August 1861.

Seeking to restore Confederate fortune in Missouri, Major General Sterling Price, of Missouri's State Guard, was gathering and drilling soldiers for an expected move into the State. Joining Price in this effort would be Generals McCulloch and Pearce from Arkansas, combining their forces for a total of more than 13,000 troops; moving to a point some ten miles southwest from Springfield and making camp along Wilson's Creek near the Wire Road. The

Confederate Army had no real way to keep the musket cartridges dry, so when rain drenched the area the night before the planned attack it was decided to postpone the attack. Lyon, who by now was in Springfield and knew of the presence of Price, decided to take the initiative.

Traveling by the Wire Road General Lyon reached Springfield by August 9 and had with him about 5,000 troops including Major Samuel Sturgis' Army Regulars from Fort Leavenworth. Also with Lyon was Franz Sigel who was with Lyon when he reduced Camp Jackson in May. Now Lyon believed that he could surprise Price and McCulloch by an unbelievably Napoleon-like attack of dividing his force in the face of a superior enemy and attacking him in a pincer-like movement from two directions, sending Sigel south in a roundabout route to get behind the Confederates without any real way of staying in contact to co-ordinate the attacks. Unaware of Lyon's presence or intentions, Price and McCulloch's forces were quietly encamped for miles along the Wilson's Creek when, early on August 10, cannon fire north of the camp opened up.

The Battle of Wilson's Creek opened with James Totten's Battery of four artillery guns booming away at the just waking Confederates. Initially surprised, Confederate officers began to rally their men as fast as they could as artillery explosions filled the camp with flame and shrapnel, scattering gear and draught animals everywhere. Moving in line of battle, Lyon's force drove the outlying Confederates toward the main camp. Union Major John Schofield reported:

Sterling Price, one-time Governor of Missouri and Mexican War Veteran, was in his fifties at the beginning of the war. Some early successes may have led him to believe that he had qualities that would lead to victory in Missouri, but when the time came he discovered difficulties he was incapable of overcoming (Library of Congress).

> With this disposition the column moved forward about one and a half miles, when at about 5 o'clock a brisk skirmish was opened along our entire front. The enemy was now discovered in considerable force, occupying the crest of a ridge running nearly perpendicularly to our line of march and also to the valley of Wilson's Creek, and lying between us and his main camp. The First

Missouri Volunteers was now sent forward and deployed in line of battle, at once advancing upon the ridge under a brisk fire, and driving the enemy from his position on our right, while the First Kansas came forward and engaged the enemy on our left, causing him to retire. Captain Totten's battery meanwhile moved forward in the center and reached the crest of the ridge.[5]

At this point Lyon could only guess and hope that Sigel and his force would be simultaneously attacking the Confederates in their rear. With much luck and fortune Sigel had begun to engage, also taking Price and McCulloch by surprise. The firing could be heard on the hill in which Lyon had now crested, but Lyon moved no further as the Confederate Arkansas Pulaski Artillery stalled his advance and the Confederate infantry took line and began to return an intense rifle fire with the Yankees, as smoke now hung heavily over the hill. The fighting soon turned to the Confederate advantage as Sigel's attack stalled as well and then fell apart as McCulloch's men attacked and overwhelmed Sigel's small force, sending it in disorder from the fight.

On the hill, General Lyon moved nervously along his line and then committed his last reserves, hoping to break the enemy's line.

> Early in this engagement, while General Lyon was leading his horse along the line on the left of Captain Totten's battery, and endeavoring to rally our troops, which were at this time in considerable disorder, his horse was killed, and he received a wound in the leg and one on the head. He walked slowly a few paces to the rear and said, "I fear the day is lost." But upon being encouraged that the troops could again be rallied and regaining his confidence, Lyon believed that the disorder was only temporary. He passed over to the right of the center, where our line seemed to be giving way, obtained another horse, and, swimming his hat in the air, led forward the troops, who promptly rallied around him. A few moments later, Lyon reeled from his saddle and fell off his horse and was carried from the field dead from a gunshot. His death was known at the time to but very few, and those few seemed to fight with redoubled valor.[6]

Major Samuel Sturgis now took command of the Army of the West and after five hours of heavy fighting retired the rest of the Union Army off the field at Wilson's Creek and headed them back to Springfield. General Price reported:

> A severe and bloody conflict ensued, my officers and men behaving with the greatest bravery, and with the assistance of a portion of the Confederate forces successfully holding the enemy in check. Meanwhile, and almost simultaneously with the opening of the enemy's batteries in this quarter, a heavy cannonading was opened upon the rear of our position, where a large body of the enemy, under Colonel Sigel, had taken position in close proximity.... The action now became general, and was conducted with the greatest gallantry and vigor on both sides for more than five hours, when the enemy retreated in great confusion, leaving their commander-in-chief, General Lyon, dead upon the battle-field, over 500 killed, and a great number wounded.... In conclusion, I beg leave to say to your excellency that the army under my command, both

officers and men, did their duty nobly, as became men fighting in defense of their homes and their honor, and that they deserve well of their State.[7]

After Wilson's Creek the contest for the state moved toward the area of Southeast Missouri in an area that continued to be unsettled and in question by federal control. Here at the alluvial head of the Mississippi, M. Jeff Thompson was operating against federal forces. Recruiting a force of Confederate cavalry operating for the Confederacy, Thompson and Ulysses S. Grant, commanding Union forces in that area, sparred for control with Thompson constantly moving in his rear and disrupting Union lines of communications and supply. In St. Louis John C. Frémont, Commander of Union Forces in the Missouri Western District, was scrambling to stem any momentum that the enemy forces might maintain. The famous explorer and self-promoter managed to acquire a political appointment and now wanted to prove his acumen. With Lyon's demise, at Wilson's Creek, Frémont became even more disconcerted when Price moved his Missouri State Guard north and subdued the Union Garrison at Lexington, Missouri, along the Missouri River. Frémont needed some sort of win, so he turned to Ulysses S. Grant and appointed him commander of the Southeast Missouri Military District.

Grant proved to be marginally successful in Southeast Missouri due to the fact that one M. Jeff Thompson, known locally as the "swamp fox," continually raided Grant's supply lines, going as far north as the Big River, burning bridges and confiscating necessary materials and then disappearing from the scene, even capturing some federal troops in the process. Grant put in motion a plan to interdict Thompson in a series of troop movements that had the purpose of squeezing Thompson and his movements. Thompson avoided them all and in October 1861 turned his outnumbered troopers at Fredericktown and stymied his attackers, escaping into the region of the Mississippi alluvial plain often referred to in that region as the Nigger Wool Swamp. General Frémont in St. Louis wanted Thompson interdicted and sent this order: "Thompson is at Indian Ford of the Saint Francois River, 25 miles below Greenville, with about 3,000 men. Colonel Carlin has started with force from Pilot Knob. Send a force Cape Girardeau and Bird's Point to assist Carlin in driving Thompson into Arkansas."[8] Thompson reported to his superiors, "I cannot be cut off.... I may be driven southwards."[9] Thompson was right; he could not be caught and seemed to disappear in the face of superior Union forces.

In St. Louis, General John C. Frémont, Commander of the Missouri Military District, was impressed with Grant's earlier aggressive actions and appointed him to command Union forces at Cairo, Illinois. A central supply point near the confluence of the Ohio and Mississippi rivers, Cairo was a muddy and worn river port on a flood plain that was often covered in water. Here Grant decided on what his next action would be to dislodge the Confederates from the head of the Mississippi alluvial valley. At the Iron Banks, near the town of Columbus, Kentucky, the Confederates, under General Leonidas Polk, had emplaced an impressive array of fortifications armed with a number of heavy artillery. When the U.S. Navy tried to run down those fortifications the fire power of the Confederate guns forced the Union timberclads to back off.

Grant now decided that the best way to neutralize forces like Thompsons was to eliminate the Confederate defenses by attacking the Confederate camps opposite Columbus at a river landing near Belmont, Missouri. Grant reported the composition of his force: "The troops composing the present expedition from this place will ... be followed by the First Brigade, under command of Brigadier General John A. McClernand, composed of all the troops from Cairo and Fort Holt. The Second Brigade, comprising the remainder of the troops of the expedition, commanded by Colonel Henry Dougherty, will follow. The entire force will debark at the lowest point on the Missouri shore where a landing can be affected in security from the rebel batteries. The point of debarkation will be designated by Captain Walke, commanding naval forces."[10]

That point would be a few miles above Belmont and just out of range of the Confederate guns at Columbus. In the early morning hours of November 7, 1861, Major General Leonidas Polk was informed that Union Gunboats were approaching Columbus. Across the river from Belmont was Camp Johnston, which housed mostly Tennessee and Arkansas troops under the command of Brigadier General Gideon Pillow, who was ordered back from a movement toward Clarksville to return and defend the camp. Lying on a river flood plain, Camp Johnston was approachable by land even with heavily wooded surroundings interspersed with corn fields and muddy sloughs. Grant disembarked his force well above the camp and must have moved south through the river bottom with the intent of attacking Camp Johnston.

The Battle of Belmont was fought by Tennessee and Arkansas troops on the Confederate side and mostly Illinois and some Iowa troops on the Union side. Landing on the muddy Mississippi banks, the steamboats threw out their gang planks and the soldiers and horses of Grant's Command moved off from the shore and headed out, weaving their way over muddy roads. Knowing from reports that the Confederates had reinforced the camp, Brigadier General Grant commenced his assault on the camp at about 9:00 a.m. As Grant put it in his *Personal Memoirs*, "his forces fought the enemy from tree to tree and foot by foot," finally driving Pillow's forces out of the abatis around Camp Johnston over the riverbank on the other side of the camp. Once Grant's force entered the camp the troops looted tents and burned most of everything else.

Pacing nervously on the opposite bank, at Columbus, General Polk was moving more forces across to support Pillow and drive off the federals. General Cheatham moved his reinforcements across the Mississippi waters in wooden steamers arriving and linking up with the scattered forces of Pillow's men blow the river banks. Moving between Grant's forces and his transports, General Cheatham started for Camp Johnston. Grant believed he had completed what he had set out to do and in his memoirs recorded, "I knew there was a small camp ... at Belmont, immediately opposite Columbus, and I speedily resolved to push down the river, land on the Missouri side, capture Belmont, and break up the camp and return."[11] His judgment was sound, even with the quick reaction of the Confederates at Columbus.

Seeing the steamboats ferrying more of the enemy across the river Grant soon began to extradite his force back toward his awaiting flotilla protected by Commander Walke's gunboats. Cheatham and Polk were too late and moved on Grant's forces from rear and flank while Grant's forces were still in a bit of confused order. "Meanwhile the enemy was pushing reinforcements across the stream ... and the Union forces began to fall back to their transports. It would seem that the troops, yet unaccustomed to war, had been somewhat disordered by their victory, so that the return was not accomplished as rapidly as was desirable, the enemy pressing down upon the transports."[12] Cheatham and Polk turned on the retreating federals coming up on their embarkation but held off in a tentative manner as Grant's men were removed onto the transports.

Here, at the embarkation, Commander Walke could now bring to bear his guns on the looming Confederates. "At this moment the gunboats, from a favorable position, opened upon them with grape, canister, and five-second shell, silencing them with great slaughter. When the transports were under way the two gunboats followed in the rear, covering the retreat."[13] Grant said in his memoirs that he had cut his way into Camp Johnston and would be able to cut his way out, and he did just that. As a matter of fact, as the Confederates made their way toward the site, it was Grant who literally was the last man to board the steamship, making his way up the gang plank with shots whizzing by. This was Grant's way to make sure his men were looked after before he left the field.

Confederate Major General Leonidas Polk breathed a sigh of relief as he watched the Union flotilla slowly move up the Mississippi. The fortifications and gun emplacements arranged by engineer and artillerist General

John McCown had deterred the U.S. Navy but only for the moment. Soon Polk would have to abandon Columbus and would be given command to send General McCown down the river to fortify Island No. 10 and New Madrid, Missouri, thinking that there, too, the U.S. Navy could be deterred from moving farther south. Grant's strategic vision of reducing the Confederate river defenses would prove to be accurate and by taking the offensive initiated a response in the Trans-Mississippi that forces there could not remain idle for long.

The situation in the Trans-Mississippi was an interesting one. Grant had failed to corner the Swamp Fox, M. Jeff Thompson, but had kept the Confederate command off balance. Eventually the U.S. Government would increase its control over the Missouri populace, but that control would be tentative. Areas of Missouri would become more unresponsive to Union control. It is not unreasonable that control over the state could possibly be lost. It was just a matter of how best the Confederates could gain and then maintain control; one way was to make the Union Commands in St. Louis and the western border drain resources the Union could ill afford. Events would now dictate actions and those actions would lead to desperation on all sides.

The focus now once again shifted from Southeast Missouri to Southwest Missouri near the actions of 1861. In January 1862 General John C. Frémont, at his office in St. Louis at the Missouri Military District, had decided to send Federal troops under Samuel Curtis to drive Sterling Price and his Confederate force out of Southeast Missouri. Centered in Springfield, Price had remained there since the victory at Wilson's Creek, but could not really garnish support from Confederate forces just across the border in Arkansas. The united forces of Benjamin McCulloch and Sterling Price, which had so effectively sent the Union Army retreating at Wilson's Creek, did not see eye to eye on military matters in the area. In fact McCulloch loathed the idea of even working with Price, disparaging Prices Command and belittling the Missouri Troops under Price.

With orders in hand, Samuel Curtis made his way with the Union Army of the Southwest into Southwest Missouri, forcing Price to now abandon Springfield and move further down the Wire (Telegraph) Road into Northwest Arkansas, forcing a linkup with the Arkansas forces under McCulloch. Securing Springfield, Curtis then decided to head the Union force into Arkansas, making his way to rest stop on the Wire Road called Elkhorn Tavern. Price reported, "The enemy had taken position in the Boston Mountains, a high range that divides the waters of the White River and Arkansas. General Price had rallied the forces that had fought at Carthage, Wilson's Creek, and Lexington.... The circulation of all manner of extravagant falsehoods on his way induced the whole country to leave their homes, and for fear we would kill them thousands joined his ranks. General McCulloch brought at least eleven regiments to the field and General Pike five."[14] Curtis now concentrated his men at Elk Horn Tavern, securing his lines of communication and supply from Springfield.

For the Confederate Army the need for a unified command was obvious in the face of the quarreling Price and McCulloch. Sent to unite and augment the command was Major General Earl Van Dorn, who was highly regarded in the higher Confederate Command under Albert Sidney Johnston, who had the ear of the Confederate President. It was believed that Van Dorn, who arrived on March 3rd, could ultimately unite the commands and immediately plan to move against Price. Moving through the Boston Mountains, the forces had to contend with ice and snow, which had a particularly bad effect on Van Dorn, who had already been suspect of many of his units' effectiveness from the time he took over command of the Arkansas and Missouri forces. On March 7th Van Dorn came in view of the federals at Elkhorn Tavern from Pea Ridge, which loomed north of the Tavern along the Wire Road.

Van Dorn's plan was simply to get his force between Curtis and the Union Army and his supply base at Springfield. The Confederate Army of the West consisted mainly of Arkansas, Missouri, Texas, Louisiana and the Indian Territory troops and with Price's forces in the van, headed around Curtis' Army of the Southwest. On the Confederate's southern flank, Union forces, under Sigel, came under attack when Van Dorn detached McCulloch's men, splitting his force and hoping to destabilize Curtis' lines. With the rebel yell mingled with Cherokee Indian war whoops, McCulloch's command smashed into the Union line, momentarily driving it in and stunning the federals.

Hoping for a double envelopment, Maj. Gen. Earl Van Dorn moved Price's Missourians down off Elk Horn Mountain into the gap and onto the Wire Road for attacking Curtis' rear. General Curtis' left flank now became his right as he adjusted his front from rear to facing an attack from the north instead of what he thought would be from the south. Caught in a pincer-like attack that Lyon's had tried at Wilson Creek, Samuel Curtis utilized his genius of terrain and his calm manner to adjust his force in an orderly manner to meet the attack. "The approach by Bentonville brought the enemy to my extreme right … which crosses Pea Ridge some 3 miles northwest of the main Telegraph road. I ascertained in the morning this flank movement of the enemy, which I perceived was designed to attack my right flank and rear."[15] For a moment it seemed that Van Dorn and the Confederates had gained the advantage and was on the cusp of possible victory. The determined attack of Price now drove the Union forces back and past Elkhorn Tavern.

Just as a seeming defeat of the Army of the Southwest was looming, the attack of Maj. Gen. McCulloch collapsed when Brig. Gen. Osterhaus, of Sigel's Command, turned the tide on the butternut and grey. Bringing his artillery to bear the Union artillery fire distressed the Indian contingent of McCulloch's Command and those units fled for cover inside the wood line. When McCulloch rallied and counter attacked, the Yankees were ready and slammed the force with heavy rifle fire along with the artillery fire, killing a number of Confederates, including McCulloch and other officers. This had the effect of destroying the morale of that force and scattered it from the fields around Leetown. The double envelopment had now failed and with it Van Dorn had to concentrate where he had been successful, moving the remaining force he had at Elk Horn Tavern.

On March 8, 1862, General Samuel Curtis massed his artillery on the open fields south of Elkhorn Tavern straddling the Wire Road. "The roar of cannon and small-arms was continuous, and no force could then have withstood the converging line and concentrated cross-fire of our gallant troops. Our guns continued sometime after the rebel fire ceased, and the rebels had gone down into the deep caverns through which they had begun their precipitate flight. Finally our firing ceased. The enemy had suddenly vanished."[16] Curtis was right: The Army of the West was broken and forced to retreat as its dead and dying littered the ridges and hollows. One soldier described the scene: "Great God what a scene is presented. The mingled trunks of men are thickly scattered around."[17] The Battle of Pea Ridge (Elkhorn Tavern) was over.

This was not the last drama in which Price and Curtis would play—their contest was only beginning. The Army of the West now retreated through bitter winter weather that took its toll on the defeated ranks of Price and Van Dorn. Making for the Boston Mountains and the Arkansas River, what was left of the Confederate forces went into winter quarters with an uncertain future. Most of the Confederate infantry would be ferried across the Mississippi to join the Confederate forces under P.G.T. Beauregard and Albert Sydney Johnston to contest the moves of the Union armies now under the command of U.S. Grant, who was making his way up the Cumberland and Tennessee Rivers. What was left would have to constitute a force able to fight for control in Arkansas and Missouri.

The war would shift focus to other areas, but for the Tans-Mississippi West the war was not over and that uneasiness in Missouri proper was only beginning. With many of the Confederate infantry detailed elsewhere in the Confederacy, Price decided that he could still influence events in Missouri by acquiring permission from the Trans-Mississippi command to allow raids of mounted cavalry. With the removal of Van Dorn's Army of the West to support Albert Sidney Johnston's moves in west Tennessee, the Military Authority in St. Louis decided on a plan to arm and defend the military districts of Missouri by creating a militia force. The Provisional Missouri Militia and the better trained Enrolled Missouri Militia would now become the main avenue for defense against possible action by Confederate Forces on the border and within the state. The response to this action was that Confederates decided on a course of expeditions (raids) that would recruit within pro–Southern areas and at the same time disrupt communications and confiscate Union military stores. The ultimate objective was the possibility of taking control of the state and reducing, if possible, the Union military stronghold of St. Louis itself.

1

"Our Once Happy Land"

In early September of 1864 William S. Rosecrans looked out over the gabled roofs and false fronts of the City of St. Louis and paused. From his military headquarters on 10th and Locust, he was beginning to get concerned for the District of Missouri. He was expected by authorities in Washington, D.C., to continue to ferry Union forces to battlegrounds in the Southern theatre. There had been rumors for days of Confederate Forces gathering to make a move on Missouri and possibly St. Louis itself. Rosecrans was responsible for a region that, in some areas, had been favorably disposed to support the South. In fact, Missouri had been constantly at war with itself since the Kansas-Nebraska Act set off a border war well before the Civil War broke out in 1861. Neighbor was set against neighbor. There were expulsions of whole towns and farm families in western Missouri near the Kansas border and this only increased the animosity toward federal authority.

One of the ways federal authority thought it could maintain control was to simply intimidate the local people by implementing what would become a series of orders that stripped citizens of much of their civil rights. In other words, the Constitution of the United States, for some, simply ceased to exist. One particular order was Order No. 11; this order was implemented by Federal Military Officials in 1863 and was referred to as Expulsion Order No. 11. Thomas Ewing, the Union General in charge and later commander at Fort Davidson in 1864, was the instrument of the order.

> Order No. 11 devastated much of western Missouri. Several thousand people, exiled within a fortnight, streamed into the adjacent counties, where many communities were scarcely prepared and often unwilling to absorb the refugee population. An additional provision, designed to keep guerrillas from foraging upon the countryside, empowered Union troops to seize the grain and hay crops of displaced families. Soldiers and bandits plundered abandoned properties and set many farmsteads ablaze. Once the flames jumped to the adjoining tallgrass prairies, fire quickly consumed much of Cass and Bates Counties, an area that came to be known as the "Burnt District."[1] Exempted were those persons who could demonstrate Unionist loyalties to the satisfaction of local military commanders.

Order No. 11 was probably not the only reason for Price's incursions into Missouri, but it highlighted the oppression. Price was a Missourian and many soldiers and officers in Price's Army were probably well aware of the actions now being visited on their fellow citizens in and around "Little Dixie." In January 1864 Lizzie Brannock of the "Burnt District" wrote to her brother from Chapel Hill, MO, highlighting what had occurred since the order was implemented: "Dear Brother Edwin. Yesterday I was most pleasantly surprised in reviewing a letter from you whom I had almost given up … thus far you have survived in this most horrible reign of terror which has been so long desolating our once happy land."[2] Many families had sons and fathers serving in the Confederate armies and the actions of federal officials now exacerbated their feelings.

At one point, as described in her letter, Lizzie and her neighbors witnessed a raiding party of presumably irregular Union cavalry under the command of a man named Jennison, who would later be part of the Union force confronting Price in 1864, as they "burned 150 houses, helpless women and young children … were taken out and left standing in the snow while all they owned on earth … was destroyed before their eyes."[3] The War had come home to the people of Missouri and specifically to people who had Confederate leanings. For many this order simply confirmed their fears that the U.S. Government would not protect certain people and only reinforced their allegiance to the Southern cause. The Charles

William Rosecrans's excitable personality and nervous energy served him well at the Battle of Stones River, but not so much at Chickamauga. General Halleck appointed Rosecrans Commander of the Missouri Military District, particularly St. Louis; here "Old Rosy" was concerned that the Confederacy was on the verge of taking the City (Library of Congress).

Jennison that Lizzie spoke about would later be court-martialed for his depredations and dishonorably discharged from the Army in 1865.

The line between Union and Confederate supporters became increasingly blurred as opportunists took advantage of a situation in which a certain element within society could just take what they wanted. Lizzie recognized the increasing tensions early on in the conflict and the threats many families faced every day, writing, "the next spring 1862 we went into Cass Co ... but the Kansas troops would give us no rest anything that was in Missouri was to be destroyed and taken, yes brother we are what is called Rebels."[4] Lizzie in her rancor remarked that yes, she was a Rebel, when she saw and experienced the increasing injustice they were all subjected to. She also went on to point out in her letter that they "would have burned us out but for proving that we were union and had never done anything against government."[5] Again this incident occurred in 1862 and Lizzie was clever as to not indicate what government she was actually loyal to.

This dramatic letter from a young woman in western Missouri, describing events in their family life up to 1864, truly defines the picture of life in much of Missouri. Her heartfelt writings gave Lizzie an unwittingly heroine quality in a war where the pen could transcend even weapons. It can be said that the actions of Kansas Jayhawkers and Missouri Bushwhackers only fed the tensions that brought so much misery to so many people all over Missouri; when Lawrence, Kansas, was attacked in August 1863, the Federal Military Authorities, under General Thomas Ewing, implemented General Order No. 11. This order literally allowed for the persecution and removal of long-standing citizens of particularly Southern extraction. War brought consequences and this was a different kind of an attack: an attack on citizens' constitutional rights, particularly their individual rights.

The war was problematic to many Missouri Confederates. Most Missourians sympathetic to the Confederate cause never owned a slave, but joined in the conflict anyway. There were reasons for this and soldiers like M. Jeff Thompson explained it this way: "I never fought the North because I hated the North. I did not desire to be one iota freer than I was under the flag of the union; but there was an abstract principle of States rights and four thousand million dollars' worth of African slaves that I thought could only be saved out of the Union."[6] This issue over slavery was one that brought about a debate as to just how far the Federal government was willing to expand its control over the states. This was a polarizing issue for many Southerners, and Patrick Cleburne, a Division General from Arkansas, saw through the Federal Government's intent when he stated that the federal government was merely using the slavery issue as a pretense "to establish sectional superiority and a more centralized form of government, and to deprive us of our rights and liberties."[7] Many ordinary Southerners did believe this even if they did not articulate it like Cleburne who, late in the war, went farther and suggested freedom for blacks who would serve in the Confederate Army. This was rejected by the Confederate government.

From the beginning of the Civil War, when President Abraham Lincoln asked for 75,000 troops from the states, Missouri was at odds. The governor of Missouri, Claiborne Fox Jackson, was dismayed when he received the President's request. Jackson vehemently refused to acquiesce to the President, stating that the call was unconstitutional. Jackson was from the Little Dixie area and knew this act would galvanize some from that area and all over the state to resist. Events of 1861 would force Jackson to flee with a rump government of Missouri legislators to Arkansas as Union forces took control of most of the state.

One of the Federal tools for acting against the elected state government was the *writ of habeas corpus*. The Constitution of the United States gave the executive power to act against what was deemed rebellious actions. As Commander in Chief of the Armed Forces of the United States, the President had the right to take actions to alleviate dissent. President George Washington used such power to put down the Whiskey Rebellion in the 1790s. Secession of states from the Union was problematic and was considered by some legitimate. This was not the view of President Lincoln and he looked to the constitution to end it.

M. Jeff Thompson was born in Virginia and moved to Liberty, Missouri, in 1847. At the start of the Civil War, Thompson was appointed a Brigadier General and Commander of the 1st Division of the Missouri State Guard, which comprised the southeastern corner of the state. A natural at independent command, his dashing exploits confounded Union authority as he raided stores and burned bridges in southeast Missouri. He rose to take command of Jo Shelby's "Iron Brigade" during Price's Expedition (courtesy Wilson's Creek National Battlefield; WICR 31436).

When the case of *Ex-parte Merryman* was argued before the Supreme Court of the United States, Lincoln's argument of extraordinary power was overturned. Lincoln's response was simply to ignore the ruling of Chief Justice Taney and implement martial law. Supreme Law of the Land was securely in the hands of the office of the Presidency in 1861. In order to keep border states like Missouri, with leanings towards the South, the right of habeas corpus was suspended. In December 1862, the order was sent to the commanding officer of the Department of Missouri:

> GENERAL: As an insurrection exists in the United States and is in arms in the State of Missouri, you are hereby authorized and empowered to suspend the writ of *habeas corpus* within the limits of the military division under your command, and to exercise martial law as you find it necessary, in your discretion, to secure the public safety of the authority of the United States.
>
> A. Lincoln[8]

The year 1862 was a pivotal for the State of Missouri which would define it for the rest of the war. S. Elliot Morison wrote that it was a crucial year for the nation. For Missouri, nothing could have been truer and it was in 1862 that things began to coalesce in a way that would eventually bring Sterling Price back into Missouri in 1864. The Southern sympathizers in the Little Dixie area of the Missouri River Valley had a smaller cousin in the area centered on the rich river-bottom farmland of the Bootheel of Missouri between the St. Francis River and the Mississippi River. Here was the initial defensive line for the Confederate States in the west on the Mississippi River at New Madrid, Missouri. The Grand Strategy of Confederate General P.G.T. Beauregard of the Army of Tennessee was originally to move on Paducah, Kentucky, Cairo, Illinois, and then on St. Louis, Missouri. With the willingness of Albert Sidney Johnston, who had the ear of President Jefferson Davis and was in nominal command of all western Confederate forces, Beauregard was prepared to do just that until the news of Van Dorn's defeat at Pea Ridge, Arkansas. Beauregard always failed to take into consideration just where the Confederacy would find such forces for his grand strategy.

It had become a blunt reality: The Army of the West failed to deal a fatal blow to the Union Army of the Southwest at Pea Ridge. That victory presented opportunity for Union forces to adjust its focus down the Mississippi River, at New Madrid, but it also presented opportunity for the Confederates to deal a blow at Union intentions in the broad Mississippi Alluvial Delta. Van Dorn had to remove his Army of the West across the river to support the Army of Mississippi, taking Price and the Missourians with him. Price, before leaving with Van Dorn, had a conversation with those forces left in Arkansas to stem Union efforts there. One of those was Joseph Porter, whom Price agreed now had the opportunity to raid Missouri and cause as much disruption as he could while recruiting and avoiding Union forces where he could.

In early 1862, New Madrid and Island No. 10 became the fortified bastion that would prevent Union troops and transport from moving south toward Memphis, Tennessee. Along with Island No. 10 it was thought that the federal forces could be blunted. Federal authorities decided that the area must be taken. With the fall of both Fort Henry and Fort Donelson in Tennessee in February, the time presented itself to move on the now outflanked New Madrid and Island No. 10. With the loss of Columbus, Kentucky, by the Confederates, New Madrid and Island No. 10 took on a whole new importance and the scramble was on to fortify and prepare it as a temporary capital for Missouri and military stronghold.

The Bootheel Section of Missouri was a land of antebellum homes of cultured Southern families located throughout the rich bottomland of the Mississippi and St. Francis Rivers. The Hunter family of New Madrid occupied a plantation home just north of the city. From here they plied their farm and sold mercantile goods on the river and across the land. They grew cotton and tobacco and hemp. If the Federals decided to move on the area their home and land was directly in the path of the enemy. In February of 1862 the Hunters and other families watched as Confederate engineers began the urgent work of heavy gun emplacement directed on the river and toward the landward side of the city.

At New Madrid, the Confederates constructed Fort Thompson, which was located on the west side of the city along the Plank Road. On the eastern side of the city near the mouth of St. John's Bayou, the Confederate engineers constructed, in haste, Fort Bankhead; here 12 heavy guns now festooned the works and were readied for action should a force by land or even water come its way. Down river, the Mississippi River itself gave a geographic advantage to the Confederates as it made a serpentine bend to the north towards New Madrid. Here in that bend was located Island No. 10 and it was here, in the earthen ramparts, that massive 32-pound cannons were installed to fire at any craft daring to run the channel; it presented the Confederates the opportunity to fire point blank at their adversary. New Madrid had now become the Western Strategic line for the Confederacy. Because of this belief in its invincibility, it was decided that New Madrid could be used as the de-facto Missouri State Capital.

In command of the nearly 10,000 Confederate forces, New Madrid and Island No. 10 was Brig. Gen. John P. McCown from Tennessee, who was experienced in the use and placement of artillery. He had been the artillery engineer at Columbus, Kentucky, during the Union attack at Belmont. Along with

McCown and in command of Fort Bankhead was Brig. Gen. L. M. Marsh and in charge of the forces at Fort Thompson was Col. Edward Gantt. In command of the Confederate cavalry was Brig. Gen. M. Jeff Thompson, who had been considerably active against Grant's Union forces in Southeast Missouri the previous year and acquired from his enemies the sobriquet the "Missouri Swamp Fox" because of his ability to elude enemy forces. Thompson was a proponent of maneuver and quick strikes at portions of his enemy's forces. He did not relish the fact that he and his men might be cornered in defenses even though Fort Thompson was likely named in his honor; Thompson did not put much faith in static defense. As Thompson looked around from the forts along the river, he could see no tactical advantage.

Sitting below the bluffs of the Commerce Hills, at the terminus of Thebes Gap near the head of the Mississippi Valley, is the small town of Commerce, Missouri. In February 1862, the river levee of the town became the hub of activity as barges and steamers off loaded troops and munitions that almost overwhelmed the populace of the town. Major General Henry Halleck, commanding all Union forces in the Missouri district, had decided to break Confederate control in Southeast Missouri and along the Mississippi. He now tasked the Army of Mississippi and its commander Brig. Gen. John Pope to do just that: "I was recalled to Saint Louis from Central Missouri on the 14th of February, 1862, and on the 18th General Halleck pointed out to me the situation at New Madrid and Island No. 10, and directed me to organize and command a force for their reduction."[9]

John Pope's success came early on in the war and quickly became problematic. A pompous man with political connections in Illinois, he had success at New Madrid, Missouri, and Island No. 10. Pope was later given command of a Union Army in Virginia, where his success ended (Library of Congress).

New Madrid was not only the important choke point on the Mississippi River—it was also the terminus of the river road leading to St. Louis only 175 miles north. The Confederate forces and government always had an eye in the direction of St. Louis as it was always a focus for possible operations. Pope was wasting no time and his force of more than 20,000 troops fell into ranks and moved out from Commerce on February 28 down the river road heading south. Pope remembered the 50-mile journey as one of wading through mud and rain over a flat terrain all the way to New Madrid. He also thought that if there was any good time to engage his army it would have been while on this journey, for the area he was traversing was along the old aggradation of the Mississippi River. "I can only account for the fact that the enemy attempted no opposition to our march by their belief that the country at that season of overflow was entirely impracticable."[10]

Confederate Brig. Gen. M. Jeff Thompson troopers were watching Pope's progress and on the 3rd of March reported to Brig. Gen. McCown of Pope's near arrival. Soon after this Thompson's troopers and the Army of Liberation pickets were driven back to the earthen forts around New Madrid. McCown had less of a force facing Pope, which is likely why he did not attempt even a delaying movement against this force. He did have an instrument at his disposal for just such action in the person of M. Jeff Thompson and his Cavalry group. With this and some infantry regiments he could have attacked a portion of Pope's army and crippled or at least delayed his progress. Instead, now at the mere presence of the Yankees, M. Jeff Thompson, probably to his satisfaction, was given order to leave and escort the Confederate State Legislature of Missouri out of New Madrid to points south in Arkansas. Brig. Gen. Pope said in his official report:

> I found the place occupied by five regiments of infantry and several companies of artillery. One bastioned earthwork, mounting 14 heavy guns, about a half a mile below the town, and another irregular work at the upper end of the town, mounting 7 pieces of heavy artillery, together with lines of entrenchments between them, constituted the defensive works. Six gunboats, carrying from 4 to 8 heavy guns each, were anchored along the shore between the upper (Fort Bankhead) and lower redoubts (Fort Thompson). The country is perfectly level for miles around the place, and as the river was so high that the guns of the gunboats looked directly over the banks, the approaches to the town for several miles were commanded by direct and cross-fire from at least 60 guns of heavy caliber.[11]

An immediate assault was soon thought impractical.

Ensconced within the fortified position of Fort Thompson, Brig. Gen. McCown and Brig. Gen. Alexander Stewart studied the Federal forces before them. The concern was with how long the bastions could hold out. Unknown to either Confederate commander was Pope's concern as to whether to assault the fortifications with his troops or begin to dig in. "Finally on the 7th a general demonstration against the Confederate works was ordered. General Stanley's Division was ordered to move on Fort Thompson while Col. W. H. Worthington's Brigade was to move on Fort Bankhead and occupy the trenches. John M. Palmer's First Brigade was to support Worthington. The Confederate's discovered the feint and the gunboats opened up.... Now caught in the crossfire between the Confederate gunboats and heavy guns in the forts, the force ... withdrew from the town without engaging."[12] Pope now decided that a frontal assault on the Confederate position was tantamount to total destruction of his force.

The fortification of the Confederates would have to be reduced and in order to do this Pope decided to bring up artillery in response to the enemy. "On the 11th the siege guns were delivered to Colonel Bissell, Engineer Regiment, who had been sent to Cairo for the purpose. They were at once shipped to Sikeston; reached here at sunset on the 12th; were placed in battery during the same night within 800 yards of the enemy's main work, so as to command that and the river above it, and opened fire at daylight on the 13th, just 34 hours after they were received at Cairo. One brigade, consisting of the Tenth and Sixteenth Illinois, under Colonel Morgan, of the Tenth, was detailed to cover the construction of the battery and to work in the trenches."[13] Soon after this both sides began a desultory fire.

The failure to take on Pope's Army of the Mississippi before he got to New Madrid was simply surrendering the initiative. M. Jeff Thompson was correct: he was not going to be caught inside the forts. The Confederate forces could still be supplied by river from the opposite bank but so could the Union forces by land. For a week McCown exchanged artillery duels and pickets, skirmishing with the federals. In his official report, he related the siege: "March 10, heavy pickets skirmishing all day, March 11, I placed two 24-pounder siege pieces opposite Point Pleasant." For McCown forces the placing of siege pieces opposite Point Pleasant was the turning point for the siege of New Madrid.

All the people of New Madrid could do was hunker down and listen as the cannons boomed and artillery shells whistled over the tree tops; "the enemy planted some batteries during the night, with rifle pits supporting the batteries. They opened fire upon our transports, hitting all that approached Fort Thompson. The enemy's guns were 24-pounders and one 8-inch gun. Commander Hollins, from his gunboats, and we with our guns from the works, returned the fire, repulsing one heavy advance upon the fort (Fort Bankhead) at the mouth of the bayou."[14] When Point Pleasant fell to Union General Plummer and McCown had to place cannons opposite that place, the Confederates were cut off downstream from the city.

McCown now had a decision to make. On March 13th McCown recorded: "By a careful examination of their works I became satisfied that they were making regular approaches to cut off communication with the lower fort (Fort Thompson). I was also convinced that our gunboats could not stand against their land batteries and that unless the fleet dropped below Point Pleasant it would be cut off. Commander Hollins and General Stewart concurring in this opinion, I ordered the evacuation of New Madrid."[15] On March 14–15, under cover of night, transports moved back and forth between Fort Bankhead and Fort Thompson as the confederate forces removed themselves from New Madrid.

As daylight slowly approached on the 15th, Union soldiers began to assemble as they prepared for an assault on the Confederate works around New Madrid. As Brig. Gen. Pope and his staff viewed the 400 yards between them and their objective and preparations were under way, a white flag of truce was seen fluttering from the ramparts of Fort Thompson and a party of Confederates approached the Union entrenchments. For nearly a year the Bootheel of Missouri had been a part of the Western Department of the Confederate States of America, but now it was surrendered to the United States of America. It had been hoped that New Madrid would have been part of a spring board for an attempt on the City of St. Louis. The Confederate high command of Maj. Gen. Albert S. Johnston, Maj. Gen. Pierre T. Beauregard and President Jefferson Davis, considered it possible.[16] A combination of defeats soon quashed the dream. "This ruled out any chance of cooperation in an advance against St. Louis."[17] Pope and his men cheered at the site of New Madrid's surrender. For the citizens of New Madrid, their future was now changed.

The hope of the Confederacy maintaining a position on their western flank and on the Mississippi River laid on Island No. 10. This was Brig. Gen. McCown's back up even though he faced a river fleet of Union gunboats and now in his rear the Army of the Mississippi. Island No. 10 was a fortified earthen rampart heavily festooned with heavy artillery. Brig. Gen. McCown reported on March 16th: "the Federal fleet advanced in line of battle and remained at long range."[18] It would be from this point, a few miles upstream, that the flotilla would now constantly bombard the island for the next three weeks with 13-inch mortars on reinforced hexagonal rafts.

Brig. Gen. John Pope got busy after the fall of New Madrid. He expected flotilla Commander Foote to assault and pass by Island No. 10. Foote decided to do no such thing until he at least softened up the batteries there, which he set about doing so for weeks. Pope sent a flurry of requests for Foote to advance, going so far as to go over Foote's head and ask Maj. Gen. Henry

Halleck to push Foote. In the meantime, in New Madrid, he set about cutting a canal in Wilson's and St. John's Bayou, hoping to reinforce and supply his command. As soon as this was done he would move his force across the Mississippi River and assault Confederate forces at Tiptonville, Tennessee, and completely isolate Island No. 10 from resupply.

For the Confederate forces a combination of events conspired against them for the continued defense of the Madrid Bend. The Confederate high command of Beauregard and Albert Johnston needed troops in Corinth, Mississippi, to counter Union forces moving on the Tennessee River. On March 23rd Brig. Gen. McCown was relieved and his forces at Island No. 10 reduced to 4,000. His replacement, Brig. Gen. William MacKall, was a protégé to Beauregard and it was hoped he would bring vigor to the command, but it was not to be. Instead, "MacKall arrived at Madrid Bend and found his new command disheartened, poorly armed and the Confederate gunboats in the vicinity useless."[19]

Under constant bombardment for two weeks and with no reinforcements coming, the Federals were about to up the ante on the fortress. For MacKall, the news was dim; "a note, signed 'One of Jeff. Thompson's men,' and dated April 1, gave notice that the canal would be completed the next day, the 2d. On the same night (actually April 4), during a violent storm, the first gunboat ran past all the batteries above New Madrid unharmed; it was early discovered, and every gun was opened on it."[20] One of Foote's Flag Officers, Henry Walke, who had been with Grant at Belmont, volunteered to run the USS *Carondelet* past the island. Walke devised a plan in which he would fortify the gunboat with shot-absorbing hay bales to the port side of the boat, between him and the fortress. Tied to a barge with bales of hay packed heavily all over it and around the gunboat itself, the *Carondelet* raised steam in its boilers and readied for full speed.

Could the Confederates under Brig. Gen. MacKall fulfill the orders Maj. Gen. Pierre Beauregard had ordered Leonidas Polk and McCown to do? "His instruction were that they were to be 'held at all costs,'" which in soldier language meant that those guns were worth their weight in blood.[21] For MacKall and his troops, on Island No. 10, the strategic situation for the South had changed considerably since Beauregard spoke those words. In fact Beauregard and his senior Maj. Gen. Albert Sidney Johnston were desperate to concentrate as much Confederate force as they could to fend off a Union thrust up the Tennessee River. At the same time the U.S. flotilla was running the island, the Battle of Shiloh in Tennessee was in the offing.

On the night of April 4, 1862, the warm air of the previous day was giving way to the rumble of thunder as a cold air mass moved in from the northwest.

Flag Officer Walke and his sailors on board the *Carondelet* could plainly see lighting streaking across the night sky, cracking the evening with a violent display. The craft was making good headway at full steam and silently passed the tip of Island No. 10 undetected. This hopeful passage did not last long, with rain now streaming down on the scene, the gunboat's flues now betraying its position.

Steam boilers tended to be noisy and when the flues vented some of the burnt ash could explode with the sound of a shotgun. With that sound and the accompanying flame that spewed forth from the stacks the Confederates were now alerted and took to the heavy guns in earnest. The gunboat and the fort's guns now blazed away at one another. Silhouetted against the flashes of lightning the *Carondelet* presented a tempting target that the Confederates missed more than hit. The gunboat ran the gauntlet and arrived with some minor hits, some even landing on the barge hay bales. The deed was done; the fate of Island No. 10 was sealed.

> The position of the enemy, though thus powerful against attack, was one of great isolation. From Hickman a great swamp, which afterward becomes Reel-foot Lake, extends along the left bank of the Mississippi, discharging its waters into the river forty miles below Tiptonville. A mile below Tiptonville begins the great swamps, extending down both sides of the Mississippi for a distance of sixty miles. The enemy therefore had the river in his front, and behind him a swamp, impassable to any great extent for either men or supplies in the then high state of the river. The only way of receiving help, or of escaping, in case the position became untenable, was by way of Tiptonville, to which a good road led.[22]

John Pope could now envelop the island fortress. The Union forces began moving across the Mississippi River downstream from Island No. 10. Mackall was probably not aware that on April 7th the Confederates had suffered defeat at the hands of U.S. Grant at the Battle of Shiloh (Pittsburg Landing, Tennessee). When Union forces moved on Tiptonville, Tennessee, MacKall's supply base, his now meager force of about 4,000 was looking at a siege situation. Mackall decided to surrender his command and the heavy guns on the island were spiked. April 7th and 8th were bad days for the Confederacy; the possibility of launching an offensive for regaining Missouri needed re-evaluation and maybe something on a lesser scale. The grand design of Beauregard had to become something that Sterling Price could mold into continued action, actions that the Trans-Mississippi Command could implement with the idea that St. Louis could still be the objective.

2

Union Militia

Sterling Price was forced to remove his command from Missouri after having success there in 1861 in order to augment Van Dorn's and McCulloch's Army. His victory at Wilson's Creek and Lexington, Missouri, bode well for 1862, until his command was defeated at Pea Ridge (Elk Horn Tavern, Arkansas) in late February 1862. Because of these setbacks, February, March and April 1862 were difficult times for Missouri Confederate forces and Southern sympathizers. Price believed that things could be turned around and was looking for a campaign of some type to bring Confederate presence back into the state. Price decided that a campaign of recruitment complete with showing the flag might be the idea.

Maj. Gen. Sterling Price was a native former Governor of Missouri; he had left his home in Keytesville, Missouri, to command Missouri forces in defense of the Confederacy in Missouri. The late events of the war were distressing and he and Colonel Joseph Porter had decided that an excursion of Porter's command into Missouri would help bring more Missourians into the war on their side. Joseph Porter was from Lewis County, Missouri, and in April 1862, Price and Porter agreed for his departure from Price's command. Col. Porter anticipated recruiting a number of men when he arrived in Northeast Missouri, but it is presumed that he had few troops with him when he entered the state.

It was believed that Porter's forces would help tie down Union forces and that Porter would encounter unprepared Union Militia. "In April, 1862, Confederate Colonel Joseph Porter of Lewis County received orders to proceed to his home territory to enlist cavalry and bring them south…. Missouri's Little Dixie could fill Confederate ranks fighting in Tennessee and Arkansas."[1] In July 1862 Porter and his Missouri Brigade entered into Missouri, moving in the direction of Little Dixie in Northeast Missouri. It would be here that he found a considerable number of people to join his command.

The last time Porter had been in Northeast Missouri he had been under the command of Colonel Martin Green, in the summer of 1861, when tensions between pro-South and pro-Union factions clashed in Scotland and Clark counties.² On the Des Moines River at Athens, Missouri, these tensions climaxed when Confederate forces under Green (Missouri State Guard) were asked for support by locals against Union occupation of the town by (Missouri Home Guard) forces under David Moore. Here on August 5th, just days before Wilson's Creek, Col. Martin Green moved on the Union troops camped in Athens.

Joseph Porter was a Lt. Col. under Green and on the morning of August 5th was bringing up Confederate forces just outside Athens on a low rise some 400 yards from the Federals looking down Thome Street. Col. David Moore had his force of over 400 effectives form ranks on Spring Street, near the center of town. Immediately Green's artillery opened up on Moore's men and the battle was joined with desultory rifle fire. With over 1,000 troops (about the size of a Civil War Regiment), the Confederates outnumbered the Union forces. The main problem for Col. Green and Lt. Col. Porter was that their troops were inadequately armed—some had no arms. The battle lasted about two hours and ended when Moore's men fixed bayonets and charged the wavering Confederates, who had been slowly advancing.

Pro-Southern Athens was now left to the mercy of growing Union influences and resentment eventually detrimental to the town's existence. It was in this area of Northeast Missouri that Porter now was back and the Union officials were taken off guard and fairly alarmed. By June Col. Porter was moving easily over Lewis, Marion, Knox, Clark, Scotland and Schuyler counties, recruiting as he went, eventually increasing his force to over 400 men. This incursion of Porter was soon to be a test for the Union Officials and the need to establish militias to counter such activities. Coupled with this was the fact that Porter was near the Iowa border, which presented concerns of extending the conflict even farther north.

At the same time that Porter was recruiting and raiding in Northern Missouri, Military and State Government Officials in St. Louis had decided to act to counter "Guerrilla Warfare" in the state. "Accordingly Brig. Gen. John M. Schofield, the commander of the Missouri State Militia and also the United States military commander of the District of Missouri, was authorized to organize the entire militia force of the State for the purpose of putting down marauders and defending the peaceable citizens of the State."³ This authorization did not cover those citizens who may have sided otherwise as the Governor of Missouri does not define in his Special order No. 101:

HEADQUARTERS STATE OF MISSOURI, ADJUTANT-GENERAL'S OFFICE, St. Louis, July 22, 1862. The existence of numerous bands of guerrillas in different parts of the State, who are engaged in robbing and murdering peaceable citizens for no other cause than that such citizens are loyal to the Government under which they have always lived, renders it necessary that the most stringent measures be adopted to punish all such crimes and to destroy such bands. Brig. Gen. John M. Schofield, in command of the Missouri State Militia, is hereby authorized to organize the entire militia of the State into companies, regiments, and brigades, and to order into active service such portions of the force thus organized as he may judge necessary for the purpose of putting down all marauders and defending the peaceable citizens of the State.[4]

Note that Governor Gamble means only loyal citizens to the government.

Soon to follow on the heels of this order was the organization and implementation of the Enrolled Missouri Militia statute. General Order No. 19 was merely the action of the Federal Government to prevent having to deploy Union Army Divisions that were needed elsewhere in the main theatres of the war. What the authorities missed was the fact that Missouri was at war already and that it was a divided government, with the originally elected government of 1860 now exiled, by martial law, wanting to regain control. General Schofield issued in part: "An immediate organization of all the militia of Missouri is hereby ordered, for the purpose of exterminating the guerrillas that infest our State.... The militiamen who shall assemble at any post will be immediately enrolled and organized into companies, elect their officers, and be sworn into service, in accordance with the militia laws of the State, under the immediate superintendence of the commanding officer of the post."[5] This would include not only infantry but also cavalry units.

For Colonel Porter his actions, by June, had brought to his ranks nearly 50 recruits. Ironically it is not certain just when Colonel Porter arrived in this area of Missouri and subsequently brings to question the ability of federal authorities to monitor such actions. This fact alone helps to explain why the federal authorities decided to bring to the forefront the need for Enrolled Militia. It was in June when Porter captured Union troops near the Salt River Bridge that his actions were finally noticed. Joseph Porter was satisfied with his success thus far; he had appeared and had established a Confederate presence in an area of the State of Missouri that was considered, by some, to be pacified.

Summer of 1862 was a precarious time for Missouri. The idea for an Enrolled Missouri Militia was problematic and not really entirely reliable. A more well trained force was required and in July the Provisional Enrolled Missouri Militia was born. "The EMM was a part-time force which lacked uniforms and were only called to duty in times of emergency. The loyalties of the EMM were suspect at times. Therefore, the state also created the Provisional enrolled Missouri Militia (PEMM). Authorities only enrolled 'Unionists' into the PEMM. It was a full-time force with the soldiers paid by the state but the Federal government outfitted and supplied the PEMM."⁶ Confederate Col. Porter seemed to be everywhere and these actions of implementing EMM and PEMM could be largely due to his activities.

Moving across Scotland, Schuyler and Lewis counties, he now attracted a number of young men looking for action. Porter's force was soon recognized as the 1st Northeast Missouri Cavalry. Skirmishing with elements of the 2nd and 11th Missouri State Militia, near Cherry Hill in Schuyler County, Porter remained active, moving again in Scotland County with Memphis as his target. Federal forces were now aware of his force and had become activated. Under the command of Col. John McNeil, Federal forces in Palmyra began to assemble. "He determined to pursue Porter and not to give him time to drill or even fairly organize his forces, and to fight him whenever the opportunity offered."⁷ Realizing that Porter was headed toward Memphis, in Scotland County, he sent troopers to locate and to intercept Porter. When McNeil arrived in Newark he decided to await his commissary stores slowly coming up. He decided that some elements of his command could move on and ordered the Second Missouri Cavalry (Merrill's Horse), under Capt. John Y. Clopper, and a detachment of the Eleventh Missouri State Militia, under Maj. J. B. Rogers, to make contact with Porter's 1st N.E. Missouri Cavalry.

John McNeil had a cold-blooded dislike for Southerners. As he came into command, he refused to recognize Confederate soldiers in uniform and executed ten of them in retaliation for the death of one Union citizen. McNeil was known as the "Butcher of Palmyra" (Library of Congress).

Sunday, July 13, 1862, was warm and easy as people of Memphis watched the Missouri Home Guard make their usual rounds. Early in the day they heard a short-lived smattering of gunfire before seeing the Confederate banner of the 1st N.E. Missouri cavalry entering the town and Confederates rounding up the State Militiamen. Among the captured was one Dr. William Aylward. He was a prominent village leader and was considerably pro–Union and Captain of the Home Guard in an area of many pro-Southerners. His arrest would make for some contentious argument for what happened in Missouri for the rest of the war.

At Memphis Col. Porter was joined by a partisan guerrilla by the name of Tom Stacy. The rest of Porter's command did not look favorably on this connection and often referred to Stacy's men as the "Chain Gang," probably in reference to their surly appearance and manner. It was during this time, for Porter spent only a few hours in Memphis, that Dr. Aylward was either hanged or strangled (probably by Stacy and some of his henchmen) simply because of his influence in the area and his political leanings.[8] We do not know of Col. Porter's reaction to this event; it is doubtful he would have approved but it was difficult to keep many of the young recruits from acting out. By this time his command was something like 200 effectives and some may have not had any firearms. After leaving Memphis Porter and his force moved southwest along the Middle Fabius River; they camped near Southern sympathizer homesteads, literally living off the land.

McNeil's forces (Clopper and Rogers) were now closing in. Col. Porter was very familiar with the area of Peirce's Mill in Scotland County. He decided to set a trap for the forces pursuing him at an area known to locals as Vassar Hill, a mile or so from the Mill. On the morning of July 18th, at the bridge crossing the Middle Fabius River, Porter stationed a couple of riders to attract the oncoming federals coming down the road and then lead them off Vassar Road at the base of the hill to a point where the dismounted force of Porter's 200 men would be waiting in concealment. The Union force of about 300 troopers, Second Missouri Cavalry (Merrill's Horse) and Eleventh Missouri State Militia, came rambling down the road on horseback and immediately gave chase to the outriders, following them over the bottomland off the main road.

At the tree line just out of site of the federals, with muskets, shotguns and pistols at the ready, Porter's men watched in amazement as the federals came at a gallop down the trail, firing wildly as the decoy riders disappeared into the woods. The Merrill's Horse riders came within a hundred yards then, at Porter's command, the dismounted troopers of the 1st N.E. Missouri let loose a barrage of gunfire that dismounted almost all of the Merrill's Horse. Capt. Clopper regrouped what he had left and tried again to ride down the firing line. Col. Porter had his men withdraw back to another position and when the federals came on once again they fired; although this time they fired too early and with little effect. At about this time the 11th Missouri State Militia caught up and joined the attack. Captain Roger's men dismounted and began a desultory fire with Porter's men that lasted about two hours, at which point the opponents disengaged and Porter remounted his men and moved off to the south. The federals did not pursue, for their losses were about 30 dead and wounded. Porter's losses were about 3 killed. Rodgers was livid that Clopper impetuously attacked without his support and had not dismounted his men to form line and make less of a target.

Union Captain Clopper claimed victory, but the obvious victory went to Col. Porter and his men who had set a clever trap for Clopper and disengaged unmolested and without pursuit. Col. McNeil was flabbergasted at the news; coming up from Newark he had Clopper and Rogers continue pursuit even though he was unsure of Porter's 1st N.E. Missouri trooper's whereabouts. "The Federal commander was totally bewildered. Porter's extraordinary celerity and long and hard marches confused him. Asked where Porter was, he replied, 'How can I tell? He may be at any point within 100 miles. He runs like a deer and doubles like a fox. I hear that he crossed the North Missouri, going south, to-day, but I would not be surprised if he fired on our pickets before morning."⁹ For Colonel McNeil the frustration in dealing with some of the local population and now Porter only increased his animosity. McNeil came to believe that enforcement of order, even if it involved summary execution, was necessary.

Porter's force was too small to engage the combined force of McNeil; he now decided to move further south with the thought of going across the Missouri River by way of Callaway County. Moving through Shelby County Col. Porter made his way back to Lewis County and on Sunday July 20th stopped off, for a short time, at his family home northeast of Newark in Lewis County. After visiting for the day Col. Porter left his family and with about 300 men moved off toward Florida, Missouri, skirting Shelby County. Near the small hamlet of Santa Fe Col. Porter's N.E. Missouri Cavalry skirmished with a small Federal detachment in the same way that he handled Clopper's troopers at Vassar Hill. Federal authorities now had a good idea of Porter's N. E. Missouri Cavalry's intentions and most importantly his directions.

Moving from Audrain County on July 26th Porter entered Callaway County hoping to move across the Missouri River near Jefferson City. With a force of about 200 to 300 men armed with mostly shotguns and older muskets Porter was looking for ground in which he could deny the federals the initiative. At about this time 75 Southerners from the area, under the command of Alvin Cobb, a militant Southern proponent, joined in with Porter's Command. Moving along the Auxvasse River, Porter's N.E. Missouri Cavalry was foraging around the location of Moore's Mill near modern Calwood, selecting the ground in which to spring a trap on pursuing federals much like he did at Vassar Hill.

Oden Guitar received word from Brigadier General Schofield, commanding the Military District of Missouri, that Colonel Porter was nearby Columbia. "On July 27 I received at Jefferson City, of which post I was then in command, a dispatch from General Schofield, ordering me to send without delay two companies of my regiment to join Lieutenant-Colonel Shaffer, Merrill's Horse, at Columbia, advising me that Porter was in the north part of Boone County with a large rebel force."[10] Complying with his orders Col. Guitar moved on reports of Col. Porter's last known position. Moving toward the Auxvasse River, Col. Guitar left Jefferson City and headed north and then east, joining up with a section of artillery and a battalion of 3rd Iowa Cavalry.

It had been a hot July and the 28th was no different. Col. Porter had been moving down the Auxvasse River for days looking for suitable ground, giving his horses and men a chance at water while avoiding Federal columns. When he came upon Moore's Mill, Porter decided that it offered adequate positioning for his forces to take on the Federals, who were now closing. Col. Oden Guitar and his advance cavalry had covered the Auxvasse River and had slowly closed the gap with Col. Porter's N.E. Missouri Cavalry south of Moore's Mill. Realizing that he may have missed the enemy he had his columns move south down the old St. Charles Road. About one mile east of the Mill elements of the 3rd Iowa Cavalry came upon Porter's men who engaged the Cavalry from cover on the east side of the road.

The Battle was now joined and soon, Porter had his forces formed in line of battle. A Confederate soldier remarked, "After marching about a mile in double quick time, we were formed in line to face the enemy, who were advancing rapidly."[11] The thickets and brush was soon covered as Confederates filled the area and moved forward to engage the federals as close as possible. It was at the height of noontime as these two armies now came to grips under a blazing sun. Porter pressed the federals as soon as he came into line, hoping to panic his enemy into flight. For a time the battle favored Porter and Cobb's men fought like the furies, inflicting casualties on the Union horsemen.

Guitar reacted swiftly to events and moved to blunt Porter's attack.

> During this time the rebels kept up a continual fire, chiefly upon the center of our line. Our fire was by volleys and mostly at random. Major Caldwell coming up, I ordered him to form his men upon the right of our line, the object of the enemy seeming to be to flank us in that direction. To do this he was compelled to advance his line into the woods seventy or eighty yards east of the road. Here he was met by a strong force of the enemy, who greeted him with a shower of shot and ball. Our little column wavered for a moment under the galling fire...[12]

Porter had moved Alvin Cobb's Company across the road with the assignment to flank Guitar's right. Cobb was moving successfully when Guitar decided to deploy artillery.

Alvin Cobb was a hard-crusted confederate who disliked all things that had to do with staying in the Union. He had lost one hand and in its place he had a hook, giving him an even more fearsome look about him. He took to his job of killing Yankees proudly and at Moore's Creek he set to this task as his company moved across the road to strike the enemy's right. By 1:00 o'clock not only was the weather hot but so was the exchange of gun-fire between the Confederates and Union opponents. Colonel Joseph Porter watched as the events unfolded and believed that if he could strike Guitar's forces quickly he might fold him up and panic the rank and file; if Cobb could turn Guitar's right flank he could very well do just that.

Being quickly engaged at the woods Colonel Guitar brought up what forces he had at his disposal. Colonel Shafer and his 500-man force was still a mile or two off in the rear coming up so Guitar deployed the 200 men he had immediately available. There was one element that Guitar had that Porter did not and that was two sections of artillery. Early on in the conflict Guitar placed one of those artillery pieces forward on the road to fire canister and grape at the surging Confederates. "As soon as I saw our line steady I ordered forward one gun of the section to our center, which rested upon the road, here so narrow that the piece had to be unlimbered and brought forward by hand. I ordered Lieutenant Armington to open with shell and cannister upon the left of the road, which was done in fine style, silencing the rebel force completely for a time."[13] Now Porter's men winced as artillery shells whizzed over their heads.

Even though the N.E. Missouri Cavalry numbered only about 300 men, Porter pressed his attack. Cobb moved his force forward against Guitar's Federals and this did not escape Guitar's notice: "I now discovered a large body of rebels crossing to the west side of the road, evidently with the view of flanking us...."[14] The battle was now at its height and the artillery and rifle fire was taking its toll. A Confederate soldier remembered as the carnage increased, "It seems to me that our company was directly in front of the enemy's artillery. I have always thought it was our fire that disabled the battery and killed nearly all of the horses and a number of those in charge. It was just before our charge that Perry Brown fell, on my immediate left, with part of his skull torn away by a grape shot."[15]

It was a visceral fight between these two sectional adversaries. The Confederates disabled the one gun and were moving forward on the federals when Colonel Shafer's Cavalry arrived in support of Guitar. With 500 dismounted horsemen the federals now gained the upper hand in the fight. "I now ordered an advance along our whole line, which was promptly responded to, and with steady step the enemy was soon driven back. Tired of crawling through the brush, and catching the enthusiasm as they moved, the whole line, raising a wild shout of triumph, rushed upon the enemy, completely routing and driving him from the field."[16] The day was now suddenly favoring the unionists; the Confederates gave way and finally broke. A wounded confederate witnessed the advance:

> Soon the reinforcements arrived for the enemy, and we were forced to fall back to a gully. Their fire was continuous and very heavy, the minie balls flying in our faces, and the smoke of their guns seemed to be within twenty or thirty yards.... My right arm was fearfully shattered almost from the shoulder to the elbow. Another bullet, which I still carry, buried itself in my thigh, and a third grazed the skin under my left arm, tearing a hole in my clothing and haversack, through which you could pass your hand. I stepped back to a gully in our rear, and the next thing I remember was a Dutchman peeping around a tree at me with a shout of glee to see the damned secesh hors de combat.[17]

Porter now made haste and withdrew his force before it could be overrun.

Fortunately for Porter, Guitar did not pursue his force from the field. Ironically Guitar believed that he was outnumbered by Porter, but the reality was Porter was outnumbered by Guitar and it was one of the reasons he did not immediately pursue. With less than 300 men Porter moved over to the east side of the Auxvasse River and backtracked north to Marion and Shelby counties. "'I can raise 1,000 men in Monroe and Marion counties alone on this issue in 24 hours,' Porter said to Cobb, as they were discussing Schofield's order."[18] The order they were talking about was probably the Enrolled Missouri Militia, which singled out Confederates as partisan guerrillas, thereby creating an environment in which they could be easily executed by Union authority and not be considered equal combatants in relation to Union forces. This presented a problem and upped the ante vis-à-vis prisoners and exchanges. Porter continued his recruiting with his return to Northeast Missouri and found that many young men were eager to join his ranks; most of these young recruits, however, had little to no training and many had no arms at all. These new recruits could be targets for execution if captured.

With Porter's return to the North Missouri District he now became the responsibility of Colonel John McNeil of the 2nd Missouri Cavalry, who had just missed him at Vassar Hill in Scotland County. McNeil was determined to have him, and his opportunity came in early August as Union Cavalry was constantly on his heels, just missing intercepting him several times. "I had hung on the trail of the enemy from the time I struck it, on the 29th of July ... and continued pursuit of the enemy over a most difficult country, following his devious and eccentric windings through brake and bottom and across field, often where no wheel had ever turned before. He had destroyed bridges and obstructed the fords by felling trees. Notwithstanding this we kept well up with him, driving in his pickets, beating up his camps, and left many of his men prone upon the track."[19] In early August Porter's N.E. Missouri Cavalry found themselves approaching Kirksville.

In 1862 Kirksville, Missouri, was a small town and county seat of Adair County. Very few Civil War Battles had been fought in the form of house to house fighting and was not really sought, but Porter forced many people to leave as he and his men occupied many businesses and homes in and around the courthouse. Col. McNeil described the area as follows: "We came up … at Kirksville about 10 o'clock Wednesday morning, August 6, and learning that he had expelled the people from the town, concluded that he would occupy the houses and defend the place. Kirksville is situated on a prairie ridge, surrounded completely by timber and corn fields, with open ground on the northeast, from which direction we approached."[20] McNeil had one advantage that Porter did not: He had brought with him five pieces of artillery and immediately put them to good use firing into the woods and cornfields.

For Porter his units were hoping to surprise the unionists as they moved through the town and enveloped them from the flanks. With little more than 2,000 men, many without arms and no artillery, Colonel Porter's N.E. Missouri Cavalry would experience the opposite of his expectations. Col. McNeil had with him about 1,300 men and he deployed them to flank the waiting Confederates. To ascertain the exact position of enemy forces in the town, McNeil sent a section of the Merrill's Horse under Lt. Cowdrey to make a reconnaissance. Cowdrey and his eight men rode into the courthouse square, quickly fleeing from the square after drawing fire to verify to Col. McNeil the enemy's disposition.

House to house fighting was a rarity in the American Civil War and the fight at Kirksville was unique. With the Artillery opening up on fields and buildings in town, McNeil advanced against the defenders. Lt. Col. Schaffer was in charge of the federal right with the Merrill Horse and Major Caldwell of the 3rd Iowa Cavalry was in charge of the left. Dismounting, the Union forces advanced and engaged the Confederates, routing them out of the houses and with deadly artillery fire put to test the poorly trained forces on the Confederate flanks. The fighting lasted about five hours and the civilians who did not leave the scene hunkered down in their cellars to avoid the onslaught. One of the older residents, a Mrs. Cutts, was shot as some Confederates fled from her home and as she was exiting her basement cellar. Porter's left wing stood for a time, but with his right turned Porter's forces became panicked and fled in mostly disorder. It was Porter's last attempt to bring off another Vassar Hill.

Of those Confederates captured, Colonel McNeil, whom it could be surmised detested secessionists and paroled previous combatants, decided to make an example of at least a dozen or so and shot them.

> Thursday, the next day after the battle, quite a number of "oathbreakers," as they were called, were tried by a Federal drum-head court martial, convened by McNeil, in Kirksville, and 15 of them were convicted of violations of their paroles, and sentenced to be shot. McNeil approved the proceedings and the order, and the poor fellows were executed the same day. Their names, as can best be learned now, were William Bates, R. M. Galbreath, Lewis Rollins, William Wilson, Columbus Harris, Reuben Thomas, or Thompson, Thomas Webb and Reuben Green, of Monroe county; James Christian, David Wood, Jesse Wood and Bennett Hayden, of Shelby; Wm. Sallee and Hamilton Brannon, of Marion, and John Kent, of Adair.[21]

The actions of Colonel McNeil showed a heavy hand that would be his signature and that would bear a bitter fruit for a state already torn of its social fabric.

As torn as Northeast Missouri was, the torn fabric was never more evident than in western Missouri and the border with Kansas. Here the genesis for the war was made early on (before 1861) and the continuing strife made the Kansas authority act by mustering militia units. In particular Colored Militia units were formed in Kansas to patrol the border. Kansas Jayhawker State Senator Jim Lane decided to recruit black soldiers to join his Kansas forces before federal efforts. In August 1862 the 1st Kansas Colored Infantry was formed from many escaped slaves and some free blacks. Many of the escaped slaves were taken from raids in Missouri by Lane himself before the war broke out and now they provided a useful tool for Kansas authority.

William D. Matthews was a volunteer member of the 1st Kansas Colored Infantry Regiment who took part in the campaign against partisans at the Battle of Island Mound in Missouri. He became an officer and later recruited former slaves into the 1st Kansas Colored Volunteer Infantry Regiment at Fort Scott and commanded artillery at Fort Scott during Price's raid in 1864 (courtesy Wilson's Creek National Battlefield; WICR 13033).

By October 1862 Guerillas operating from the Missouri counties adjacent to Kansas became a haven for operations against Kansas homes and towns. A hot bed of activity was centered in Bates County, Missouri, and it was decided to send the 1st Kansas Colored Infantry to intercept and clear out guerrilla activity. Late in October more than 250 soldiers and officers were sent into the county by way of the Fort Scott Road. The force arrived at the home of a known Southern sympathizer and it was decided to occupy it, calling it Fort Africa. After skirmishing for a couple of days with the local pro-South sympathizers, the Colored troops soon came into battle with a more organized enemy at a place called Island Mound.

It was at Island Mound that the black soldiers acquitted themselves quite well with fierce hand-to-hand combat with the Southern guerrillas who outnumbered them probably two to one. As the units engaged each other a prairie fire was started around the combatants. The colored unit fought on through the smoke as reinforcements arrived and helped turn the tide, sending the Confederates from the field. Holding the ground won that day, the Colored Regiment pursued the rebels next day only to find their base of operation on the Marais des Cygnes abandoned. This area would continue to be contentious and after the implementation of Special Order No. 11 the situation would become even more desperate as many local people left their homes as refugees. When Price came through the area in 1864, it had already been laid waste.

3

Confederates

Porter now lost most of his effectiveness in Northeast Missouri but there was one more act in this tragedy to play out before his exit from the area. Porter had at Kirksville over 2,000 troops, the most he would ever have, but many of them had no standard issue weapons. For many of these young soldiers this was their first taste of combat. Colonel Joseph Porter had with him about 100 men who could be described as actual Confederate soldiers as recognized by the standards of the day. With each engagement many of these recruits would simply disappear, as Porter would constantly be forced to move from place to place outrunning Union forces. "Porter himself, at the head of a considerable number of his men, went ... to Whaley's Mill, on the South Fabius, where, on Monday, August 11th, there was a virtual disbanding of the Confederate forces, many going home, many striking out for Illinois and Iowa, and a few determined spirits accompanying the undaunted chieftain, who, the same night, crossed the Hannibal and St. Joe, and went into Monroe to join Cobb, then reported in the Salt river hills, near Florida."[1] By September 1862 Porter's N. E. Missouri Cavalry consisted of about 400 troops as they moved on the Missouri town of Palmyra.

The day of September 12 was clear and warm as Porter's column of men approached Palmyra from the west. Col. Porter was aware that there were Southern sympathizers being held at the Courthouse and jail at the town square. Colonel John McNeil's thoughts were on how he could finally bag Porter and end this incursion that had tasked his time and tried his patience with these local Southern sympathizers. McNeil "marched up from Paris and Hunnewell to Newark and then to Monticello (Lewis Co.) in order to be where he could better direct operations against Porter. Lewis and Marion were full of armed bands of Confederates, and there was the greatest alarm among the Federals. Even Hannibal was thought to be in danger."[2]

At Palmyra there was a small garrison of about three squads of Missouri Enrolled Militia that holed themselves up in the jail and store-buildings near the Courthouse when Porter's N. E. Missouri Cavalry entered the town. After a brief exchange of gunfire and Porter enveloping the center square of the town, Union forces surrendered. Porter lost one man in the raid and he freed the Confederates in the town jail while taking a Palmyra citizen by the name of Andrew Allsmen hostage. Allsmen was an ardent unionist citizen and very vocal opponent of any Southern cause; by taking Allsmen, Porter was probably hoping to send a message to unionists that they could be touched by the Confederacy. This action set up a brutal response by Union Military Authority.

Once again McNeil had missed Porter and when he arrived at Palmyra he was in a furious temper. His ability to defeat Porter at Kirksville only added to his anxiety for it was there that he had his best opportunity to corner him and now once again he was in the wind. What McNeil did now was a determined pursuit of Porter's N.E. Missouri Cavalry in southwest Lewis County, in an area very near Porter's home. At a place near Whaley's Mill Porter and his forces bivouacked and cooked meals. Relaxing his men Porter now had his guard down, though he did have pickets posted when McNeil's hard riding contingent of about 550 cavalry came thundering down on their location on Sunday, September 14th, causing a panicked reaction and a skedaddle on the part of the Confederates. "There was mounting in hot haste among the boys in gray, and dreading the terrible cannon which had done so much injury to them before, they retreated in most unseemly haste, with no resistance worthy of the name."[3]

This now was the end of Porter's presence in Northeast Missouri; with his forces scattered and the federals keeping up the pressure, Porter decided to disband his command and with about 100 loyal followers he made his way back across the Missouri River, headed to North Arkansas. Col. John McNeil, after pursuing and capturing a number of Porter's men from Whaley's Mill, summarily executed a number of them on the spot of their capture and Whaley's Mill was burned to the ground. One of the captured Confederate soldiers was an officer, in uniform, who presented his papers to McNeil identifying him as an officer of rank in the Confederate Army. This had no impact on McNeil, who simply went down the line and shot the officer and some other men in cold blood. After this action McNeil returned to Palmyra and set about addressing the death of Andrew Allsmen.

Allsmen was removed with what was left of Porter's forces after Whaley's Mill at a place near what locals called Bragg's Ridge. The details are unclear but according to some letters written after the war, Colonel Porter is said to have released Allsmen and allowed some men who were acquainted with him to escort him back to Palmyra. Somewhere on the prairie near Palmyra some men, probably a separated group from Porter's original force at Whaley's

Mill, encountered the returning group headed to Palmyra including Allsmen. Singling Allsmen out from the group, they shot him simply because of his ardent Union stance. When Colonel McNeil learned of Allsmen's death, after he had warned that Allsmen, a non-combatant, should be returned unharmed, it was decided by McNeil that blood would be exchanged for blood.

The incident of Allsmen's death precipitated the heavy-handed reprisal of Union Authority. Colonel John McNeil, as commander of the Northeast Missouri District, found that martial law would allow him to detain and arrest at will. With a number of Confederates captured, McNeil, who disliked all pro–Southerners, decided an example would be made. At the county jail one officer and nine enlisted men, whom McNeil considered guerrillas, were selected to be marched out of the town and executed at the local fairgrounds on a clear day in October 1862. They were allowed to write their last letters before being most foully murdered. Captain Thomas A. Sidner, one of the selected prisoners wrote, "Bye to you all this morning.... I am to be shot at one o'clock."[4] None of them had any direct relation to the killing of Allsmen but were held as an example of what would happen to any Southern sympathizers who acted out. From that day on, with the threat of Union reprisal against property and person, the people of Northeast Missouri settled into an unsettled atmosphere with suspicion and skepticism of each other.

Colonel John McNeil now moved on and was never held accountable by federal authority. In fact federal authority signed off on the action. The high-handed measures taken by McNeil were approved to some extent by the U.S. Government and its extension of Marshal Law, for it ended any more Confederate activity in Northeast Missouri. Military action now relocated to the southern and southeastern areas of Missouri. Here Sterling Price, John S. Marmaduke and Joseph Shelby, all natives to the State of Missouri, had plans to keep Missouri in the Confederacy in some way. All of them had homes and businesses along the Missouri River in the middle of the state. "Lt. Gen. Edmund Kirby Smith, the new Confederate commander of the Trans-Mississippi Theater (all those forces west of the Mississippi), then directed a second Missouri raid in the spring of 1863." If anything Colonel Porter's Raid showed that insertion of Confederate forces was indeed possible and should be encouraged inside Missouri.

One of the results of Porter's raid was the rise of partisan rangers on the part of Confederate sympathizers that gave the federals reason for the suppression of individual freedoms. The execution of Confederate soldiers who disregarded their paroles and re-enlisted into units such as the Confederate 1st N. E. Missouri Cavalry angered Union officials such as Maj. Gen. Henry

Halleck who considered it outlaw behavior against the norms of civilized warfare.[5] Halleck had authority from Lincoln to exercise martial law he saw fit. Confederate officials in their respective Military regions such as Arkansas and the Southwest Military District disregarded such acts by Union authority. The Act, implemented under the Congress of the Confederate States of America, recognized the formations acting in Union territory as militia units and therefore valid in this internecine conflict. Union and Confederate governments were at loggerheads.

The spring rains of 1863 had Union officials hopeful that Confederate operations against Missouri could be avoided because of the poor condition the local roads would probably be in. The Confederacy had not given up on Missouri, but operations would be problematic. In the Confederate Capital of Richmond, Virginia, President Jefferson Davis decided to make some changes in the high command of Confederate forces in the Trans-Mississippi west. President Davis wanted to gain some momentum with his forces in the west and appointed Lt. Gen. Kirby Smith to do just that. Smith was considered a premier choice. "Not yet thirty-nine, he ranked second among the nation's seven lieutenant generals, and Lee himself had lately said that he would be pleased to have him as a corps commander..."[6] It was an assignment that Smith did not expect.

Despite a spectacular victory in Kentucky, Edmund Kirby Smith thought he was being demoted when selected to command the Confederate Trans-Mississippi West. Once there, he had the ear of Price and thought that actions against Union Forces in Missouri would prove beneficial—he was partially right. Smith convened a committee to investigate Price's actions (Library of Congress).

Believing that he was being sent into oblivion, as he saw this assignment, Smith did not realize at first the importance of the task before him. Lt. Gen. Smith was briefed by the President of the Confederacy of the importance of the assignment and the urgency that he, Kirby Smith, had in vigorously prosecuting a war against the federals in the west. Leaving Richmond, in early 1863, Smith made his way to Tennessee to confer with Gen. Pemberton in order to acquire Major General Sterling Price, then assigned to Pemberton's command. Price, a well-known Missourian and former governor of that state, had won battles at Wilson's Creek and Lexington, Missouri, and was well liked by the troops. Smith was hoping that these victories could be built upon. For the North overall command of the Missouri District was in transition. Brig. Gen. Samuel Curtis and Lt. Gen. John Schofield had differing ideas on how to cope with the deteriorating situation in Missouri. With Porter's raid in 1862 and the brutal treatment of combatants by Union Colonel McNeil, a number of guerrilla forces started to emerge, in the aftermath, which would give the internecine strife an even uglier look.

Even with the success of driving Porter out of Northeast Missouri the Federal Military Authority in St. Louis was anything but agreed on what policy and actions should be taken. The conflict was between Maj. Gen. Samuel Curtis and Maj. Gen. John Schofield. It was a divided command, with Schofield having the ear of the Missouri Governor and Curtis being the victor at Pea Ridge, Arkansas, and seeking more action in the western part of Missouri and Kansas. "Curtis wanted to hold all available troops within the borders of the state in order to use them in putting down troublemakers of all sorts, armed and unarmed; Schofield on the other hand believed in taking the offensive to the Confederates to his front in Arkansas."[7] The Lincoln administration decided that the best way to put things in order was to send the aging William Voss Sumner, formally of the Army of the Potomac, to command the Missouri District. Unfortunately Sumner died en-route and it was finally decided to give Schofield the command of the Missouri Military District and maintain Curtis's command of the forces in Kansas and the border area.

Offensive action hoped for by Schofield came in the form of Confederate action on the border with Arkansas, specifically in the Ozarks of southern Missouri. From their camps in the Boston Mountains, forces under Brig. Gen. John S. Marmaduke were staging. The condition of Confederate control in southwest Missouri was all but eliminated by the battles of Pea Ridge and Prairie Grove. These actions, as devastating as they were, did not prevent further actions on the part of Confederate forces. In fact it spurred the need to keep the federal forces pinned, as much as possible, in Missouri in order to prevent the continuing reinforcement of Union forces in mid and west Tennessee. The border of Arkansas and Missouri was in a fluid military state as actions began to develop, it was just a matter of who would take action first.

In December 1862 the Confederate Command in Arkansas decided that the time was ripe to move against Union fortifications in southwest Missouri. The officer picked was Brig. Gen. John Sappington Marmaduke, a scion of a former Missouri governor, "a bachelor just past thirty, tall and slender, quick tempered and aristocratic in manner.... He had studied in Harvard and Yale before his graduation from West Point."[8] Maj. Gen. Hindman's orders to Brig. Gen. Marmaduke were to strike the enemy in his flank and get into his rear areas. This would be done in order to prevent the federals from following up their victory at Prairie Grove by the continued movement towards the Arkansas River.

With 2,000 effective cavalries, 1,000 of which were under command of Colonel Joseph O. Shelby, Marmaduke made his way into Missouri, coming down from the Boston Mountains of Arkansas and on January 6th, Confederate forces overwhelmed Union forces at Fort Lawrence on Beaver Creek. While at Fort Lawrence Brig. Gen. Marmaduke became aware of an even greater opportunity. "I learned that Springfield, Missouri with its rich army stores was weakly garrisoned, though strongly fortified, and, if surprised, I thought it could be captured. I determined to attack it."[9] Brig. Gen. Marmaduke soon ordered all his forces to converge on Springfield. Colonel Joseph Porter, recently returned from his expedition to northeast Missouri, was one of those elements away from the main colum. "Dispatched to Colonel Porter ... and ordered him to move support as rapidly as possible."[10] For some reason Porter failed to receive the dispatch and he continued to operate away from Marmaduke's command, working his way back toward Springfield.

John S. Marmaduke, the son of a prominent Missouri family, was a West Point graduate. His success was limited in the Trans-Mississippi West, but no one could question his ability (Library of Congress).

Col. Porter had moved on the federal garrison at Hartville, Missouri, and as Marmaduke and Shelby moved on Springfield, Porter attacked and took possession of Hartfield. At Springfield Brig. Gen. Marmaduke drove federal forces out of some installations, confiscating a number of needed provisions and stores for the Confederates. Marmaduke again made an effort to contact Porter in order to support him, but again failed to contact him whereupon he decided not to continue his attack on the night of the 8th of January, in Springfield. Porter, for his part, was unaware of Brig. Gen. Marmaduke's requests but was moving west toward Springfield when he met up with Marmaduke's main forces at Marshfield. "January 10, a junction was made with Porter ... who had captured ... and destroyed the forts at Hartville, and had also burned the fortifications at Hazelwood."[11]

The Civil War in the mid-west developed a unique way of warfare different from the large infantry battles in Tennessee and Virginia Theatres. Many of these encounters in Missouri were fought by mostly dismounted cavalry. This allowed for smaller armies, particularly Confederate armies, to move rapidly with smaller numbers and attack Union forces scattered throughout the military region. This action at Hartville brought Brig. Gen. Marmaduke's nearly 2,000 mounted cavalry against some 1,000 Union troops under the command of Colonel Samuel Merrill. With the ability to move swiftly unbeknownst to the opponent, a cavalry force could strike swiftly and inflict defeat and confusion on the enemy. At least this was the optimum intention.

Hartville, Missouri, sits before a low rise of hills just west of the Gasconade River in south Missouri. It became aware to Brig. Gen. Marmaduke that a Union force had now reoccupied Hartville and now presented a danger to his left flank as he sought to move back south into Arkansas. As the Confederate force made its way south they came across a Union picket line some five miles west of Hartville and soon became actively engaged. Colonel Merrill was actually moving to support Brig. Gen. Brown at Springfield when, at Hartville, he became aware of Col. Porter's action there and Marmaduke's movement back toward the area. Hunkering down around the courthouse building Merrill expected to make a stand.

What developed was a battle that pitted Merrill's Union forces against Porter's Confederates, both of whom had faced off at the battle of Moore's Mill in July. The action began in the late morning of January 11, 1863, and lasted until late afternoon. Moving up on the town from the south and west, Brig. Gen. Marmaduke decided it was best to deal with this force in order to protect his rear on the way back to Arkansas. "A little before daylight the advance encountered a Federal force coming from Austin via Hartville, to Springfield, and hearing that a strong cavalry force was in my rear, I deemed it best not to put myself in battle between the two forces, bur to turn the force in my front and fight them."¹² Once his decision was made he ordered Porter's men to execute the attack on those Union forces just outside and in Hartville.

Colonel Porter was the right choice for he already knew the ground and presently deployed his command of dismounted troops. By midafternoon the federals began to give ground under Porter's artillery fire and dismounted cavalry and rapidly fell back and out of the courthouse square. Colonel Porter and some of his command pursued on horseback into the square, believing the enemy was now in full retreat. When it was realized that a rear guard was just off in the brush near the courthouse, Porter gave the command to dismount to exchange fire with the skirmishers. A volley of rifled musket fire roared between the two lines, sending whistles of bullets into the air. It was about this time, as Col. Porter was dismounting his horse, that he was struck in his hand and upper thigh, incapacitating the Colonel; he was removed to a wagon semi-conscious with a tourniquet around the leg wound.

Successfully eliminating a threat to his withdrawing south, Brig. Gen. Marmaduke made his way with his force back into the Boston Mountains on the other side of the border with Missouri. It was a difficult march. It was January and the winter weather had now closed in as the Union military forces could not. Colonel Joseph O. Shelby, one of the brigade commanders remembered it. "During the march from Hartville to Batesville, the men suffered much, and some in my brigade are badly frozen, yet the cause demanded sacrifice, and it was made."¹³ One of those sacrificed was Colonel Joseph Porter, who would die a month or so after the Confederates returned. He would never see his wife or kids again in Lewis County, Missouri, and was buried in Oaklawn Cemetery in Batesville. The trail of Marmaduke's course back from the raid was literally traced in blood in the ice and snow.

The Southern command in Arkansas was pleased with Marmaduke's operation in Missouri. Lt. Gen. Theophilus Holmes, before being replaced by Lt. Gen. Kirby Smith, wrote, "This expedition was gotten up by General Hindman to divert the enemy from their attack on Van Buren and to force them to retire from the valley of the Arkansas. It was perfectly successful, and made them fall back into Missouri."¹⁴ It surely brought consternation to federal authorities in St. Louis and Washington, D.C., and made those authorities realize that their guard could not be relaxed. Missouri was vulnerable to confederate raiders and the concern continued to be just how large or determined those future attacks would be.

The wait for those future attacks would not be long. Lt. Gen. Holmes did express his concerns that a confederate attack into Missouri would need to be sustained and relayed his thoughts on February 27, 1863, when Marmaduke decided on another assault in southeast Missouri. "If you go alone, and are forced to return, you would leave our friends there to a merciless foe ... please remember that you are entrusted with the entire defense of the northern frontier."[15] With this Marmaduke made his decision to try and dislodge Union forces at Bloomfield and then make his way quickly to Cape Girardeau, attacking the Union forces and removing the Union stores.

Cape Girardeau, Missouri, sits on the west bank of the Mississippi River just above Thebes's gap 100 miles south of St. Louis. In 1861 federal authorities moved quickly to secure the river town under the command of Ulysses S. Grant. Grant believed that to secure the somewhat pro–Southern town a series of forts would need to be built on the western outskirts of the city's boundary. Newly minted a Brigadier General, Grant entrusted the construction of four earthen forts to Lieutenant John Wesley Powell, a West Point graduate with excellent engineering skills. Powell's forts, from north to south, were simply named A, B, C and D, with batteries in which to cover the main roads leading into the town from the west. As events were to prove, they would be well positioned.

When Kirby Smith became Confederate Commander of the Trans-Mississippi West he came on the heels of Marmaduke's successful raid on Springfield in Missouri. Lt. Gen. Smith understood that some actions must be taken to relieve pressure on Confederate forces in other theatres and that more success could be built upon in the west, and that the initiative still lay with the Confederates. Theophilus Holmes was more reticent about Confederate possibilities in Missouri but gave John S. Marmaduke the go ahead on his next campaign before Smith arrived. Holmes would share in some command but Edmund Kirby Smith was now in command of the Trans-Mississippi theatre and remained there.

In late April 1863, Brig. Gen. Marmaduke made his way into southeast Missouri with 5,000 troopers. His command consisted of Joseph Shelby, also a native Missourian, who now commanded a division and had passed his Brigade command to Colonel G. W. Thompson, with Col. Burbridge. The rest of his command included Colonel Carter who commanded his and Greene's Brigades. Brig. Gen. Marmaduke's initial target was the destruction or capture of Brig. Gen. John McNeil's Union forces at Bloomfield. "If successful in capturing McNeil's forces, I anticipated that my whole command could be well armed and finely mounted."[16] With this as his objective he sent Col. Carter towards Bloomfield and Col. Shelby towards Fredericktown further west, believing that if McNeil withdrew he could intercept him.[17]

Finding that Union General McNeil had hastily departed Bloomfield after burning his stores, Brig. Gen Marmaduke realized that he had an opportunity to catch the hare and possibly the rich store of supplies at Cape

Girardeau. McNeil never received the orders that had him retreat to Ironton; they had been intercepted by Jo Shelby's command at Fredericktown on April 22nd. The stage was now set as the columns of Marmaduke's command converged on Cape Girardeau. "On the 25th, I received dispatches from Carter that he had pursued McNeil to within 4 miles of Cape Girardeau. I immediately ordered Shelby to make a night march ... in order to form junction with Carter."[18]

Brig. Gen. John McNeil believed he faced a force of more than 8,000 troops. As he made his way into and around the forts and batteries surrounding Cape Girardeau, John McNeil had under his command 1,700 troops. The command at the Cape was now anticipating attack. This was not John McNeil's first go around with Confederate opposition. It was this John McNeil who had faced off with Col. Joseph Porter in Northeast Missouri in 1862. He knew he was not well respected by the Confederates, even vilified because of his actions there, and expected very little quarter if defeated, but he also knew that the fortification at his disposal was a good one. McNeil did have crack military units at his disposal including the 1st Nebraska Volunteer Infantry Regiment, which had seen action at the Battle of Shiloh. Once in the Cape, McNeil immediately began to send telegraph messages to the 16th Corps command in Columbus, Kentucky, for arms and reinforcement.

Moving east up Jackson Road Col. Shelby ordered Col. G.W. Thompson's force to drive in Yankee pickets. At about 10:00 a.m. on the 26th Shelby deployed his forces in line of battle, just three miles from Cape Girardeau. He had Shanks's battalion to the left of the road; on his right was G. W. Thompson's battalion. On the right of Thompson, unlimbered was Collins's battery of artillery. Next to the battery was Jeans's battalion facing off against the main Union lines. Fort B and Battery B soon began to roar with cannon fire but it had little effect on the Confederate forces except to move Collins's battery farther to the right of Jeans's battalion. "The enemy's fort's and batteries continued to play upon our battery for more than one hour without intermission, and now and then swept the woods with shell and shot, canister and grape, while the minie balls came hissing a treble to the music of the roar."[19]

Between Jackson Road and Battery B formed the 1st Nebraska Volunteer Regiment. A veteran regiment, the 1st Nebraska had fought at Ft. Donelson and at Shiloh. At Shiloh the regiment was part of Brig. Gen. Lew Wallace's command part of Thayer's brigade when on Shiloh's second day helped drive in the Confederate Army's left flank. Under the leadership of Captain William Baumer, his regiment covered the approaches to Cape Girardeau along the Perryville and Jackson roads. Confederate Colonels Jeans and Gordon's brigade advanced assiduously up the hill, moving east, driving in Union pickets and soon encountering heavy fire from the 1st Nebraska's main line. One Nebraskan soldier recalled "the troops ... advanced so close to each other that they shouted out insults."[20] Between one and two o'clock in the afternoon the volley's cracked and reverberated between the lines as both Union and Confederates fired volleys at one another. Brig. Gen. Marmaduke soon decided that his forces needed to fall back and by 3:00 o'clock the firing ceased.

That afternoon the units under Shelby withdrew through the commands of Carter and Greene's men who supported Shelby's attack. With Cape Girardeau so well protected Marmaduke had decided that a full attack would be futile. Brig. Gen. McNeil was unsure of Marmaduke's intentions and still believed that the Confederate forces outnumbered his and on the 27th wired the 16th Corps command: "COLONEL: At the urgent solicitation of Brig. Gen. John McNeil, commanding at Cape Girardeau, I have this morning sent him two regiments of infantry, a section of artillery, and 100,000 rounds of ammunition ... he had been attacked ... with four brigades, 8,000 men, and repulsed him, but would be attacked again."[21] Ironically Marmaduke came to believe that McNeil now outnumbered his forces and was soon informed that a Union force was making its way from Ironton toward his rear. Brig. Gen. Marmaduke now decided to make his way back to Arkansas by way of the Bloomfield Road.

With his force of 5,000 men Marmaduke's army made its way down through the Morehouse Lowland, between the Commerce Hills and the Salem Plateau, just southwest of Cape Girardeau. Brig. Gen. John McNeil was counting on Brig. Gen. Vandever cutting off Marmaduke and catching him between the two Union forces. It was exactly what Marmaduke was concerned with. "On the morning of the 27th, I found myself between two forces ... either outnumbering my force, and both prepared to attack me simultaneously."[22] Marmaduke decided to move his Confederate force down to the White Water River to Bloomfield and cross the St. Francis River very near Chalk Bluff, Arkansas. Fortunately for the Confederates, Brig. Gen. Vandever was tardy, complaining to McNeil that he needed to rest his mounts. Even though Marmaduke had a force of 5,000 men he did not believe he could take on the federals because of the inferiority of his weapons and lack of weapons for some, made more acute because of his failure to take the Union stores at Cape Girardeau.

Moving south through river bottoms and forested hills, Marmaduke's rear guard was made up of Col. Shelby's Brigade under the command of Col. G.W. Thompson. Making a brief exchange of gunfire at the Castor River crossing, Thompson decided to make a show at the small town of Bloomfield. Col. Thompson was acquainted with the acts of McNeil in northern Missouri, noting, "we patiently awaited the approach of the enemy, determined to win a victory upon the grounds so recently deserted by the criminal outlaw and tory leader, General McNeil."[23] For his part Brig. Gen. McNeil kept up the pursuit to just north of Bloomfield finding the Confederates in force inside the town. Exchanging fire with some Union cavalry late in the day the Confederates removed south of town by 10:00 o'clock the next day and McNeil moved to pursue.

By now Brig. Gen. William Vandever had reinforced McNeil on April 30th and was in close proximity of Marmaduke's Confederates as Marmaduke came to Arkansas at Chalk Bluff above the St. Francis River. With Vandever in overall command of the Union forces he soon deployed to try and bring the Confederates to bay. On May 1st Vandever came into contact with Marmaduke's rear guard and maintained constant contact all the way to the east side of the St. Francis River, "engag[ing] them in constant succession, they taking position after position for 20 miles. Night found me in position 2 miles from Chalk Bluff."[24] By this time Marmaduke had successfully extradited his forces across the swollen river and had made ready to engage the federals.

Brig. Gen. Marmaduke had not expected the well-executed federal pursuit, but was confident in his ability to counter it, setting up Shelby's Brigade. Colonel G.W. Thompson, commanding Shelby's Brigade, positioned his force on the flats before the river, gradually following the rest of the army as it made its way over the St. Francis River and setting up sharp shooters on the Bluff on the other side of the river. "Noon passed and the evening wore on to near its wane.... Soon however, the firing increased in the advanced of my center, and as it advanced became more constant and determined, until within about 300 yards of my lines, when it became severe and obstinate."[25] Having Captain Collin's Battery with him, Col. Thompson soon had his artillery pieces open on the advancing Yankees; soon the fire of dismounted troopers and Collin's artillery forced the federals to pause.

Col. Vandever was intent on closing with the Confederates and set out to that purpose. On May 2nd, with Brig. Gen. John McNeil commanding, the federal army moved on Chalk Bluff. "I advanced the artillery on the bluff-north side of river-the enemy having crossed ... and being posted on Chalk Bluff.... The enemy immediately opened with artillery and small arms."[26] Soon the 1st Nebraska and 37th Illinois parts of the 1st Wisconsin and 2nd Missouri State Militia became heavily engaged with the Confederates on the other side of the river, exchanging rifle fire for rifle fire and artillery firing into the trees on the bluff which was giving the Confederates cover. This action by Marmaduke stymied the Union pursuit but it came at a cost to the Confederates as they drove the Yankees out of rifle and cannon fire. Thompson and his Brigade soon moved off firing artillery from the bluff as his men began to withdraw. Brig. Gen. McNeil, the scourge of most Confederates, lamented that Marmaduke was "allowed to make a successful retreat."[27] This was probably a reference to the fact that Brig. Gen. Vandever was tardy earlier on in the pursuit.

Marmaduke had won a tactical victory at Chalk Bluff but it was also where he had suffered the most casualties. Though this did not help in the realization that Marmaduke failed to take Cape Girardeau and destroy McNeil's Command, it did not detour further action. These raids did divert some Union forces away from the buildup for attacks against Confederate forces in Arkansas and against the campaign against the Confederate stronghold at Vicksburg, Mississippi, something that would prove pivotal over the next year for both the North and the South. One fact was clearly understood: Missouri was becoming more vulnerable and Union authority in St. Louis was concerned.

4

Months of Discontent

The summer of 1863 was a series of setbacks for the armies of the Confederacy; Vicksburg fell in July despite attempts by Maj. Gen. Sterling Price to take pressure off with his attack on Helena, Arkansas, and the Army of Northern Virginia had retreated from Gettysburg in the east. Brig. Gen. Marmaduke's raid notwithstanding the theatre of action, on part of the Confederate command, centered on the lower Mississippi Valley; by June 1863 the last fortified Confederate bastion on the river at Vicksburg was being besieged. Union forces under the command of Maj. General Ulysses S. Grant had moved on the city from the eastern land approaches and had put the Confederate Army under Maj. Gen. Pemberton up against the Mississippi River. In an attempt to take the initiative General Holmes and Kirby Smith decided to take the Union forces in Helena.

If Vicksburg were to fall, what would be the Confederate fallback position on the strategic waterway? This question was asked "in mid–June an excerpt from a letter the (Confederate) Secretary of War had written ... after Pemberton was besieged, suggesting that he urge the Trans-Mississippi commanders to 'make diversions.'"[1] The town of Helena sits in the heart of the Delta of the Mississippi flood plain along a slight rise of hills on the west side of the river half way between Cape Girardeau and Vicksburg. Already in federal hands, it was also fortified with earthen forts on the west side of town very similar to what Cape Girardeau had, in overall command was Maj. Gen. Benjamin Prentiss of the District of East Arkansas. In Command of the Union forces in Helena, Arkansas, on June 2, 1863, was Frederick Salomon of Wisconsin. "He was educated to the profession of a civil engineer and architect and served for some time in the Prussian army, being a Lieutenant of artillery when he left Europe, in 1849... He immediately commenced, and completed in less than thirty days, a line of a line of fortifications around Helena."[2] Centered on Fort Curtis, these fortifications and rifle pits where built in a semi-circular pattern and were designated north to south batteries A, B, C and D.

With over 7,600 troops at his disposal Maj. Gen. Sterling Price made his way from Little Rock, Arkansas, towards Helena. Theophilus Holmes had assigned Price to command a Brigade along with the Brigades of Col. Fagan, Walker and Brig. Gen. Marmaduke. This force arrived before Helena on and around July 3rd. Held up by bad roads made worse by incessant rainstorms, the element of surprise was long lost. Coupling this predicament was the fact that Holmes's army did not have any supporting artillery. Marmaduke in April had brought artillery when he tried to invest Cape Girardeau, but his was not the case this go around.

The 28th Wisconsin was supporting Battery B on the morning of July 4th when through the early morning haze "they saw the enemy covering the surrounding hills."[3] Generals Holmes and Price were still confident that they could still reduce the Union force at Helena, even in their earthen redoubts and set about positioning their forces. Price's men would assault Battery C and Fagan would support in attacking toward Battery D. For Marmaduke his and Walker's assignment was to take Batteries A and B and their assault was slow in developing. Maj. Gen. Sterling Price sent his troops forward, driving the pickets of Company G 28th Wisconsin back towards Battery C. Soon the federals found that the fire of the guns had not blunted the onrushing Confederates. Removing the primers of the big guns in the battery the federals withdrew towards the earthen walls of Fort Curtis.

The Confederates had taken the enemy redoubt and were jubilant, but the celebration was short lived as now the guns of Fort Curtis and to the consternation of the Confederates the Union Navy had the gunboat USS *Tyler* at anchor in the Mississippi River with its 8-inch guns trained on the approaches to the batteries. Battery C was placed on the ominously named Graveyard Hill and it would soon live up to its name as the *Tyler* opened up with half fuses that exploded overhead on Confederate forces on Hindman and Graveyard Hills. "So demoralized were the attackers by the sudden deluge of heavy-caliber projectiles that, according to one blue officer, two groups of about 250 men each responded 'hoisting a white flag.'"[4] The Confederate command had not taken into consideration the Union Naval Force and it cost them, denting their attack on Helena.

From the early morning attack that started around 5:00 a.m., lasting to just past 10:00 a.m., the Confederates worked to make their way into and through the enemy. On Price's right flank Fagan's Brigade made its way on to Hindman Hill not far from his former home only to be stymied by the persistent cannon and rifle fire. Sent there by Maj. Gen. Holmes in support of Price, Holmes reinforced Fagan in hopes of breaking the enemy lines. The support of Fagan's assault on Battery D was cut down as the troops made their way up the rise to the battery[5]; it was a fruitless assault and the casualties now mounted. For Marmaduke and Walker disagreement on their assault only added to the fact that with no artillery support their assault from the very beginning was flawed as they tried to dislodge the 4th Kansas Infantry. By early afternoon Holmes and Price broke off the attack after losing nearly 1,500 in dead and captured, mostly at Battery C and D. For Theophilus Holmes, this repulse at Helena coupled with the fall of Vicksburg on July 3rd, would end his command and leave the road to Little Rock, central to Confederate control, open to Union designs.

Joseph O. Shelby hailed from Waverly, Missouri, where he had operated a plantation and hemp business building ropes along the banks of the Missouri River. Shelby proved to be one of those unique individuals, rare in history, who had no military training but a natural ability to adapt to it. In many ways he could be ranked with Nathan Bedford Forrest and John Singleton Mosby as one of the premier cavalry commanders that served in America's Civil War. Union cavalry commander Alfred Pleasonton, who had served in both eastern and western theatres and against J.E.B. Stuart, had this to say of Shelby when he came up against him during Price's Missouri Campaign: "Shelby was the best cavalry general of the South."[6] Still a colonel at the time of the attempt to take Helena, Shelby would be the answer to counter Union advances in Arkansas.

Lt. Gen. Kirby Smith decided to change the command in Arkansas and relieved Theophilus Holmes and replaced him in his command with Maj. Gen. Sterling Price, in late July 1863. By then the Union forces under Maj. Gen. Steele's advance upon Little Rock had forced Price to evacuate the city, concerned that he was outnumbered 2 to 1. In reality the forces were almost equal but Price failed to counter with Marmaduke's cavalry and surrendered the river crossings, giving Price the fear of being bottled up like Pemberton at Vicksburg. Moving further into Arkansas, Maj. Gen. Sterling Price was looking for opportunities to mitigate the fortunes of the Southern forces in the Trans-Mississippi and to take some pressure off of Confederate forces there and hopefully in Tennessee. One of these options would be presented by Shelby himself. The seed for Confederate action was planted back in April 1862 at Little Rock when the Confederates planned for future action. "Smith conferred with Holmes (now dismissed) Thomas C. Reynolds, Confederate Governor of Missouri, and Missouri political general Sterling Price. A paramount topic of discussion was the recapture of Arkansas and the conquest of Missouri. Smith approved in principle a plan to secure Arkansas as an invasion route to Missouri. Pursuit of this objective served as both a political payback to the Arkansans and Missourians,"[7] but events modified the plans and Little Rock as a stage for action was now gone.

4. Months of Discontent

In September 1863 events presented opportunity for the Confederate Trans-Mississippi west for action against Union-occupied Missouri. In the western theatre William S. Rosecrans's Army of the Cumberland was stymied by the combined forces of the Army of Tennessee under Braxton Bragg and the First Corps of the Army of Northern Virginia under James Longstreet. At Chickamauga Maj. Gen. Rosecrans was forced to retreat back into Chattanooga Tennessee. Under siege Rosecrans desperately telegraphed Washington, D.C.: "We have no certainty of holding our position here." This was of grave concern to Lincoln.[8]

Seeing an opportunity to reduce the pressure on his forces in Arkansas and putting more pressure on the Union armies in Missouri, Price was, in an indirect way, keeping more pressure on Union armies in Tennessee. Price met with Jo Shelby and the decision was made to unleash his cavalry against Union forces soon after Chattanooga, Tennessee, was besieged. "From Arkadelphia, where he ended his retreat in mid–September, Price launched Shelby on a raid into his home state, hoping thus to discourage Schofield from reinforcing Fred Steele for a follow-up push from the Arkansas River to the Quachita."[9] In late September 1863 Shelby put his columns in motion and headed toward southwest Missouri "with 600 troopers, a section of light artillery, and 12 ammunition wagons."[10] It was a bold move with hopeful expectations.

Joseph "Jo" Shelby was a self-made man in business who shined as a soldier, officer and strategic tactician. He would ride into battle with a black plume in his hat so all his men could see he was with them; Shelby was basically in command of the Army of Missouri from Westport on. Afterward, he became a key figure in helping heal the wounds of the Civil War (courtesy Wilson's Creek National Battlefield; WICR 31493).

The weather in the area of southwest Missouri was pleasant and dry by late September and early October. Most importantly the roads were hard and dry so Shelby, with his almost 700 troopers, could move swiftly in their entrance to Missouri at Neosho on October 4th. The common practice of the

Union forces in the small towns and county seats was to make their force concentration on the County Courthouse usually in the center of the town. Once confronted with force the federal forces would fall back on the fortified building and make like a fort defense within the walls of the building, simply because it was usually the best built. Unlike the previous incursion of Marmaduke in April and even at the attempt to take Helena, Arkansas, under Holmes and Price, Col. Jo Shelby brought artillery with his cavalry.

This one element was a key factor for Shelby's success as he now engaged the small Union force holed up in these buildings. Firing on the courthouse building, with his artillery, the advantage that the Union forces believed they had was soon extirpated and the Union troops surrendered after a brief fight. Paroling most of the federal troops and confiscating the Union supply depot of needed weapons, Shelby now saw his way open to move north toward the Missouri River and possibly even head to the State Capital at Jefferson City to raise the Confederate flag. The exploit of Shelby's advance soon spread around the area as the Confederates burned courthouses, cut telephone lines and sent panic among Union authorities throughout the counties in southern and southwest Missouri.

With a black feathered plume in his hat, so he could be easily recognized by his troops, Colonel Joseph Shelby earnestly made his way towards the Union-controlled town of Greenfield and set about burning the fortified courthouse after capturing the small garrison. The same was done to Stockton and Humansville where Shelby briefly skirmished with the Union defenders before they surrendered. At each opportunity, particularly at Greenfield, Shelby looted the Union depots and commissary stores, where his men could equip themselves with shoes, uniforms and weapons. Ironically by his men dressing and mixing uniforms they at times appeared as Union soldiers. If it was not for the butternut shirts and patched grey pants, Shelby's men appeared as a Union cavalry unit. To counter the confusion Col. Shelby had his men put red sprigs of vegetation in their hats to distinguish them from the Yankees.

By the time the Confederates reached Tipton, Missouri, where he tore up Pacific Railroad tracks, Shelby was forty some miles from Jefferson City and his ranks had now swelled to over a thousand men. Shelby's success was now starting to catch up with him. Shelby had to decide to move on the Missouri Capital or to continue his raid to the Missouri River near Arrow Rock. Reports came in to Shelby that convinced him that his force was too small to take the capital and confirmed that the federals knew of his whereabouts and were now planning to catch up with him. Col. Shelby believed that despite the awareness of his force by the enemy he could deal effectively with them. Shelby never shied from a fight.

There was just a tinge of color in the trees along the Missouri River when Col. Shelby's Cavalry Brigade reached Boonville, Missouri. It was still fair weather for military campaigning and Union forces under the command of Brig. Gen. Egbert Brown were moving swiftly toward the river town hoping to corral the clever Confederate colonel. Elements of Shelby's forces came into contact with Brown's Union force just outside Boonville. Shelby, after assuring the Boonville citizens that he would not treat the town as he did other towns on the way, immediately made his way west along the Missouri. Making for Arrow Rock, on the Santa Fe Trail, three Union Cavalry Columns converged on Shelby and his force just east of Marshall Missouri at the road crossing over the Salt Fork.

On October 13, 1863, Union military forces finally caught up with Jo Shelby. Shelby had jettisoned his wagons and munition train, having his men load up with what was left, and was travelling light knowing full well he would probably have to cut a path through the enemy. For Brig. Gen. Brown he believed the converging forces could surround Shelby and kill or capture his force; Brown had about 1,800 troopers at his disposal and Shelby's ranks had grown to about 1,300. Coming in from the east, west and north the Yankee columns spread out to envelope Shelby's force along the Salt Fork. Shelby would have none of it. Instead of deploying his troops, Shelby put his troopers in column in order to punch a hole in what he thought would be the weakest spot in the Union Force.

Plunging headlong into what would turn out to be Union Missouri Troopers, Shelby, with his plume in full view and at the head of his column of men, broke through the Union cordon taking many of the federals by surprise at his unconventional attack. The federals made a counter charge and struck near the back of Shelby's column splitting it in two. The idea Shelby had was that he could concentrate his firepower en-masse from the column of troopers firing from all sides as they shocked one portion of the enemy's line. It worked in the fact that Shelby did indeed escape his pursuers even though he lost his artillery.

With his force now divided, Shelby made his way south to the town of Carthage near the Arkansas border. On the 19th and 20th of October Shelby briefly contended with Union General Thomas Ewing, the originator of the infamous Special Order No. 11, and slipped his pursuers once again. By early November he reached Washington, Arkansas, having caused approximately a million dollars in damage to the Union authorities. "I have arrived safely with my entire command.... I have fought five battles had daily skirmishes; traveled 1,500 miles."[11] Shelby also goes on to say that the pro–Southern population of Missouri required a "strong presence of a Confederate army to make them volunteer."[12] The Confederates were also pleased that Shelby had also tied down Union forces from being sent from Missouri to help relieve the siege of Chattanooga, Tennessee.

About the same time Colonel Joseph O. Shelby was moving north near Neosho, Missouri, another less conventional war-fighter was making his way south for targets of opportunity. William Quantrill was truly a northern antagonist with a dislike for anything federal or pro–Union. Coming off his raid into Kansas and the burning of the town of Lawrence, he now set his 300 men on a route that would bring them to the federal military post at Fort Blair. Moving southwest across the Missouri-Kansas border toward Indian lands, Quantrill decided that the fort had to be reduced.

Fort Blair was strategically located on the old military road. The road was constructed in the late 1830s into the 1840s to connect the major posts of Fort Leavenworth, on the Missouri River, and the established post at Fort Scott with Fort Gibson in Oklahoma Indian lands. It would expedite the movement of troops and military supplies to these posts and facilitate travel to Arkansas, particularly Fort Smith and points in Texas and Oklahoma. The prize was just too tempting for Quantrill and his band to pass up and Quantrill believed he had the element of surprise. When the motley force came upon a couple of soldiers out taking rifle practice and then immediately dispatching them they probably did not realize where they came from, but when a teamster was encountered on the military road they knew what was up ahead and deployed to the fort's outskirts.

In charge of the post was Lt. James Pond of the 3rd Wisconsin Cavalry. Pond was in charge of part of the 3rd Wisconsin, the rest under detail to Maj. Gen. Blunt coming down from Fort Scott. The rest of Ft. Blair was garrisoned by the 2nd Kansas Colored Infantry. The fort was approximately 100 feet wide and 200 feet in length, constructed of logs three to four feet high. Within the breastworks, firing pits were dug and the dirt cast over the sides to form an embankment outside the walls. Within the compound, a small wooden blockhouse was centrally located. Pond was not overly impressed with the size of the fort and thought it was vulnerable to attack—he was soon proved correct.

It was a clear sunny day when at about noon time, with the predominantly black soldiers who had stacked arms preparing to eat lunch, a sharp and crisp rifle fire emanated from the woods north and west of the fort. Springing to action the infantry soldiers took to their arms to man the rifle pits and the four-foot-high inner walls. A sharp exchange of musketry was joined as the combatants bore down on one another. Quantrill was confident of prevailing until Lt. Pond, who had never really manned an artillery piece, took control of firing a 12-pounder. Howitzer in the direction of the woods and prairie where the Confederates were concentrated. At about the time the artillery was giving the rouge band second thoughts of their endeavor news came to Quantrill that a column of blue coats and wagons were now approaching on the military road just 500 yards or so away.

Major General James B. Blunt was entirely unaware of what was happening up the road at Ft. Blair. Possibly this was due to the unusual phenomenon called acoustic shadow or the escort party was simply too lax to think that any enemy was nearby. Quantrill, now aware of the wagons, broke off his attempt on Ft. Blair. Moving out on open ground some distance from the head of the Yankee column, dressed in a motley array of blue uniforms, the unsuspecting Blunt sent a rider forward, believing that the post had sent out an escort guard for the general. Quantrill deployed his cavalry in position, straddling the military road. When the outrider realized that it was a hostile band of rebels, he immediately reined in his horse and galloped back toward the wagons.

It was too late for the train as the Confederates came at a trot and then broke into a gallop to the surprise of the federals. The 14th Kansas Cavalry, providing escort, immediately bolted and fled. The 3rd Wisconsin Cavalry, the companies detached from those at the fort and much better disciplined, manned a brave but brief defense. Quickly, the entire train was overrun by the screaming and rabid action of Quantrill's command. "The whole rebel line advanced with a shout, at which the remainder of Company A (14th Kansas) broke, and could not be rallied. In the meantime a full volley was fired by Company I, Third Wisconsin."[13] It was a rout and it soon turned into every man and every woman for themselves. Blunt managed to escape along with the young woman who abandoned her carriage and made off on a horse surrounded by screaming Confederates as the federals were gunned down in all directions.

There was no quarter here on the prairie and the Union lost some 90 soldiers, the Confederates barely a dozen. Quantrill broke off his idea of reducing Ft. Blair and moved on south toward Texas. He sent off a report to Maj. Gen. Sterling Price, the only official report he would ever write, and was highly amused with himself in the fact that he had bested Blunt where Marmaduke and Shelby could not. Lt. James Pond praised the action of the colored troops of the 2nd Kansas Infantry at Ft. Blair. He believed that their marksmanship kept the enemy at bay, not allowing them to creep up to the fort's walls. As for Pond his presence of mind and authority, particularly manning the cannon and directing his meager force won for him the Nation's highest military award: the Congressional Medal of Honor. For Maj. Gen. Blunt he lost his command of the western district out of Ft. Smith, where he was headed, and pretty much out of favor with the Union Command.

5

Arcadia Valley Confluence

The rewards of Shelby's expedition were arguably a mixed bag. For someone like the young Lizzie Brannock the war took another turn for the worst for her brother-in-law and husband, who were both captured at the Battle of Marshall while serving in Shelby's cavalry. As Lizzie relates, "my husband and his brother Thomas came in with Shelby ... he thought that he would get to see us once more but at Marshal Bro Thomas was wounded in the left cheek ... and my husband would not leave him so they were both taken prisoner ... they are now in St. Louis Gratiot Street Prison Mc Dowel College and in good health and tolerable spirits."[1] Lizzie Brannock is one of the many examples of what was happening to families all across the land and her frustrations were shared by the Confederate Commanders Theophilus Holmes and Sterling Price. As successful as Shelby had been in tying down some Union forces, his raid had done little to stem the tide of fortunes in the Trans-Mississippi West.

Losing territory in Arkansas, the Confederates had fallen back. Control of this state now consisted of the southwest area and portions of the Boston Mountains in the north. Price's command consisted of little more than about 7,000 men and the region commander Edmund Kirby Smith had to deal with a Union advance up the Red River towards Sabine Crossroads and the Western Confederate Capital at Shreveport, Louisiana. It is probable that Maj. Gen. Sterling Price and the exiled Confederate Governor of Missouri had the ear of the Trans-Mississippi West Commander Edmund Kirby Smith, who still believed that the objective of the Confederate forces was to still acquire Missouri. This attitude set up a contentious relationship with Maj. Gen. Richard Taylor, who believed that General Smith needed to concentrate Confederate forces in Louisiana and deal a major blow to Union forces under Nathaniel Banks. The focus of action should be in the bayou and along the Red River in Louisiana.

Richard Taylor was the erudite son of General Zachary Taylor, hero of the Mexican war and short-lived President of the United States. Taylor had served under Jackson and Ewell in the Valley Campaign of 1862. Now he was in command of the Confederate forces in South Louisiana and his biggest concern was the seeming indifference that Lt. Gen. Smith had for the defense of the area of his responsibility. When Smith met with the Missourians, before the fall of Little Rock, Arkansas, "Smith approved in principle a plan to secure Arkansas as an invasion route to Missouri."[2] This did not play well with Taylor and when Smith failed to reinforce his command when Major General Nathanial Banks began to move up the Red River toward Shreveport, Taylor did not hesitate. Highly outnumbered, Taylor's army surprised Banks near Mansfield, Louisiana, at a place called Sabine Crossroads, a stretch of land between the Red and Sabine Rivers, and routed his force, sending Banks reeling back down the waterway.

Banks's push up the Red was supposed to coincide with the Union force of Maj. Gen. Steele's thrust out of Little Rock to hopefully squeeze Price and his force between his and Banks ascending force coming up from Shreveport. Taylor put an end to that and had won a resounding victory in spite of Kirby Smith's reticence and his slow support of Taylor. Now it was Price's opportunity to change the tables on Steele. Price's force was now made up by mostly Cavalry units but he had the services of two very well qualified commanders in John S. Marmaduke and Joseph O. Shelby. Although Price had a little more than 5,000 troops, his opponent General Steele did not realize that he had superiority over the Confederates when he launched his Camden Expedition from Little Rock in March 1864.

Launching an offensive in the spring presented Steele some unanticipated difficulties. Moving from rain to dry weather the roads soon became problematic, not to mention that crossing rivers like the Saline and Little Missouri slowed Steele's columns. With Brig. Gen. Jo Shelby's cavalry nipping at his flanks and rear Steele tentatively made his way to the Little Missouri River by the 3rd of April. Paralleling that river, he made his way down toward Camden, skirmishing with Maj. Gen. Sterling Price's forces at Prairie D'Ane before arriving at Camden. It was here that Steele finally decided that the effort to reach Banks, down on the Red, was not going to succeed. "Steels was down to roughly the same number as Smith, having suffered 2000 casualties in the past month."[3] Now he had had enough and made for Little Rock, fending off Kirby Smith and Price at Elkins Ferry, eking out a Pyrrhic victory.

The failure of the Union Campaigns of the Red River and Camden buoyed the spirits of the Confederate authority in the Trans-Mississippi West and talk began again of the possibility of striking at Missouri. In January 1864 there took place a change in command in St. Louis and Maj. Gen. Schofield was replaced with Maj. Gen William S. Rosecrans. Rosecrans's reassignment came on the heels of his removal at Chattanooga, Tennessee, when U.S. Grant was assigned to reverse Union fortunes then under siege.

Grant believed that to defeat the confederacy the concentrated effort needed to be in Tennessee, Georgia and the Atlantic Theatre in Virginia. He gave little thought to the problems across the Mississippi and the command there was pretty much on their own as to how to deal with any contingency that might occur. Grant believed that events in the Trans-Mississippi were secondary. Grant goes on to say that it was necessary to do this because of the presence of Nathan Bedford Forrest and his operations against him in Mississippi and Tennessee: "Forrest, a brave and intrepid cavalry general, was in the west with a large force; making a larger command necessary to hold what we had gained."[4] This played well into the hands of Lt. Gen. Edmund Kirby Smith, who now saw opportunity to try and reverse Confederate fortunes as Union officials tackled Confederate operations east of the Mississippi.

St. Louis, Missouri, was a very wealthy city in 1864. From the exclusive and spacious antebellum homes of Lucas Place to the fine hotels that were near the levee, the commerce of the city never missed a beat during the war. In fact more money was being made and the well to do citizens both pro-North or pro-South were benefitting. The city buzzed with activity made even more hectic with the presence of the Union military which had its military headquarters in the middle of downtown. As he made his way out of Army Headquarter at Locust and 10th after handing over the command of the area to William S. Rosecrans, John Schofield was relieved that he no long had to deal with the uppity behavior of the prominent St. Louis citizens, of which many resented the occupation of their city by the federal forces.

Ironically those same citizens who so resented the government where also making a profit from those very entities they would look down upon. It was a source of frustration to Union authority that those pro-South sentiments held by so many prominent citizens were financially benefiting. "The calamity under which the State was suffering had been brought upon her by the influence of prominent and wealthy persons, thousands of whom were living in the state, and even in the city of St Louis, enjoying the protection of the Government, and many of them growing rich upon their country's calamity. These persons even yet did not hesitate to talk and act treason whenever they could do so with impunity. They even persuaded young men to join the bands of outlaws … and furnished them with arms and money."[5] In this report Maj. Gen. Schofield would provide an unwelcomed solution.

In Schofield's undated report in late 1862, probably written sometime in January 1863, he vented on the citizenry of St. Louis and proposed a tax on the prominent and most wealthy residents. Schofield reported, "For these reasons, after consultation with the governor of Missouri, 1 determined to assess and collect from the rebels of St. Louis County the sum of $500,000, to be used in arming, clothing, and subsisting the enrolled militia when in active service and in providing for those families of militiamen and volunteers which might be left destitute."[6] Schofield was alarmed at the way many St. Louisans avoided serving in the Union Army by using substitutions from those who could not afford otherwise.

> Many reputed loyal men, but more mindful of their comforts than of the salvation of their country, would willingly pay a high fee, which the really loyal poor man could not, and thus throw upon the shoulders of his poor neighbor the burdens, of which the latter was willing to bear his share but not the whole. Finally it was determined to take the high ground that none but those of approved loyalty should be required or permitted to bear arms in defense of the State. I have had no reason since to doubt the correctness of the principle thus established, or the wisdom of the policy pursued under it.[7]

In a letter to President Lincoln, dated October 20, 1863, Maj. Gen. Schofield explained the role of the enrolled Militia and the need for it by his actions as commander of the St. Louis District. He explained its importance and the continuing need for it. "The services of the Enrolled Militia have been of great value, not only during the summer of 1862, when they were first organized, but also during the present year."[8] When Maj. Gen. William S. Rosecrans took command in January 1864 he assumed command of all Union forces in Missouri and all enrolled Militia in keeping with Schofield's request and Lincoln's concurrence with his wishes. The Missouri Enrolled Militia would continue to be an important element in facing any possible Confederate actions.

In Arkansas the reverses of fortune in the Camden Campaign gave impetus for renewed action of Confederate forces under Lt. Gen. Edmund Kirby Smith. With Arkansas occupied in places by Union forces it was simply a question of what form would an attack north into Missouri would take. By summer 1864 Jo Shelby began to operate in the Boston Mountain area. It was beginning to be excepted that cavalry operations, by the Confederates, was a more effective form of warfare and offered better flexibility in order to meet Union threats. The successes of Confederate cavalry against Union forces, in occupied Confederate territory, were apparent in the operations of commanders such as Nathan Bedford Forrest, in Tennessee, John Singleton Mosby, in Virginia, and increasingly Joseph O. Shelby, in Missouri and Arkansas. The continuing problems of Union commanders like Schofield and now Rosecrans, in St. Louis, was preventing pro-Southern populace in acting against, what they probably considered Union occupation. Encouraged by the successes in Louisiana and Arkansas and the possibilities in Missouri, the Trans-Mississippi Department looked once again for action in Missouri.

By 1864 military operations by U.S. Grant and William T. Sherman were beginning to stare the Confederacy in the face. Those Union armies in Virginia and Georgia were driving into the heart of Dixie towards Atlanta and Richmond. With the Western Theatre of the Trans-Mississippi considered by the Union Command as secondary in importance to the main theatre, Lt. Gen. Edmund Kirby Smith and Maj. Gen. Sterling Price could now act on what both had wanted to do since the beginning of the year. The genesis of the Missouri campaign was percolating since April of 1863, when Smith met with Theophilus Holmes, then commanding the Arkansas district, Missouri Governor in exile Thomas C. Reynolds and Missouri Maj. Gen. Sterling Price. "A paramount topic of discussion was the recapture of Arkansas and the conquest of Missouri."[9] More than a year later this thinking had not changed; in fact it had only grown larger and was soon to become an actionable plan.

The stage was now set for a Confederate offensive unlike those fought in Tennessee, Georgia and Virginia. From the time the Union forces were turned back on the Red River in Louisiana and retreated back to Little Rock, thoughts now came to fruition as to a campaign in the Trans-Mississippi West, but not until late summer of 1864. Limited in arms, materials and troops, Lt. Gen. Edmund Kirby Smith rose to action in August. The pressure on the large Confederate armies in the east prompted, with a little nudge from Richmond, the need for action and the hope that action would slow the movement of Union forces east; Smith counseled with Price. Actually it was Price who offered up the idea of a move into Missouri and his plan was unorthodox; since there were a lack of infantry and infantry units for use in the theater, it would be done with a large force of cavalry.

In the American Civil War the use of dismounted cavalry, particularly by the Confederates, became the point of the spear for operations in Tennessee, Virginia and specifically in Missouri. The ability of cavalry units to get in behind enemy lines to disrupt communications, destroy telegraph and railroad lines and to loot military stores confounded Union authority and tied down Union infantry units to deter such actions. This was the design of Maj. Gen. Sterling's Price's operation in August 1864. This was not all in his instructions from Smith: "You will make immediate arrangements for a movement into Missouri, with the entire cavalry of your district ... and impress upon them that their aim should be to secure success in a just and holy cause."[10] Kirby Smith also went on to point out that the troops should not act in a vengeful manner, but this was more of a guideline and not so much an order.

Price believed that he would be coming up against a strong federal force, being that he had very little intelligence to tell him otherwise and that this misinformation would lead to some operational mistakes. In fact the authorities in St. Louis didn't have any idea. Indeed St. Louis had very little defenses or preparations for actions by the Confederates against the city. Basically the Department of Missouri concentrated on establishing the Enrolled Militia and the Provisionally Enrolled Militia. The federal forces in and around the city were considered adequate to prevent any serious threat. This thinking, however, was beginning to lose weight as further incursion by Confederate forces continued vis-à-vis the raids of the previous year.

When Maj. Gen. William S. Rosecrans took command of the Missouri Military District, replacing Maj. Gen. Schofield, he found that the Enrolled Missouri Militia was well established. "The services of the Enrolled Militia have been of great value, not only during the summer of 1862, when they were first organized, but also during the present year. The ten Provisional Regiments which the governor organized for continuous service, and placed under my command, enabled me to relieve an equal force of United States troops and send them to General Grant."[11] By early 1864 Rosecrans was concerned that the troops now transiting by St. Louis to the Eastern Theatre may well be needed there to counter any Confederate operation.

In July Maj. Gen. Rosecrans deemed it necessary to ask for troops and in a series of letters to Secretary Stanton, in Washington, D.C., that "authority be given." Stanton readily agreed and Rosecrans started action to build "a force of Missouri volunteers for the defense of the State."[12] What Rosecrans soon realized was that he needed a force for St. Louis as well. In the spring of 1864 Rosecrans was informed that an invasion of the state was imminent in a report he expressed his concern "it is known through the lodges ... and other rebel sources that Price intended a great invasion of this State."[13] What soon materialized in September was one of the largest Cavalry forces ever assembled moving to the Missouri border.

The only force that could prevent Sterling Price from concentrating his army was Maj. Gen. Frederick Steele's Army of Arkansas. Steele believed that Price was actually going to operate against his command and did not think it was possible for him and an army to operate in Missouri; "it is my opinion that he intended to join Shelby, who has about 5,000 armed, and operate on my communications.... I cannot understand how they can subsist on the march to Missouri."[14] Steele had underestimated the confederate's resolve and missed all the signals. Brig. Gen. Shelby had already been operating in the Boston Mountains and had prepared the way for Price and his Army of Missouri to meet at Pocahontas, Arkansas, on September 17th to formalize his command and designate his Lieutenants.

By September 1st Maj. Gen. Rosecrans was scrambling to sound the alarm and request forces from the Federal Government in Washington to divert Union troops to aid in his defense of the Military district there, particularly St. Louis. On the 3rd of September, Rosecrans requested the XVI Corps for deployment in Missouri. On its way to reinforce Sherman's Army approaching Atlanta, the XVI Corps had already passed St. Louis and was near Cairo, Illinois, when word reached XVI Corps Commander Maj. Gen. A. J. Smith to take transport and move back up the Mississippi River to St. Louis. The request was interesting considering that Rosecrans really believed the area was defensible—why was there a need for an Army Corps to be diverted for its defense? The fact that the city did have the Arsenal, Benton Barracks and gun emplacements that ringed the city, did not calm Rosecrans's fears; the reality, for Rosecrans, must have been that the fortifications were not enough with their limited garrisons and that his concerns were that the approaches to the city, outside the ring, must have been lacking.

With the focus on having the Enrolled Militias and the Provisional Enrolled Militia the actions by Maj. Gen. John Schofield were more of a concentration against the pro–South guerrilla activity than the concern of a major Con-

Commanding the XVI Corps, A. J. Smith and his command was slated to be sent to Georgia and Sherman's Command, but instead the Corps was redirected to St. Louis as concerns of Price's intentions grew. The unit was instrumental in blocking Cabell's command at Franklin and then in the pursuit of Price's Army (Library of Congress).

federate military operation against the state let alone St. Louis. Now the realization was that a series of actions had to be taken to prepare the city for confronting an unsuspected enemy. Therefore in pursuant to General Order No. 176 DEPARTMENT OF THE MISSOURI, 1864, General Rosecrans issued an address to Missourians. In it he said, "invited citizens not in the Enrolled Militia to join the militia organizations called out in their localities, or report to the nearest United States commander for such duty as they could perform during the continuance of the 'raid.'"[15] Rosecrans did not stop there.

For the defense of the City of St. Louis he used the power of Military Law and suspended business activity in the city; "he directed a partial suspension of business in the city of St. Louis to facilitate the work of organization for local defense, St. Louis, Mo., September 26, 1864... Such business as is necessary to supply the daily wants of the people—public administration, banking and printing offices, manufactories which cannot be stopped without great damage—are exempt from the operations of this order."[16] For the city Rosecrans came up with what was called Military Exempts and had these citizens put under the military command of Colonel B. Gratz Brown. By September 29th the process of organizing and arming the Exempt Force had reached a point that General Rosecrans justified the general resumption of business. Rosecrans may have thought better had he known just how close the Confederates came.

It was a day of anticipation as the newly minted Army of Missouri moved out. It was Price's intention to move over the state line and move his army of about 12,000 in a three-prong movement heading toward Fredericktown and the St. Francois Mountains. Not unlike Stonewall Jackson and his valley campaign in Virginia, in 1862, Price and his Generals would use the mountain terrain as a means to shield his movement and keep the federals off balance. The Army consisted of these three divisions: Maj. Gen. James Fagan with four brigades, including the brigade of the battle-hardened William Cabell, Maj. Gen. John Marmaduke with two brigades, one of which was a veteran brigade under Brig. Gen. John B. Clark, and the experienced Brig. Gen. Joseph Shelby with his "Iron Brigade" heading up the third Division.

Ironically the District Commander in St. Louis, William Rosecrans, was unsure of the whereabouts of the Confederates. Rosecrans already knew the enemy was on his way, but he was not sure just where. He described his dilemma this way, when he learned that Price was at Batesville: "From this point midway between the Mississippi and the western boundary of the state there are three practicable routes of invasion. One by Pocahontas into the southeast ... another by West Plains and Rolla ... a third by Cassville north through Springfield and Sedalia."[17] It is revealing that the thoughts of the

Union command of the possible routes of invasion were influenced by the previous raids in 1862 and 1863 and this influenced just where to concentrate federal forces which were spread fairly thin.

The Arcadia Valley lies within the confines of the St. Francois Mountains and the Ozark Plateau. Rough and somewhat isolated, the district was the focus of the Iron Mountain Railroad which had its terminus located at the Iron Mines at Pilot Knob. Situated in the valley, with Shepherd Mountain to the southwest, Pilot Knob to the east and Cedar Mountain to the north, was the Federal earthen hexagon Fort Davidson. Armed with 32 pdr siege guns and 24 pdr howitzers, the fort was exposed in the plain by the heights of land; "all parts of the hill-sides toward the fort, except the west end of Shepherd's Mountain are in musket range. The fort was always conceded to be indefensible against any large army having serviceable artillery."[18] Under the command of Major James Wilson, 3rd Missouri State Militia Cavalry, the fort had only a small force of about 300 troops. The Iron works, the railroad and the supplies at the garrison became an attractive target for Price.

Before the expedition, Wilson and the Missouri Cavalry had been trying to enforce Union control in the area south of the valley and had earned the enmity of many pro–South families in the area. One in particular saw Wilson as his own personal enemy and would seek him out when Price's army came up. Tim Reves was an active partisan in the area and was unapologetic for his action vis-à-vis targeting pro–Union types. The lack of any kind of authority and suspension of most people's rights in the areas along the border only increased

Born in Prince George's County, Maryland, on May 3, 1834, Maj. James Wilson entered the Union Army on May 11, 1861, and was promoted to the rank of major on May 5, 1862. There is a belief that he ran into conflict with pro-Southern citizens in southeast Missouri, one of which finally caught up with him outside Union, Missouri. Captured at Pilot Knob, Wilson was taken as prisoner; his death triggered a retribution signed off on by Rosecrans and Lincoln (www.findagrave.com).

the tension just as it did along the Burnt district in western Missouri. When Confederate commander William Cabell's Brigade reached this area he testified to its volatile state of affairs: "The woods were full of bushwhackers ... burning houses and destroying the property of all southern sympathizers.... It was truly a sad sight to see those noble women, both old and young, looking on the destruction of their homes.... The mounted militia were soon stopped in their cruelty to these good people."[19] Cabell goes on to say that when he cornered two-thirds of these "cruel monsters" they were killed.

Now aware of Price's whereabouts even at the surprise of the Fort Davidson commander, Rosecrans acted to intercept Price's Army of Missouri. Rosecrans still concentrated his forces at Rolla and Sedalia, but he sent A. J. Smith and some of his XVI Corps; "General Ewing was ordered to concentrate the troops in the southern part of his district at Pilot Knob.... On the 26th General A. J. Smith, with two of his, was ordered to a point on the Iron Mountain Railroad."[20] That point would be in Desoto, Missouri, located on the rail line, making it a place where Smith could move against Price or retreat back to St. Louis, if need be. Brig. Gen. Ewing moved on from there and now took command of the garrison at Fort Davidson and prepared for a possible engagement with the Confederates.

From the beginning of the movement of Price's Army initially made good time. Brig. Gen. Shelby was in Patterson and Maj. Gen. Marmaduke was in Fredericktown by the 25th all moving up from Poplar Bluff. When Rosecrans was informed of the advance on Fredericktown he realized Price's intention. Ewing now had a force of over 1,500 men at hand. Brig. Gen. Shelby with his division was out and gathering information on Union strength in the area. He informed Price of the strength of Union forces at Pilot Knob and suggested against attacking into the Arcadia Valley. Maj. Gen. Fagan believed that the Fort could be taken and counseled attacking it to gain its stores and munitions. Price's last great victory was attacking a fortified federal position at Lexington, Missouri. Price agreed with the attack and moved Fagan's and Maj. Gen. Marmaduke's forces toward Shut In Gap and the Arcadia Valley.

Brig. Gen. Jo Shelby was tasked to move around the St. Francois Mountains and raid and then get behind federal forces and interdict the Iron Mountain Railroad. Shelby actually wanted the whole of Price's forces to move now against the federals in St. Louis. Shelby believed that the Union command was in a state of panic and that there was little in his way or in Price's way at that moment. What Shelby probably did not know was that Maj. Gen. A. J. Smith's Union troops were slowly arriving and concentrating near St. Louis. If Shelby did know this he also knew that the federals could be outflanked with speed and that he could get the whole Confederate force between St.

Louis and Smith's Corps before they could get between him and the city. To Jo Shelby's disappointment, Price and Fagan would have none of it.

By the time Brig. Gen. Ewing arrived at Pilot Knob, Major Wilson's command had grown to nearly 1,500 men, including some of the local citizens living in the valley. Included in this ad hoc command was the 47th Missouri Infantry regiment, which had been recently organized under the command of Colonel Thomas Fletcher a local county official from Hillsboro, Missouri. A mix of cavalry, infantry and artillerymen, it was this force which would have to confront the oncoming Confederates if they decided to enter the Arcadia Valley and take the post's stores and munitions. Ewing had no doubt of the enemy's intentions and had Major Wilson take a force to cover the approach to Shut In Gap. A defile in the mountains, Shut In Gap provides for a narrow passage between weathered metamorphic outcrops that cuts a path where Stout's Creek crosses the bedrock some five miles from Fort Davidson. If Wilson could arrive before the Confederates he could possibly position rifleman in the passage and slow the enemy advance.

On the morning of September 26th Price's Headquarters, with Fagan's and Marmaduke's Divisions leading, headed down the Fredericktown road toward Ironton. With a force that now totaled about 1,500 men and Brig. Gen. Ewing, a protégé of William T. Sherman and the author of the infamous Order No. 11, in command, Brig. Gen. Ewing decided to intercept the lead elements of the Confederate force. Knowing the enemy was somewhere near Fredericktown, Ewing decided to send Major Wilson to Shut In Gap. Major James Wilson was, at the time, in command of the sub-district there at Ironton and commanded the force at Fort Davidson before Brig. Gen. Ewing arrived. Wilson had been active in routing out so-called pro–South citizens and had run afoul of a number of families in the region, and had gained the enmity of Tim Reves, a considered active guerrilla, who would soon attach himself and his partisans when Price's Army of Missouri arrived.

With Maj. Gen. A. J. Smith setting up at Desoto on the Iron Mountain Railroad, with a minimal force of about two brigades, Ewing decided to make contact with Price's Army and delay him. "Major General Smith ... was kept fully advised by telegraph of my information, movements, and purposes, until 11 O'clock Tuesday forenoon, when the line went down."[21] The line went down because Brig. Gen. Jo Shelby and his brigades were moving toward Mineral Point from Farmington, which he occupied on September 5th, disrupting communications, cutting wires and tearing up rail track in the direction of Desoto, Missouri. This movement of getting in between Ewing and Smith made Ewing, in Pilot Knob, realize that Fort Davidson was a target.

In St. Louis Maj. Gen. Rosecrans was confronted with a series of problems that seemed to stretch his resources. Rosecrans wrote, "The safety of Saint Louis was vital to us" as the activity of roaming bands of partisans was continuing to distress local authorities. Rosecrans refers to such activity aggravated by the appearance of Price's forces. "Previous to and pending these events the guerrilla warfare in North Missouri had been raging with redoubled fury."[22] All forces were now on alert and military action was now imminent as Brig. Gen. Ewing peered over the earthen ramparts of Fort Davidson, straining to hear gunfire from between Shepherds and Pilot Knob Mountains. Shut In Gap was only about five miles from the fort and Major Wilson was deploying his troops as the sound of horses was heard nearing the Gap.

Moving in a trot the Confederate horsemen, the vanguard of Brig. Gen. Fagan's Division, arrived at Shut In Gap in the early morning hours of September 26th. Sitting astride the Fredericktown Road, just west of the Gap, was Wilson's troopers. Price's Army got to the gap before Wilson could occupy it. Heavily outnumbered, Wilson's force of 300 troopers could do little except fire a few wild shots at the enemy before making towards the rear in the direction of Arcadia. Moving swiftly, Major Wilson and his troopers would fall back at intervals, reign in their horses, and turn and fire at their pursuers, all the while the Confederates closing the distance. By the time Wilson reached Stouts Creek, his positon was threatened at being overrun.

By now Brig. Gen. Ewing heard the intense pistol and rifle fire coming from the gap between Shepherd Mountain and Pilot Knob. Acting quickly Ewing now ordered the 14th Iowa Infantry to move across the plain at the double quick and close with Wilson's Troopers to provide support for his beleaguered command. "Both commands met Price's advance in Arcadia Valley ... where with

One of the two West Point graduate's in Price's Army of Missouri, William Cabell, or "Old Tige" (Tiger), was an extremely capable Lieutenant who believed that the expedition was badly managed under "poor generalship." He looked after his men until his capture. After the war, he wrote his Official Report on the expedition (Library of Congress).

Captain Dinger's company, Forty-seventh Missouri, (Company E) then on duty there they made a stand. I re-enforced them with a detachment of the Fourteenth Iowa, Captain Campbell commanding, and a section of Montgomery's battery, Lieutenant Simonton commanding … placing the whole under the command of Major Wilson."[23] At about 5:00 p.m. Wilson actually pushed Fagan's forces back toward Shut In Gap, with the help of Simonton's two artillery pieces until Brig. Gen. William Cabell's Brigade, the largest in Price's Army, arrived and moved swiftly to force Wilson and his Cavalry back across Stout's Creek near Ironton, wounding Wilson slightly.

As the night came, rain began to fall and the firing ceased, the combatants took positions on opposite sides of Stouts Creek. Wilson could expect no more reinforcements from Brig. Gen. Ewing; he would have to face the Confederates with what he had at his disposal on the 26th. During the night Ewing readied his batteries of artillery for the fight that was sure to come the next day. At the General's disposal was the most modern implements of death at that time. The Hexagonal fort had four 32-pounder siege guns, three 24-pounder howitzers and three 3-inch ordnance rifled cannons. Included in this was a number of field artillery positioned on platforms within the walls of the earthen fort. All these guns had a picked field of fire that would rain shot and shell on Confederate movements in the valley's plain and mountain ingress. With local militia and 47th Infantry under the command of Colonel Fletcher manning the interior walls and parapets, the federals waited in anticipation.

The battle was joined in earnest on Tuesday, September 27th, early in the morning. One of the first contacts was made against Simonton's Battery deployed in front of the Iron County Courthouse, when Cabell's infantry charged the guns as they beat a hasty retreat. One of the Confederate artillery pieces actually struck the courthouse façade as the federals fled taking Co. E with them. Brig. Gen. Ewing now decided to redeploy his forces in the face of a strong Confederate advance. "While they were trying to force the gap I ordered the detachment of the Fourteenth Iowa to take position on the east end of Shepherd Mountain, and ordered Wilson to fall back with his cavalry along the side of Pilot Knob, thus commanding the gap from both sides and opening a clear range from the fort."[24] Ewing was preparing his field of fire once the Confederates moved over open ground.

The immediate threat was where and how the Confederates would advance and Ewing made the effort to confront the enemy coming through the gap between the mountains. For a time the efforts of the 14th Iowa Regiment and Wilson's 3rd Missouri Militia Cavalry prevented the Confederates from moving through the gap. Realizing that the high ground around the summits of both Shepherd Mountain and Pilot Knob were not occupied by Union forces, the Confederates began to move up the backside of those mountains, even trying to use a ruse of a white flag to buy some time and asking for surrender.

General Ewing was informed of the white flag attempt and immediately ordered Wilson to ignore and keep attacking the Confederates. Eventually the 14th Iowa and skirmishers had to give ground when the Confederate forces began to appear on Shepherd Mountain, maintaining good order, when the big guns of the fort unleashed a crash of cannon fire. Ewing reported, "After an hour of lull, lines of the enemy were seen at exposed points on the summits of the two hills moving down; and almost before we could open fire on them another white was raised on a rock ... where a group of officers had been taking observations under shelter."[25] Ewing realized that the attack on the fort was now developing and ordered the guns to open fire on the troop movements moving in and around the mountains.

Major Wilson probably did not become aware that his rear had now been compromised as he moved along the trees at the base of Pilot Knob with pistol drawn. As a matter of fact Brig. Gen. Cabell's, Slemon's and McCray's Brigades came down the mountain and overwhelmed Wilson, surrounding him with bayonets before he could direct a hasty retreat. Cabell recalled, "The next morning I drove the enemy from Arcadia, capturing a major and ten soldiers."[26] Wilson was now stripped of his gear and sent under guard to the same rear (Arcadia) that he had defended so well. Much of the 3rd Missouri State Militia did elude the Confederates; Wilson, Captain Dinger and five others did not and events would play out dismally for some.

All the forces of the Confederates where now in play; Brig. Gen. Cabell was reluctant to commit his forces against the well-fortified Union position and advise his commanding general, Sterling Price, not to attack fearing heavy losses. "I was opposed to making the charge when we did and so informed the staff officer who delivered the order, as we did not give our artillery time to drive them out or to demoralize them ... my poor men were unnecessarily sacrificed."[27] Cabell was overruled by both Maj. Gen. Price and his Division commander James Fagan. In his report Cabell goes on to reflect on the battle and says, that it was poor generalship on the Confederate's part. Cabell does not specifically say it was Price's fault, but the conclusion that it was Price could be drawn. As Cabell's men were forming in the gap, between Shepherd Mountain and Pilot Knob, Confederate artillery was positioned to support him on Shepherd Mountain. It was going on one and two o'clock in the afternoon when the assaults of Fagan's and Marmaduke's on Shepherd Mountain got underway.

From inside the fort Brig. Gen. Ewing now saw the battle developing. The attack would now strike the eastern and southern side of the earthen ramparts. The nearly 1,000 soldiers he had were positioned along the parapets, concentrating along the rifle pits adjacent to and west of the rampart. The guns of the fort now roared with a thunder that shook the earth inside the fort. Located on the east side of the bastion were two 32-pounder guns on platforms 13 and 15. On platform 15 the gun was in the process of firing when Cyrus Peterson, a resident of Ironton and civilian volunteer, saw a member of the gun get hit. "At the big gun on the east side, one of the gunners was struck by a cannon ball from the battery on Shepherd Mountain. The roof of his skull was blown off; yet he was not instantly killed. Some moments after I saw the palpitating brain, ere the soul departed."[28] The roar was deafening and men could now barely hear one another.

This firing continued as the Confederates came on down the sides of the mountains in broken formation because of the vegetation and fences in their path. An intense rifle fire now played on the members of Fagan's infantry as they tried to close the distance from East Branch of Knob Creek. Staggered by the intense rifle and cannon fire, the regiment soon sought low ground at the stream bed where they took cover, advancing no farther. It was the same for Marmaduke's regiments as they, too, advanced down Shepherd Mountain, encountering the same obstacles as Fagan's men. Again, under the command of young Brigadier General John Clark, the Confederates were forced to take cover along Knob Creek falling short of the earthen ramparts because of the accurate cannon and rifle fire that had also silenced the Confederate guns on Shepherd Mountain.

Smoke now hung low in the plain surrounding the fort as the troops inside kept to manning the guns. At one point the big 32-pounder on platform 15 was put out of action when an overloaded charge caused it to recoil off of the platform. Manned by mostly black citizens from in and around Pilot Knob and Ironton, David Wilson remembered that Tom, a black man who worked for Mr. Delano, had been at that gun and had been injured when "it fell brushed along one of his legs, and bruised it badly."[29] Brig. Gen. Ewing could be seen moving along the parapet and fort grounds dispatching troops where he could to cover sectors he thought weak. In some instances many of the civilian recruits could not be used because of ineffective weaponry and everything being so well covered. At one point, just as Cabell's Brigade was preparing to move up the plain, the Confederates moved around to the fort's rear, a cavalry detachment under Colonel Thomas Freeman who charged through town only to be stopped by the federals occupying the rifle pits just north of the fort. This concentrated fire announced the last and third attempt to storm the works.

5. Arcadia Valley Confluence

William Cabell was seated on his horse as he looked out over the plain and his men forming up in ranks as they prepared to hear their officers give the word to move forward. Almost in unison with the movement of Slemon's Brigade, Cabell gave the order to attack. They came on in ordered ranks as gaps appeared in the Confederate's line as a result of the rifle and artillery. The bullets whizzed by or made a peculiar thud as they hit bodies of men moving over the ground. Soon the rebel yell filled the smoky valley as Cabell's men broke into a determined charge. Cabell was hoping that in making this attempt he would be properly supported in order to take advantage once the fort was stormed. His men were terribly exposed and being on horseback exhorting his men, Cabell presented an obvious target.

Brig. Gen. Thomas Ewing looked out over the parapet of Fort Davidson and could not help but marvel at the spectacle that now presented itself before his eyes. Moving through the smoky haze of the cannon and rifle fire was the ordered ranks of the butternut and gray with the red and blue star cross of their battle flags. Ewing described the scene: "his lines were greatly broken ... but were hastily reformed ... by General Cabell, who led the assault, and swept upon the plain in handsome style, yelling and on the double quick."[30] At 600 yards Ewing had the garrison open up on the advancing Confederates with musketry; as if this wasn't concentrated enough he also had seven of his artillery at his disposal to open up with canister.

The Confederates now had shot and canister exploding over-

Thomas Ewing had a very dim view of local Southern sympathizers. He wielded his assignment as commander in the Western District by implementing General Order No. 11. This single act, due to the ability to initiate Marshal Law, gave him the weapon he needed to inflict punishment on those Bushwhackers and anyone else who sympathized with the South (Library of Congress).

head along with concentrated rifle fire. Brig. Gen. Cabell now had his brigade in a cauldron of hell, he later recalled. "I moved to the charge on Marmaduke's right as directed. My men had no shelter, but were in open ground for 1200 yards. Marmaduke's men took shelter in a creek with high banks. My brigade was left without any support and on reaching the fort, found the ditch so deep and so wide that they could not scale it without ladders."[31] It was all true; no support came from Marmaduke or Fagan, as those units were broken in their initial assault on the fort even as Cabell's Regiments came on over the plain to the dry moat. Coming up to the edge of the moat pit Cabell was reigning in his horse and giving the commands, when his horse was finally shot out from under him. Raising his officer's sword Cabell exhorted his men to fall back as they tried to fight back from the ditch. The Union men now threw makeshift grenades into the moat, killing and disabling a number of Cabell's men as they fought on and out of the moat.

The dry moat on the south side of Fort Davidson and the hail of bullets from the fort did not relent. Many more of their colleagues lay dead or wounded as they retreated over the plain to shelter along the banks of Knob Creek. Keeping low, Cabell's men made no further attempt to storm the post and many officers believed that scaling ladders would now have to be made. Once he was able, Cabell took stock of the results: "My loss was heavy in both killed and wounded. Forty-five officers and men killed; one hundred and ninety badly wounded and a large number slightly."[32] The total for Price and his army was something like 1,000 killed and wounded. Many of the wounded were unable to crawl back to their lines and huddled together as rain began to fall in the early morning of September 28th; this was the last attempt to storm the works and now only the desultory fire from sharpshooters filled the air until nightfall.

The Union side fared better from the confrontation. The losses measured were about 75 men killed and wounded. The one thing that was a problem was the shortage of munitions to serve the artillery pieces. Brig. Gen. Ewing had some decisions to make. That evening Ewing called a meeting of his officers and staff. The discussion about whether or not they could abandon the fort eventually turned to one about how the fort should be abandoned. Under the light of the burning Iron works, which the Confederates had put to the torch, Ewing set about to withdraw his force north down the Potosi Road. Amazingly, none of the Confederate forces around the fort saw any signs in the light of the burning works that the federals were preparing their escape.

With Union and Confederate casualties now being taken into both Hotels in Ironton and Churches like the Lutheran Church in Pilot Knob, which was about a hundred yards from the fort, General Ewing appointed

Col. Thomas Fletcher to blow up the fort's magazine. Approximately two hours after the rest of the garrison, under Ewing, was making its way up the Potosi Road, Fletcher was preparing the timing charge to blow the fort's magazine. Working through the night and gathering up what his forces could take with them, Ewing's troops headed over the drawbridge and out of Fort Davidson at around 1:00 a.m. In order to muffle the sound of horses' hooves, wheels of caissons and 3-inch ordnance cannons on the drawbridge, Ewing and Fletcher covered the wooden bridge in tent canvass. Giving the Union force enough time to pass through the town and up the road, Col. Fletcher had Captain H. B. Milks rig a slow-burning fuse outside the entrance to the fort's magazine and then followed Ewing's route with his small group of troops.

During the night the Confederates had the opportunity to envelope the fort and actually encamped nearby the Caledonia/Potosi Road on the fort's north side. Amazingly Brig. Gen. Ewing and his one-thousand-soldier command silently passed by the Confederates without raising alarm in their camps. "Fletcher silently led the infantry out the sally port around the ditch, and through the north rifle pit, forming them under cover of a deep shadow at the end of the pit."[33] Price and his officers never really explained how such a large number of men and material could pass without being challenged. Not even the destruction of the magazine moved Price to action.

It was at around 3:00 a.m. in the still of the night that the quiet of the plain between Cedar, Shepherd and Pilot

Thomas Fletcher was born in Jefferson County, Missouri, in 1827. During Price's Raid at Fort Davidson, he was in command of blowing the fort's magazine and removing the rest of the command safely. Fletcher was nominated and elected the eighteenth governor of Missouri in 1864, the first native-born governor of the state, and served from 1865 to 1869. During his term, he issued a proclamation abolishing slavery in Missouri (courtesy Wilson's Creek National Battlefield; WICR 11509).

Knob Mountains shook with a roar of explosion that reverberated for miles around. The Confederates were shaken from their bedrolls as the sound rang in their ears. For people like David Wilson, it was just another event in two very eventful days, when he and Tom, the black man, decided to head out of one of the makeshift hospitals. Wilson recalled, "Down the stairs, I went with him to put him on the trail, when just as I stepped out of the hotel two or three paces from the front door, the magazine at the fort was exploded, and the debris was falling about us like hail."[34] The whole scene gave the impression that another battle was under way.

It was not until morning light that Price cautiously approached smoking Fort Davidson to investigate the event of that night. He was actually surprised to find that the fort was now abandoned and this only fueled the frustration of the futile assault in many of the Confederate command. Immediately Price had his Division Commanders order their men to break camps and form in columns to move out. It was bittersweet for Brig. Gen. Cabell, who remembered, "It made me feel sad.... We should never have attempted to take that fort by direct attack, but by getting behind them ... as there was but one way for them to get out."[35] One citizen remembered that the ranks of the Confederate soldiers passed by with expressionless faces, looking forward as they rode down the roads leading out of Ironton and Pilot Knob.

Operating up the Iron Mountain Railroad at places like Farmington since September 26th, Brig. Gen. Jo Shelby, with Colonel Shanks and M. Jeff Thompson of his Iron Brigade, had been operating behind and in front of Union forces in the District of Southeast Missouri. Tearing up track and cutting communication lines, Shelby eventually learned about Pilot Knob and had received instructions, from Price, to move back down the Potosi Road and rejoin his command. In the morning daylight on September 28th Brig. Gen. Ewing was expecting to move to Potosi and had sent "Captain Hills, Tenth Kansas ... with ten men to Mineral Point to acquaint the command there of my approach.... On starting, they, with our advance, fell upon twenty-five rebels in the town of Caledonia."[36] This now changed Ewing's plans and he decide to turn west leaving the Potosi Road and heading instead toward Webster and Rolla.

After the initial skirmish, Shelby's division reached Caledonia and met up with Maj. Gen. Marmaduke. Realizing that the skirmish with some of Ewing's forces was actually his rear guard, it was decided that Shelby should take up the pursuit of Ewing. Maj Gen. Price decided to move north towards Potosi, with the bulk of his command, still with the possibility of moving on the military stores at St. Louis. Stretched out for miles, the Grey and Butternut soldiers made an impressive sight riding on horseback and snaking down the dusty roads. In St. Louis the Federal command now believed that the Confederates had decided to attack the Union forces, desperately trying to muster there. Price, it is believed, may have decided not to attack St. Louis or was at least in doubt; he may have changed his plans but he had not, at that time, abandoned the idea of attacking St. Louis.

6

Objective: St. Louis

Complicating the situation in Missouri at the time of Price's expedition was the fact that the disruptive activity of the guerrillas in Missouri only picked up once the word got around of a Confederate Military force moving towards Little Dixie. Maj. Gen. Rosecrans had a twofold problem of how to deal with the partisan rebels and Price. In General Order No. 176, Rosecrans warned the citizenry: "'MISSOURIANS: I. After two years of barbarous and harassing war, in which every citizen directly or indirectly suffered loss of property, and many of life, you are now invaded by Price and the recreant Missourians, who, in defiance of professed principles, have been the chief cause of your sufferings and loss. They bring with them men from other States to plunder, murder, and destroy you for adhering to the Government of your interests and your choice. Prepare for them the reception they deserve. Make this raid fatal to the enemy and you will insure peace. Let them succeed and you will almost ruin your State.'"[1] Rosecrans issued this order on September 26th. Ironically it came the day before the Battle of Pilot Knob and more importantly the day before the notorious ruffian Bill Anderson rode into Centralia, Missouri.

William Anderson was the definition of what war can give birth to: a cold-blooded killer. He had a message of hate and welcomed anyone who could ride a horse well and kill Yankees. By the time of Price's Raid the various Confederate leaning partisans received word that Price hoped for cooperation and that these groups would work to tie down Union forces that would be in Price's advance. Having left Quantrill's band Captain Bill Anderson made his way back to the Missouri-Kansas Border and by the summer was causing problems for Union officials there. With a little more than 100 men, Anderson's group camped on the rolling prairie land just outside Centralia on September 26th. Looking to cause mayhem along the North Missouri Railroad, Anderson's force rode into the small town of Centralia on the morning of September 27th.

Surprising the quiet town, the renegades were soon threatening the populace as they began to decide what to loot first and who to kill. Soon the whistle of an oncoming train lumbered down the tracks, slowing to avoid a makeshift pile of railroad ties and debris in front of the depot; Anderson's men were excited that now they could cause real mayhem. To their delight they found a number of soldiers, disarmed and on furlough. Andersons's men, led by a seemly little fellow named Archie Clements, robbed the civilian passengers and separated some 22 soldiers who were roughly led off the train in front of the horrified citizenry. Once off the train the unarmed men were led down the track for a short distance and, within sight of the populace, shot point-blank near the tracks.

It is doubtful that Anderson's men might have known of the Palmyra incident of 1862. Some may have, but the actions of Union Brig. Gen. McNeil in his pursuit of Porter were probably much more known. This was now a war that could not be refined. After burning the Depot, Anderson moved his force out to the southeast of town. Early in the afternoon a Union patrol of the 39th Missouri Infantry were looking for guerrillas in the area, "about 7 o'clock on the morning of the 27th instant struck a trail which was supposed to be that of Anderson's guerrillas."[2] Reaching Centralia they were immediately informed of the dire events and told of Anderson's whereabouts. Under the command of A.V. E. Johnston, the detachment of about 140 men moved out immediately in pursuit. A few miles southeast of Centralia, Anderson set up his camp along Young's Creek. He positioned some pickets outside the tree-lined banks of the creek just in case of a pursuit. It was just a short time later that the pickets relayed that a force of men and horses were approaching their positions.

At about the same time that Price was trying to reduce Fort Davidson at Ironton, Captain Bill Anderson, on that warm September day, prepared his guerrillas to receive what he certainly believed was a federal force. Though Major A.V. E. Johnston believed that he could deal with a force equal to his own, he did not realize that a number of pro–South partisan groups had met up with Anderson and bolstered his force. "The Major determined at once to attack the enemy ... when discovering the guerillas, formed his line of battle and dismounted his men."[3] Simultaneously to Johnston forming his line, Anderson's men rode out of the swale that hid them from the federals. In ranks of two the federals fired their muskets at about 150 yards. Anderson's troops charged in at a gallop, opening fire on Johnston's lines at about 100 yards.

Before they could realize it, the 39th was overwhelmed with the sounds of the screaming Confederates who allowed no quarter from the Union men. Many Union soldiers were shot point-blank in the head as they probably tried to surrender. Major Johnston was last seen firing his pistol before being rode down by the Confederates. The whole encounter lasted less than ten minutes whereupon the Confederates rifled the bodies for valuables, clothing and boots. Bloody Bill Anderson smiled in triumph as he watched the gory scene. Making his way back to Centralia, Anderson made short work and more of a body count of the soldiers left behind by Johnston, some of whom actually made their escape by the hair of their chin. Thomas C. Tripler, Adjutant of the 39th Missouri Infantry, recorded the dismal numbers, "Recapitulation: killed, 2 officers, 114 enlisted men; wounded 2 enlisted men; missing, 6 enlisted men; total, 124. I certify that the above is a correct return of the killed, wounded, and missing in the Thirty-ninth Regiment Infantry Missouri Volunteers at the engagement at Centralia, Mo., September 27th, 1864."[4]

Brig. Gen. Joseph Shelby had been detached from the main force of Price's Army since 26th September, with orders to feel out the enemy's force, cut enemy communications and to act as a screen against any attempt to get into Price's flank. Leaving Fredericktown, Shelby's Division included M. Jeff Thompson, who had been a thorn in U.S. Grant's side early in the war and was now part of Shelby's Iron Brigade, Thompson and Shelby, two men of the same mind, who would now ride together and, as events would later prove, were instrumental in keeping Price's command together. Deception, maneuver and striking the opponent at his weakest point were the hallmark of both Thompson and Shelby. Thinking along the same lines was Brig. Gen. William Cabell. The first impetus of Shelby and Cabell was to move quickly on St. Louis, before the federals realized they were there.

In St. Louis Maj. Gen. William Rosecrans went about trying to gather a local force while he awaited Maj. Gen. A. J. Smith's XVI Corps to arrive in force in the anticipated belief that Price was headed in that direction. "Five regiments, two battalions, and several unattached companies of Militia Exempts were speedily formed in the city of St. Louis and vicinity, embracing a force of more than 5,000 men."[5] That was October 1st; in the waning days of September Rosecrans had less that number. On the 28th, believing that he may be outflanked, Maj. Gen. Smith, at Desoto, reported that he "decided to move back across the Meramec River and closer to St. Louis; "discovering the enemy on his front moving to west and north, in pursuance of his orders to hold "the most advanced position compatible with the certainty of keeping between the enemy and Saint Louis."[6]

The enemy on A. J. Smith's front was Brig. Gen. Jo Shelby's Division, tearing up rail tracks, cutting communications and reducing the Union outposts along the line. By the 28th Shelby and his cohorts were at Mineral Point and Potosi. Operating in St. Francois County, Brig. Gen. Shelby set to work on destroying the communication network vital to federal operations. This network included bridges, telegraph lines and railroads. Shelby praised Colonels Benjamin Elliot and Frank Gordon in these works. "Gordon and Elliot did their work well, as they ever do, and Elliot, after destroying the splendid bridge at Irondale ... commenced upon the track."[7] Shelby then goes on to described the art of attacking rail lines: "The whole command was deployed in a new line of battle, called the railroad line; that is, each man took position at the end of a tie, the rails were broken at intervals of a thousand yards, and then when the word was given and the united strength of a thousand hands was taxed great masses and flakes of wood and iron were torn free from the yielding bed ... away from the parent grade."[8]

Encountering little resistance, Shelby noted that the covering forces of A. J. Smith put up "but little fight." At Mineral Point Col. Gordon's column came upon a brigade of Smith's men who retreated in the direction of St. Louis, leaving the bridge to be burned and the military stores raided. This was all taking place between September 26th and 27th with Shelby unaware that Price had detailed a request that Shelby join him at Pilot Knob because of the stern resistance encountered there. Shelby, by the time he reached Potosi, was unimpressed by the Union force's response to his activities. In fact in his report he eludes to the fact that they tended to surrender, as they would at the Court House in Potosi, after minimal resistance, or retreat in other areas. Because of this and the belief that Shelby thought that the whole Army of Missouri should have moved on St. Louis, Shelby decided to detach from his command a squad of cavalry to make for the City of St. Louis and determine its strength. Shelby wanted St. Louis.

Sometime on September 27, 1864, a squad of four horsemen in butternut and grey made their way up the old Indian trails that led north towards St. Louis. The decision had been made by Maj. Gen. Sterling Price and agreed to by Shelby, in Fredericktown, that sometime after entering Jefferson County, Shelby would send a detail to St. Louis, indicating that as late as September 26th Price still intended to strike St. Louis. Shelby selected Captain Arthur McCoy and three troopers, from his original Iron Brigade, with the mission to secure the Cheltenham Post and Telegraph Office on Manchester Road just outside the city along the Pacific Rail Line. Avoiding Union pickets and staying just outside Union forts that surrounded the city, McCoy reached Manchester Road just west of their destination late in the afternoon on September 29th. To the surprise and shock of Auguste Muegge, the proprietor to the office store, in came McCoy and his men dusty and barely recognizable as cavalrymen. Slowly drawing their pistols and leaving one man outside to watching the door, McCoy began to interrogate Muegge about what kind of strength the Union had in that area. At some point McCoy and his men were distracted from their questioning because, according to Muegge, he made his escape, probably through a back door. Muegge immediately sought out Union forces, but by the time they got back to the store the Confederates had left.

When Rosecrans was informed of the unhappy incident Augustus Muegge had experienced, it only confirmed his idea that St. Louis was in peril and Rosecrans believed that the fortifications around the city were not enough. The fortifications consisted of a series of earthen forts and gun emplacements that ringed the city from the Marine Hospital and the Arsenal on Carondelet Avenue to Benton Barracks on St. Charles Rock Road, which anchored the north side of the city. The forts covered Arsenal, Jefferson, Manchester and Central Plank Road, all main roads. They were numbered from No. 1 through No. 10 with Gun Batteries A through E in between. Even with these guns Rosecrans still believed that Maj. Gen. A. J. Smith should concentrate back across the Meramec River closer to St. Louis. In fact Smith, "discovering the enemy on his front moving to west and north,"[9] then decided to leave Desoto, which the enemy then occupied on the 29th, burning the rail depot. The optimism of putting 5,000 in the field against the Confederates was woefully short of the actual numbers. On September 29th, the day that captain McCoy visited the Cheltenham Post, the total force, other than the garrison forts, was 1,500 militia and the 4,500 troops of A. J. Smith's XVI Corps. Fortunately for Rosecrans Smith's units were trickling in off their transports near Jefferson Barracks and soon his numbers would rise to over 8,000.

Price's Army of Missouri moved north out of Pilot Knob and headed towards Caledonia. Jo Shelby had been successful in reducing the Union force at Potosi and now decided to try and meet up with the main army: "not receiving orders from General Price, nor, in fact, knowing the results of operations at Pilot knob. I determined to march there with my entire command."[10] Ewing was determined to move to Potosi but on learning that Shelby was moving in his direction he turned west toward Webster. Meeting Ewing's rearguard, Shelby's Cavalry videttes skirmished briefly for some time before the advance elements of Price's army reached Caledonia. General Marmaduke reported, "my command is encamped three-fourths of a mile from this place toward Ironton.... I met General Shelby here this morning and presumed he will encamp here.... I am preparing a force to follow them as soon as my men can obtain forage, etc."[11]

Sterling Price ordered Marmaduke and Shelby to pursue Ewing and his 1,000-man force, thinking it would be of short duration. Instead it cost Price time and divided his force instead of concentrating his command for a move

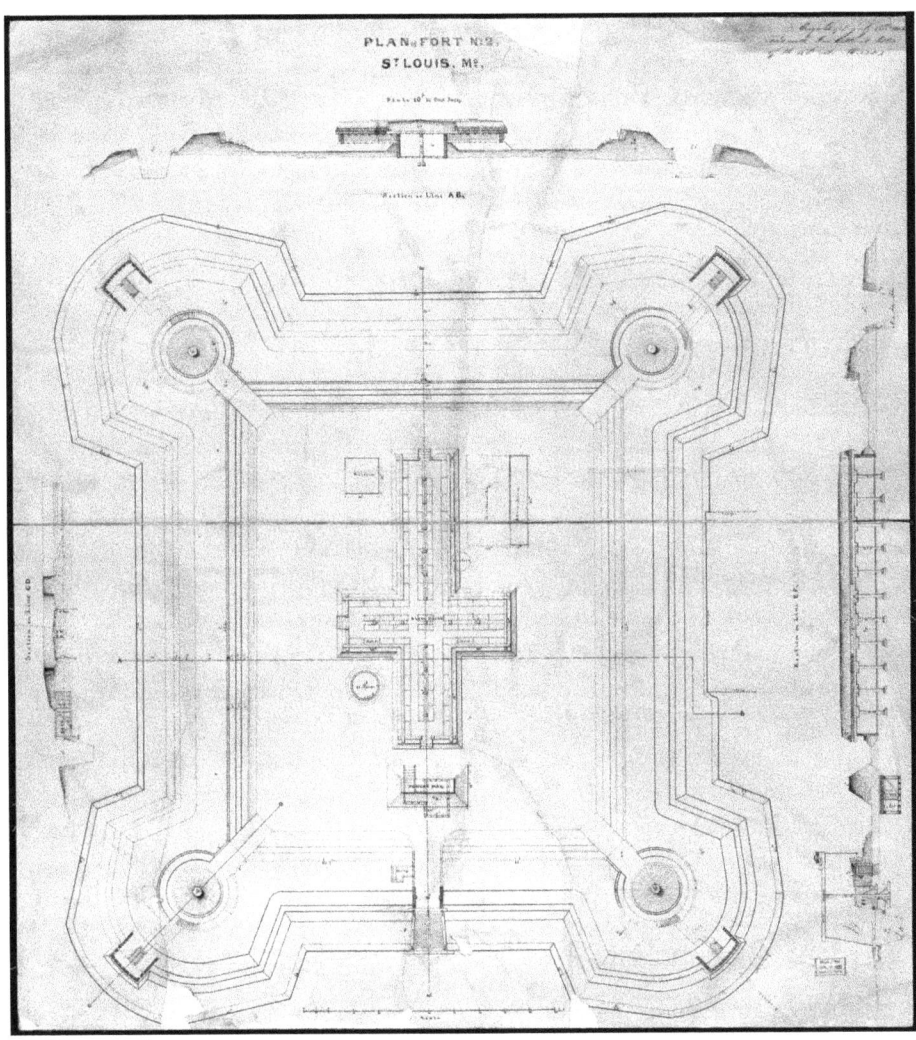

Fort No. 2: was one of ten forts in St. Louis, located at the southern end of the ring of forts. Located off Marine Ave. and Carondelet, it covered the approaches to the Federal Arsenal. Fort No. 1 was just south of No. 2, on Marine Avenue, near the Marine Hospital (Library of Congress, Geography and Map Division).

towards St. Louis. Ewing remarkably eluded Marmaduke and Shelby moving through a countryside that offered difficult maneuvering for a force as large as Marmaduke and Shelby's. One of Marmaduke's Brigade commanders, Brig. Gen John B. Clark, remembered the area this way: "owing to the topography of the country it was impossible to deploy rapidly, and in consequence failed to bring him to a general engagement."¹² By the time Ewing gained Leasburg Shelby's force was engaging his command and, according to Jo Shelby, making a concerted charge by his men before daylight made any more contact impossible and brought the fight to an end. Unwilling to commit the Confederate forces against the Union fortified positions, Shelby and Marmaduke broke off contact and moved toward Sullivan to rejoin Price's main force.

While Marmaduke and Shelby fruitlessly tried to corral Ewing, Price and Fagan, along with the Confederate Missouri's exiled Governor, moved on to the small community of Richwoods. A small town of scattered homes and small businesses, the Confederates made encampment in the area that was mostly friendly and pro-South. During the overnight at Richwoods it was decided by Price to meet up with Marmaduke and Shelby at St. Clair, after raiding Sullivan, on the Southwest Branch of the Pacific Railroad and detach William Cabell's Brigade toward the line at Franklin (Pacific, MO) The intention of the move by Cabell was to test the Union defenses and with positive results turn on St. Louis, which would determine Price's decision to move on the city and its military stores or pivot west in pursuance with Trans-Mississippi West Commander Edmund Kirby Smith's directives.

Franklin County, Missouri, sits on the northern edge of the Salem Plateau of the Ozark Physiographic Region, where it touches the Missouri River. Moving north from Richwoods, Price's forces headed toward St. Clair. Some miles from Richwoods William Cabell separated his Brigade from Price's column and headed directly north by the back roads of the Ozarks toward the small towns of Moselle and Franklin. Here, screened in the rolling hills of horse country, Cabell moved his extended dusty grey columned men on narrow twisting roads, expecting to be near Franklin by the morning of October 1st. Marmaduke and Shelby headed east toward St. Clair via Sullivan Station, where they burned the depot and tore up the tracks of the Pacific Railroad. On the night of the 30th Price was encamping just outside St. Clair, Marmaduke and Shelby on the Springfield Road just west of the town and William Cabell's Brigade camped his well-worn men around the hills nearby the Saint Patrick Rock Road Church just a few miles from Franklin.

At Union Military Headquarters in St. Louis General Rosecrans was apprised of Price's activity. "The enemy moving up by Potosi seemed to halt at Richwoods, about forty miles southwest of Saint Louis, in the hills between Big River and the Meramec, as if concentrating for an attack on the City."¹³ Even at this late point Rosecrans believed that St. Louis was going to be attacked and he positioned his available forces in response, with the forts and batteries on alert. On the 30th he ordered Major General Smith to occupy Kirkwood, which commanded the Richwoods Road into St. Louis. He also had Colonel Merrill's Horse to survey the area around Franklin and the Pacific Railroad, believing that if the Confederates moved it would now come from that direction, striking at the Pacific Railroad. Merrill's Horse now communicated, late on the 30th, that indeed Confederates were outside Franklin. Proceeding carefully, Merrill's command was alerted that Cabell had made camp in the hills around St. Patrick's Rock Church.

October 1, 1864, presented a clear and seemingly pleasant early fall day for Brig. Gen. William Cabell to rouse his troops for action. Sipping a rough cup of coffee, Cabell watched as soldiers quickly ate a meager breakfast, struck their tents and saddled their horses to form column. Later that morning in Kirkwood, Missouri, Maj. Gen. A. J. Smith had rail cars standing by in order for Wolfe's Brigade to embark. The Brigade of about 4,000 men consisted of the 49th Ill., 117th Ill., 52nd Indiana and 178th New York and they were soon loaded onto the cars and immediately rolled out along the Pacific Rail Line toward Franklin some 40 miles west. Allotted no artillery for support, the troops stood motionless as the cars jerked and the train engine began to build steam, smoke billowing along the sides.

Franklin (Pacific), Missouri, is located on the north side of the Meramec River where it makes a sharp northern bend toward the east. The town itself sits below an escarpment of sandstone bluffs, about 150 feet high, that cradles the town in an amphitheater-like bowl. In those early morning hours of that day the rail workers went about their tasks as they usually did and the townspeople were milling about their daily activities when to the south of town many observed a cloud of dust moving in the town's direction. William Cabell's troopers arrived with a thunder from the main road directly south and west. Immediately Cabell ordered the rail workers rounded up and the Depot and rail siding buildings put to the torch. The air was soon filled with the smell of burning buildings as local citizens surrendered whatever the soldiers asked for. Cabell ordered that the local businesses be spared along with the citizen's private property; the railroad was another matter and he had the local rail workers begin to tear up track east and west of town.

Cabell was also there to gauge what would be the response of the federals. Once in Franklin he had his brigade position pickets to the east of town and they managed to move over a mile to a point of land where the sandstone formation tapered down to a narrow passageway between the rock and the river. Just beyond here the Confederates burned a wooden bridge over a small creek and as they watched, heard in the distance a train whistle coming their way. The troops on the train cars could see the smoke billowing up into the air from the vicinity of Franklin and Colonel Wolfe had the train engineer slow the engine down stopping at a place the locals called Doziers Crossing.

Dropping out of the train cars, the Union soldiers formed ranks as Col. Wolfe moved forward with skirmishers in the front to screen Confederate pickets. At that narrow point the Confederate pickets picked up the blue uniforms of the skirmishers and instantly the crack of musket fire filled the air as both sides caught sight of the other.

In Franklin even as the noise of the destruction was going on, Brig. Gen. William Cabell, "old Tige" as his soldiers called him, turned his head sharply toward the east as that familiar sound of gunfire was first heard. The General immediately informed his artillery command to prepare for action. Hughey's battery was with Cabell's command that day and he had decided to locate his 4 sections of artillery on a bluff commanding the main road coming in from the east along the rail line. Hughey had sighted his guns so as to bring maximum bearing on the road where it comes around the bluffs. When the Confederate pickets fell back as Hughey knew they would, he would open up on the blue uniforms coming around the bend. Hard pressed, the pickets could

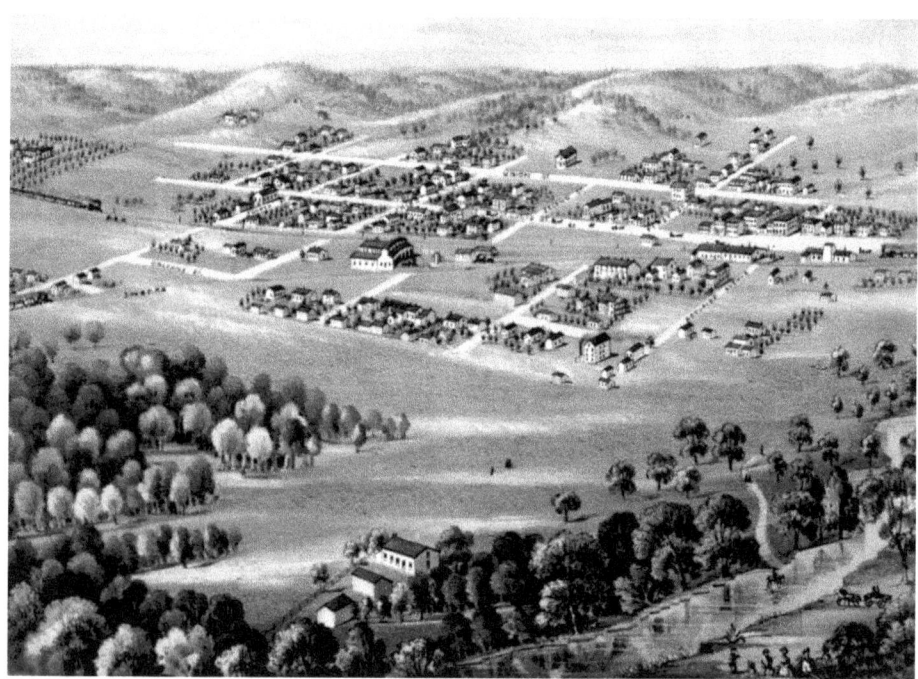

Franklin, Missouri, a railroad town founded on the Pacific Railroad line and the Southwest Branch of the Pacific Railroad, was a small town in the path of the Confederates and was attacked in the early morning hours of October 1,1864, by William Cabell's troops. All rail buildings were destroyed and the military stores were looted (Library of Congress, Geography and Map Division; G4164.P15A3 1869, R8).

no longer hold the narrow promontory and fell back toward the town and Cabell's Skirmish line just east of the burned Depot. Like water, the blue uniforms now filtered west around the bluff escarpments, making their way toward Franklin.

The cannons exploded on the bluff road just north of town. Within an instant shell and canister began to rain in on the Union soldiers coming around bluffs and along the river. The Union men now took what cover they could as their advance was halted. Cabell ordered his train and some of this command to begin the move out of town on roads leading toward Grey Summit and the St. Louis Rock Road. Cabell then ordered a part of his command to dismount and form a line of battle to meet the oncoming federals. For the better part of two hours the antagonists exchanged gunfire and the little valley was filled with smoke and the whizzing of bullets as blue and grey tried to kill one another. Slowly in that time, Hughey's men hitched up their batteries and moved off the bluff one by one, covering Cabell's dismounted infantry. Satisfied that the Union infantry was at bay, Cabell's men remounted their horses around noon and rode off in the dense smoke that filled the area from rifle fire and burning buildings.

On the same day that Cabell was dealing with Franklin, Sterling Price was meeting up with Marmaduke and Shelby at St. Clair, in south Franklin County. St. Clair was on the Southwest Branch of the Pacific Railroad, making it a target for the Confederates. To the displeasure of the local citizenry, some of whom had pro–South leanings, a large Confederate army overran their small community, destroying the railyard and buildings and vandalizing local businesses, as one citizen remembered, "Letters and papers were thrown and scattered in every direction."[14] Price had now decided that he would concentrate his army at Union, Missouri, the county seat of Franklin County and meet up with William Cabell's command. A large train of wagons and mounted men stretching for miles, now made its way north on the St. Clair Road. Along with all this were also a number of captured Union militia men, who had not been paroled and instead held for various reasons, particularly a number of 3rd Missouri Militia and their commander James Wilson.

Waiting at Union were the Enrolled Missouri Militia and the Provisional Enrolled Militia, which John Schofield and William Rosecrans had worked so hard to develop for the defense of Union interests against local guerrillas. They now had to face a genuine Confederate Army. Union, Missouri, sits on a series of hills that are dissected by the Bourbeuse River, some fifty miles west from St. Louis. It is here that the St. Clair and St. Louis Rock Road intersect at Vitt's Mill located on Flat Creek. The Union forces here consisted mainly of Co. B 54th Enrolled Missouri Militia, Co. E 55th Enrolled Missouri

Militia and Fink's Provisional Enrolled Missouri Militia. Fink's Provisional was the best trained and disciplined unit of the three and would prove so.

The citizens and county officials were abuzz with reports and rumors that the Confederates had entered the county and were on their way toward the town. Around noon, at about the same time General Cabell was leaving Franklin, a couple of horsemen rode into Union relaying the events that had occurred at St. Clair and that the Confederates were now on the St. Clair Road headed to Union. When news of this reached Captain Fink and the other Militia Officers, it was decided immediately to improvise a barricade on the road and fortify Vitt's Mill where it intersected the Rock Road. J. H. Hanneken, aide to Clark Brown, recalled that they "began erecting breastworks in the woods below Vitt's Mill in what is now Vitt's pasture to command the union side of the bridge. The breastworks were made of rails and earth…. Those who had shovels piled the dirt, and those who had none carried the rails."[15] The bridge over the Bourbeuse was only a few hundred yards from the Mill, with the St. Clair Road leading almost directly to it.

Just to the north of town, about a mile away from the mill, stands Gorg's Hill, about one-hundred-foot rise above the Bourbeuse River in sight of the bridge crossing. The St. Clair Road goes right over the top of the hill and down towards the bridge. On or about 2:00 o'clock in the afternoon the vanguard of Price's Army reached that point. Maj. Gen. Marmaduke's Division was in the lead, more specifically Brig. Gen. John B. Clark commanding Col. Colton Greene's 2,000-man Brigade. General Clark said in his report, "We arrived at Union, Franklin County, October 1; found a small body of the enemy, some 200 strong, posted in the town to dispute our entrance. Dismounting my command and opening my artillery I moved forward rapidly to the attack."[16] Brig. Gen. Clark had at his command the artillery of Hynson's Texas battery and Harris's Missouri Light artillery. Harris, who was from Missouri, immediately took up the offer to shell the Union defenders with case and canister.

Hunkering down behind their barricades, the 54th and 55th militia did what they could to avoid the shells exploding over their heads and bouncing off the mill. Residents near the river and mill soon became involved in the unfolding events. Sallie Jefferies lived nearby and recalled, "When the soldiers, reached the south hill … (Gorg's), opposite our home, the fact was known by their firing…. I could hear the shells and shots rattling on the roof."[17] It seemed that the shelling of the town was lasting an eternity and for the enrolled militia the expectation of the Confederate assault was not that long in coming. Brig. Gen. Clark had Col. Greene to dismount most of his command, except for Colonel Jeffers's and Robert Lawther's Cavalry Regiments. In line of battle, the dismounted cavalry, now working as infantry, made its way down the hill and were soon upon the river bridge plunging headlong toward the barricades.

Suddenly the Union militia men saw the numbers of their enemy and raised their muskets to send a volley of bullets at the onrushing Confederates with a rebel yell. Hanneken remembered the encounter: "Captain Detmer, in a loud, firm voice shouted 'Ready, Fire.' Then said, 'Load! Ready! Fire!' He repeated this last command the second time."[18] With the shrill sound of the artillery shells overhead and the scream of the Confederates, the militia companies broke and then ran. Seeing the collapse of the militia, Col. Lawther made for the river crossing at Flat Creek. "When arriving within one mile of the town General Clark dismounted his entire brigade.... I was ordered to proceed rapidly around on their right, cutting off their retreat.... On arriving on the Saint Louis road I observed the federals falling back. We instantly charged through the town."[19] Fink's Provisional stood their ground a bit better than the 54th and 55th militia, but when Lawther's Cavalry came on their flank they, too, took flight and the encounter was over in less than twenty minutes. Colonel Colton Greene summed up the whole: "I marched with the division through Saint Clair to Union, the county seat of Franklin County, where the enemy made a feeble resistance and evacuated the place."[20] Price's army and the train of wagons now filled the valley around the town occupying the Main Square and Courthouse.

On the evening of that Saturday, Generals John B. Clark, John S. Marmaduke and Jo Shelby took supper with the Jefferies family and apologized for firing on the home.[21] It was near midnight on the first of October when Cabell's Brigade reached Union, coming off the St. Louis Rock Road. Moving from Grey Summit he recalled: "The depot at Summit and one or two places on the road were burned or destroyed. Here I obtained a number of fresh and good horses sufficient to replace the broken-down horses in my battery, as well as the broken-down and unserviceable horses in the different regiments."[22] About the same time Cabell was making camp along Flat Creek Marmaduke's division, after that supper at the pro–South Jefferies family home, decided to move his brigade north toward the Missouri River and the town of Washington, making camp just short of that town. In Washington, like at Union, the citizens prepared for the Confederate's arrival. With Cabell's arrival, in Union, Price had now finally made his decision to bypass St. Louis and with the influence of Governor Reynolds, who was the Confederate Missouri Governor in exile traveling with Price, decided to make for Jefferson City.

With warnings from the Military District of St. Louis to the local commander at Washington, Missouri, Maj. Gen. Rosecrans raised the alarm that the Confederate forces were coming. At first it was thought that the city might have to defend itself; soon that idea disappeared as many people started for the river and transported out. The Missouri River presented a natural obstacle and the need for sacrificing the city of Washington was thought unnecessary. Coupled with that decision was the realization that the riverboat steamers, like the new *Bright Star*, must not fall into the hands of the Confederates for obvious reasons, so Washington would now surrender. In fact just as Marmaduke's forces reached the river at South Point, two miles below Washington, the *Bright Star* was making its last run down the river taking pot shots from the Confederates as it moved from the shore.

By early afternoon on October 2, 1864, the streets of Washington, Missouri, fell strangely silent. Just outside of town directly south some of the Confederate soldiers came across the Busch Brewery south of town and decided to sample the works there. Seizing as much beer barrels as they could, even the green unfermented stuff, the soldiers drank to their fill before dumping the rest in the nearby creek. In the city itself a group of citizens, under a white flag, approached the lead elements of Marmaduke's troops as they entered the town. If they expected a cordial greeting from the Confederates they were disappointed; the soldiers grimly and sternly rode by, intent on their assignment to burn the railroad storage building and depot and confiscate any military stores they could get their hands on. By 2:00 o'clock the buildings were in flames and soon the fire of one building exploded, causing the Sisters of Saint Francis Borgia Parish Grade School, which was just up the hill, to fear for it catching fire. The company of Confederates still remaining listened to the pleas of some of the Sisters; convinced, they soon exchanged their weapons for the local fire equipment and put out the fire of the building.

Marmaduke and his force headed west up the Missouri River after leaving Washington, heading for New Port. The remaining force of the Army of Missouri still in Union would not head west until the morning of October 3rd. In the courtyard of the Franklin County Courthouse was a pod of Union soldiers on the north side of the building, under guard. Among them were Major Wilson and six others of his 3rd Missouri State Militia Cavalry. Believing that they might be paroled, they were instead kept under guard and ordered to get into column with the Confederate wagon train and led west with the rest of the army. Ominously a local Union militiaman was shot dead by Confederates the day before, across from the courthouse where they were held, after being accused of killing a local pro–South supporter.

The paradox for Maj. Gen. Sterling Price was that the opportunity for the move on St. Louis had now slipped out of his hands. The experience at

Pilot Knob had a disappointing result and delayed his force. He had disregarded Shelby's advice to bypass the fort and immediately make for St. Louis. Instead Price had hoped for a quick reduction of the fort, something like Lexington in 1861, which in fact was a siege. If he had the opportunity to size up and get into the head of Union General William S. Rosecrans, he would have realized his misgivings of the city defenses and the forces to support them was unfounded. It was an ability that eluded Sterling Price and it cost him. Rosecrans demonstrated something like disbelief in his Official Report. "The rebels were now apparently at bay with 1,500 cavalry and 4,500 infantry. General Smith was not in condition to attempt offensive movements against a force of 15,000 veteran mounted rebels who could reach Saint Louis from any point in the Meramec Valley."[23] On October 2nd General Rosecrans had Maj. Gen. A. J. Smith move his command headquarters to Franklin on the Pacific Rail Line and when he learned of Price's move west, Smith headed for Grey Summit the next day. Moving west, the Army of Missouri, under Price, falling short of St. Louis, now became something less than its original intention.

7

Retribution

Major Wilson was under guard, by some officers, in Maj. Gen. Fagan's command. Moving along the old state road and nearing the western edge of Franklin County, it was just after midday on October 3rd that the Confederate guard came to a halt. Nearing a bridge over Saint John's Creek, the group of Confederates and their prisoners took a break along the state road. This group of 3rd Missouri State Militia Cavalry included Major James Wilson, Corporal William Grurly, and Privates Christopher Grotts, John Halibaugh, William Scaggs and John Shaw. Something was in the air as the group came to a halt and hoof beats were heard coming down the road. At the head of the oncoming column was the guerrilla fighter Tim Reves, who was now acting in concert with Price's forces. Captain Dinger of the 47th Missouri Volunteers remembered on that day "that he was paroled fifteen miles south of Washington and ten miles west of Union, and that Major Wilson was at the same time and place ordered by the field officer of the day of the rebel army to be turned over by the guard to Tim. Reves, and when he last saw him he was waiting there under guard for Reves to come up."[1]

Slowing to a trot, the column of men dismounted from their horses and approached the guard; after a short conversation, they took the prisoners into the tree line where a number of shots rang through the trees and gun smoke filtered up through the canopy. It is believed that some of Reves's men hesitated to shoot the youngest of the captives who may have been just a boy. Reportedly Reves would have none of it and as the youngster seemed to break down, Reves dispatched him. Reves returned to his mount and then moved off as the Confederate column continued moving to the west, down the state road. Quiet soon returned to the woods and sometime later in the month, a local man was out gathering Persimmon along the trees near the Jeffrey's farm and the old state road, he soon came across some scattered papers in the brush and after some investigating came across the remains of a number of men in, what looked like, blue uniforms. Government officials were informed of the find and a squad of Union cavalry made their way to the site and began the grisly recovery of the remains and identified Major Wilson by the papers found on his body. The information of the incident was soon passed on to Union Officials. In the woods along the old State Road, near St. John's Creek, the bodies were loaded on buckboards for transfer to St. John's German Lutheran Church Cemetery, just a few miles south. Here some of the six men executed by the Confederate bushwhackers, under Reves, were buried in a common grave. For Major James Wilson, his remains were returned to his family in Lincoln County, at Troy, Missouri, to be buried there.

In a series of correspondence from October 24th through October 29th the Union authority in St. Louis would implement the deadly effect of suspension of Habeas Corpus and Military Law. Colonel G. Harry Stone to Brig. Gen. Ewing reported: "The bodies of Major Wilson and six men, captured at Ironton, have been found about fifteen miles southwest from this place on the old State road, near Jeffrey's farm. Major Wilson was shot through the body several times.... All documents found on these bodies are in the hands of Esquire Kleinbacker, of this county, and will be forwarded to you as soon as received here."[2] Woe to the Confederates that allowed this to happen for now the wheels were turning for retribution in the form of military justice. General Ewing, convinced of the authenticity of the documents, relayed his findings to Major General William Rosecrans.

> From testimony which cannot be doubted the commanding general learns that Maj. James Wilson, Third Missouri State Militia Cavalry, and six enlisted men of his command, prisoners of war, were given up by Maj. Gen. Sterling Price to the guerrilla Tim Reves for execution. The provost-marshal-general of the department will send a major and six enlisted men of the rebel army in irons to the military prison at Alton, Ill., to be kept in solitary confinement until the fate of Major Wilson and his men is known. These men will receive the same treatment Major Wilson and his men received. The provost-marshal-general is held responsible for the execution of this order.[3]

This statement in itself opened the door for reprisal.

Special Order Number 277 was invoked on October 6th and was soon followed by Special Orders No. 279 on October 29, 1864. Six captured Confederate soldiers, who had nothing to do with the incident taken by Reves, were singled out and put before a firing squad and executed. The Office of Provost Marshall reported that on that day, "the following rebel soldiers— James W. Gates, Company H, Third Missouri Cavalry, C. S. Army; Harvey H. Blackburn, Company A, Coleman's regiment, C. S. Army; John Nichols, Second Missouri Cavalry, C. S. Army; Charles W. Minneken, Company A, Crabtree's cavalry, C. S. Army; Asa V. Ladd, Burbridge's regiment Missouri cavalry, C. S. Army; and George F. Bunch, Company B, Third Missouri Cavalry, C. S. Army—were executed by being shot to death by musketry in retaliation for the murder of six men of the Third Cavalry Missouri State Militia by Tim. Reves' guerrillas, and in compliance with Special Orders, No. 277."[4] The Special Orders sealed the fate of the six, a retaliatory measure and a warning to others, and was signed off on by Maj. Gen. Rosecrans. (See appendix for Special Orders, No. 279.)

The Confederate Army, under Price, continued moving west towards the more accommodating areas of Little Dixie. Price believed it was the best way to go and still remain faithful to General Edmund Kirby Smith's directive. The ugly truth was that Sterling Price was becoming more detached in the mission and his set back at Pilot Knob had only amplified the problem. Only officers like Jo Shelby kept the army on point. "October 1, 2, 3, and 4 I moved with my division on through Saint Clair, Union, Mount Sterling, and Linn, capturing the latter place.... Through this and other sections of the country traversed by the army."[5] Shelby would remain an energetic and positive influence for the Army of Missouri. As positive as Shelby was, the facts were that the Confederates had to forage off the land and had to requisition from the locals what they thought they needed. With an army strung out for miles along country roads, the Confederates had to traverse Little Dixie in order to replenish stores.

The Missouri Regimental Banner was recognized as the banner for all Missouri State Guards under Confederate command. A variation of this flag is believed to have been copied by women in New Orleans and then presented to General Price as his Headquarters Flag to accompany him and the Army of Missouri in 1864 (Wikimedia Commons).

7. Retribution

In St. Louis the military situation started to take form. Maj. Gen. Rosecrans was surprisingly unconvinced that Price was moving away and was eager to keep in place and build on the military forces under A. J. Smith. By October 8th and 9th more Union Forces began to arrive in St. Louis. "General Mower ... his command ... was pushed forward by water as rapidly as the low stage of the river would permit to join General Smith."[6] Brig. Gen. McNeil did not agree with General Rosecrans on Price's whereabouts, and was making his way from Rolla towards Jefferson City, convinced that Price intended to attack the State Capital. "All communication with Saint Louis being cut off, I was compelled to act in the premises without consultation with headquarters. It also became known to me that one the prominent object of the raid ... was the capture of the political capital of the State and the installation of Thomas C. Reynolds as the constitutional Governor ... with the assistance of this rebel army of occupation, would be enabled to arouse the latent spirit of rebellion which still unfortunately existed in the minds of many citizens of Missouri."[7] For Union officers like Thomas Ewing and John McNeil, the architect of the Palmyra Massacre, it created incentive to bring all force to bear on Confederates in Missouri.

Jefferson City's defenses were now somewhat bolstered by the arrival of McNeil's force, who positioned his command along the Osage River crossings, southeast of the city, to intercept the arriving Confederates. The Confederate Vanguard was commanded by Brig. Gen. Jo Shelby. He sent his old command, the Iron Brigade, under the command of Col. Shanks to destroy a bridge and then rejoin him as he forced the river crossings at Castle Rocks. With all his brigades united, Shelby approached the Osage River with caution. Rushing to cover the fords, McNeil's forces arrived just in time to contest Shelby's men. Shelby's Division formed along the tree lined banks and the artillery fired in support as the Confederates laid down; covering fire and dismounted infantry and cavalry splashed across the Osage, forcing the federals back off the banks.

Believing that he had gained the initiative, General Shelby pushed forward. Confused and pressed, the federals made an initial stand and tried to mount a counter charge when Shelby sent a strong force in support. "I immediately pushed forward Colonel Shanks with orders to press the retiring enemy hard and heavily. The federals, re-enforced, came back upon him with great vigor, and the battle raged.... Mounting Smith's and Shanks's old regiment, I sent them to his assistance. The enemy, though outnumbering, fled rapidly, and pressing on far ahead of his best and bravest, he fell in the arms of victory—a bullet through and through his dauntless breast."[8] Shelby had lost Colonel Shanks and Price's Army had the opportunity to move on Jefferson City, but would Price actually try to take it? From the time of his approach to St. Louis up to this point outside Jefferson City, Sterling Price had surmised that he was up against insurmountable odds. He believed that the Union force at both places now outnumbered the Confederates. At this point none of it was true but Priced believed it and held off Jefferson City in the hills just south of there.

Edmund Kirby Smith, in his original orders, told Price to move on St. Louis quickly. He failed to do so and now he was in front of Jefferson City and decided to move up the Missouri River to Boonville. "I determined not to attack the enemy entrenchments [sic], as they outnumbered me nearly two to one and were strongly fortified but to move my command in the direction of Kansas, as instructed in my original orders ... to arm my unarmed men at Boonville, Sedalia, Lexington, and Independence...."[9] By this time Price had actually acquired a number of recruits and needed more arms and to replenish what he already had, but the refusal to attack Union forces there was a mistake that probably was not lost to some of his Lieutenants. Brig. Gen. Cabell remembered that "I moved up with Cabell's Brigade and drove the enemy ... across the Moreau River, and made him take shelter in his fortifications. My brigade occupied the heights in full view of the city."[10] The next day the Confederate Army formed in front of the City and sidled off by the left flank. Union officers inside the entrenchments watched the enemy move away and fired their artillery ineffectively, thinking of an imminent attack and then in relief, as the Confederates moved off.

In St. Louis Maj. Gen. William Rosecrans heard of the news of Price's failure to attack and now believed, finally, that his intentions were other than St. Louis. Rosecrans now knew of Price's direction and was doubly relieved that Cavalry General Alfred Pleasonton had arrived from the east. Once under the Command of the Army of the Potomac and Commander of Cavalry under George McClellan, Pleasonton had a mixed record as cavalrymen in the Eastern Theatre and had a reputation for having a "self-aggrandizing inaccuracy ... a 'Knight of Romance.'"[11] Kept in his command after McClellan was relieved, Pleasonton made good account of himself at Brandy Station in June 1863 and the Gettysburg Campaign, but when Ulysses S. Grant took command of the Armies in the east in 1864, Pleasonton was not part of his command and Philip Sheridan was. It was Pleasonton's good fortune that there was an immediate need in the Missouri Military Department and he was at the disposal of William Rosecrans.

With Price's Army of Missouri headed west along the Missouri River, he presented a new set of problems with the Union High Command. By moving towards Boonville, Price was crossing from one military district to another, the District of Missouri and the District of the Border, and would soon find himself between two federal forces, one of which would be under Pleasonton. Arriving in St. Louis, Pleasonton was immediately ordered by Maj. Gen. Rosecrans to Jefferson City to take command of the Provisional Cavalry Division. When Pleasonton arrived on October 8th he took command of four brigades, each commanded by Brig. Generals Brown, McNeil, and Sanborn and Colonel Winslow. With this mobile force Pleasonton's orders were to maintain contact with the Confederates and, where possible, engage and impede their progress. Maj. Gen. A. J. Smith's infantry would follow but would end up moving at a slower pace to keep between Price's army and St. Louis. This was Rosecrans's intention all along and it was now up to General Samuel Curtis and his forces in the District of the Border Department to directly confront Price.

It was a welcoming scene at Boonville for the Army of Missouri when they entered there on October 9th. Price was now in the heart

Alfred Pleasonton was born in Washington, D.C., on July 7, 1824, and graduated from West Point in 1844. Originally, he was the Union Officer in command of cavalry in the Army of the Potomac. Pleasonton spent the fall of 1863 in Virginia, but the following March was transferred west. He was given semi-independent command of the Union Cavalry at the Trans-Mississippi and doggedly pursued Price's forces, sometimes confusing Curtis with his intentions (Library of Congress).

of Little Dixie and was welcomed by the town fathers. Some cheers filled the air as the dusty grey soldiers made their way to camps around the town and shared in the stores there. The journey of Price's forces to Boonville was not without incident, Brig. Gen. William Cabell reported near Gardner's Mill. "The enemy came out in strong force and made a bold attack on my brigade, but I repulsed them and drove them back with heavy loss.... Early the next morning, the 8th, moved in the direction of California, Cabell's brigade in advance."[12] The next day Cabell's Brigade was acting as the rear Guard of the

Benton Barracks was a training center and would have been the staging area had an attack ever occurred on the city of St. Louis. Benton Barracks was one of the most important Union Army training camps in Missouri during the Civil War. The 150-acre complex contained barracks, warehouses, and numerous other buildings. A number of Missouri Union regiments were organized there, including some of the state's African American units. Soon after the war, the camp was closed; it has since been demolished (courtesy Wilson's Creek National Battlefield; WICR 30837).

Army of Missouri and was the last to reach Boonville. Maj. Gen. Alfred Pleasonton was keeping up with the rear of Price's Army and where possible was nipping at the army's heals. Pleasonton was going to make sure that he would not lose contact with the Confederates and was determined to pressure Price and his Lieutenants. If Pleasonton thought he had a mixed service in the east he was going to make up for it in Missouri.

From the very beginning of Price's Expedition, the partisan bands across the state of Missouri knew that they now had an opportunity to ratchet up their depredations. Knowing that Price had entered Boonville on the 9th of October, Bill Anderson decided to make his way to that city after a flurry of activity in the region just north and east of the Missouri River in late September. On October 11th Anderson made his way to Price's headquarters where they met at the Thespian Hall in Boonville and discussed how, in Price's mind, the guerrilla could best be used in support of his upcoming actions. What Price wanted from Anderson was for him and his motley band to disrupt the North Missouri Railroad that operated east and north of the Missouri River. Price's orders were specific: disrupt and destroy the railroad and everything that was associated with it. For Bill Anderson this simply meant that he could act with impunity, even though Price warned him otherwise. Believing that Anderson would act in concert with Price's operations, Anderson would now not only attack the Northern Missouri Railroad but also use what he believed was carte blanche to spread terror among the local populace.

Anderson's men made their way east along Boonslick Road through a number of towns including Rocheport and Williamsburg and eventually ended up at the then burgeoning County Seat town of Danville, Missouri. Here Anderson and his Lieutenants decided to make an example. It was going on evening on October 14th and despite most people of Danville hoping that the war would somehow pass them by, the war with all its fury was unleashed on the town. Predominantly Unionist, with some pro–Southern sentiments, the town was garrisoned by Union troops and had a large blockhouse on the southeast corner of the town square. Most of the federal force that was stationed there was operating several miles to the east when the Anderson riders trotted into town. It was late in the evening when Anderson and his crew began to indiscriminately burn and shoot up the town, killing a number of citizens, including a 12-year-old girl. Just across the street from the town square was the Danville Female Academy, with its fine Greek Revival Architecture. Here the guerrillas believed that Union soldiers might be hiding. Threatening to burn the school buildings, Anderson's men were soon confronted by a number of the female students who insisted that many of the young women were of Southern families and insisted that the school had nothing to do with housing military units. Impressed with the young women's courage, the school was spared and the riders moved off and attacked High Hill and burn railroad property.

The operations by these guerrillas had little impact and did little to serve Price's expedition; indeed, they would have been useful had Price gone in another direction, perhaps toward St. Louis. Instead the Army of Missouri had to continually watch their rearguard as Brig. Gen. Cabell would experience. Having set up his Headquarters in the old Thespian Hall, in Boonville, Price planned his next moves. Late in the evening of the 10th William Cabell's troops were arriving into camp when Brig. Gen. Cabell and other senior officers were ordered to report to Price early next morning. Cabell reported: "Knowing that the enemy camped near us that night, I had reveille sounded early, and after they had eaten breakfast I made every preparation to receive the enemy ... giving instructions to my senior Colonel to move out with the Brigade as soon as he heard firing."[13] On that morning as Price was introducing General Cabell to the leading citizens of the town, as Cabell recalled, Boom! Boom! Boom! Went the artillery and suddenly the room went quiet. Immediately General Price turned to William Cabell: "General Cabell, you will move out your Brigade and drive the enemy back!"[14] Saluting his commanding officer William Cabell left the building and returned to his camp.

Alfred Pleasonton's Cavalry Brigades were doing their work. Brig. Gen. Sanborn was keeping pace with Price's forces and on the 11th attacked outside Boonville. "Sanborn followed the rebels ... found they were going north toward Boonville, followed and drove them into line of battle near that place."[15] The reaction was swift by the Confederates as they formed line of battle as the Confederate pickets were being driven in by the federals. Cabell remembered driving the blue cavalrymen back from the outskirts of town, even among some of the streets and houses of Boonville. General Clark also took part in the repulse and recalled, "On the 11th a picket of 100 men, commanded by Captain Hicks, of Burbridge's regiment, was attacked by heavy force of the enemy and rapidly driven in. Marmaduke and Fagan's divisions, moving rapidly ... offered battle."[16] Brig. Gen. John S. Sanborn and the federal cavalry were soon flanked by the Confederates and immediately broke off the engagement and moved off to meet up with Colonel Catherwood.

The Confederate decision was to continue movement through Little Dixie, raiding and taking federal supplies along the way. Price's options were becoming scarce, a decisive battle to destroy a federal army was becoming remote, but that idea was not entirely dismissed from some of his officers, particularly among officers like Jo Shelby. Leaving Boonville on October 12, 1864, Price's army made its way to Marshall, where a year before Shelby had made his miraculous escape and where Lizzie Brannock's husband had been captured. Along the way orders were given to Brig. Gen. John B. Clark and M. Jeff Thompson to peel off their commands for separate attacks against Sedalia and Glasgow. M. Jeff Thompson was now in command of Shelby's Iron Brigade. With the wounding of Colonel Shanks and his demise, Thompson was assigned the Iron Brigade before the move on Boonville. "I left the rear guard in charge of Brig. Gen. M. Jeff Thompson, who had been assigned by General Price, to command my old brigade."[17] Now with his orders Thompson moved south to Sedalia with 1,000 troopers and a section of artillery. Shelby finally had someone of like mind to command his old Brigade.

Sedalia was a small town set on the prairie of western Missouri. Thompson's mission was to reduce the local Union garrison, acquire what information he could and more importantly "bring back with him a drove of cattle and mules said to be in that neighborhood."[18] This order was important because of the need for mules, which for a 19th-century Army, was worth more than the vulnerable horses used by the cavalry. Learning that a large force of cavalry had passed Sedalia and that Union infantry was possibly some distance off, General Thompson immediately attacked on the 15th. Sedalia was defended by two redoubts at opposite ends of the town with rifle pits; Thompson drove in the Union pickets and after a brief initial stand by some of the federals, the dismounted Confederates rushed the pits so surprising the federals that they broke and retreated and abandoned the redoubts which were fired upon by the Confederate artillery. Thompson reported that he had orders not to damage private property, but this did not prevent his soldiers from looting and pillaging the town. "We captured at Sedalia several hundred stands of arms and many pistols, and several wagon loads of goods suitable for soldiers."[19] Paroling the Union troops Jeff Thompson made his way back to the main column, avoiding, as was Thompson's way, Union General Pleasonton's forces.

Brig. Gen. John Clark had his orders too. The reports were that the Union had a large store of supplies and material in Glasgow on the opposite side of the Missouri river. For Price's forces this would be the only attack over that river during his campaign in Missouri in 1864. Unlike Sedalia, Glasgow would prove to be a tougher nut to crack. General Clark received his orders from the commanding general on the 14th to cross the Missouri river at Arrow Rock and attack and capture the Federal Post at Glasgow. General Shelby was to support his move with two sections of artillery and a regiment of dismounted cavalry and shell the federals from the opposite bank of the river while Clark attacked. General Shelby's forces got into position early on the 15th but Clark was delayed by the difficulties crossing the Missouri. "I succeeded, after considerable difficulty, in crossing my command, but not as early as was expected.... I did not arrive at Glasgow at the appointed hour."[20] By the time Clark was across, he was still three miles from the town as Shelby opened up on the federal forces.

The Union Commander at Glasgow, Colonel Chester Harding, became aware of the Confederate presence at 5:00 a. m. when the thunderous roar of artillery opened up on the town from across the Missouri river. Even though Clark was late the cannon fire of Shelby helped distract the federals if only for a little while until Harding received word of Clark's advance in his direction. Positioning his units along a tepid creek, just south of town, Harding braced for the assault of Clark's 1,800-man force on his thinly stretched 700. Setting up his artillery just across the creek, Brig. Gen. John Clark, at about 10:00 a.m., put his forces into action. Colonel Colton Greene was given the task for the attack and described the order of battle. "My line was formed, with Greene's regiment on the right, commanded by Captain Johnson; Jeffers' on the left; Burbridge's on the right of the center; Kitchen's on the left of the center; and Davies' battalion in the center."[21] More importantly, just as he did at Vitt's Mill, Greene had Lawther's Cavalry Regiment move by the right flank around the federals and get in their rear and Jackman's force to its left.

Artillery boomed over the river bottoms as the two opponents opened rifle fire and the air filled with lead; the Confederates tried to come to grips with the federals driving them over fences and pastures toward the center of town. Colonel Harding grimaced as the battle progressed. "The troops along the creek resisted the passage of it manfully, but soon had to be ordered back, as the enemy's force was so great that he was enabled not only to pass around both flanks, but to pour through the long intervals which necessarily existed in the line."[22] Harding's troops fell back toward the center of Glasgow as Greene's dismounted infantry moved at a fast pace. Colonel Lawther's report stated that, "After some three hours fighting the Federal cavalry surrendered to me."[23] Colonel Harding soon surrendered his command and the confederate's made off with substantial federal stores and crossed the Missouri on the 17th but not before burning federal warehouses and even a steamboat captured intact on the river.

Notwithstanding the Confederate operations at Sedalia and Glasgow, the Union command in the Department of the Border was not idle. In fact the Union had the right man in place, one who had been successful against Confederate arms, Major General Samuel Curtis. The victor of the Battle of Pea Ridge, Arkansas, had no illusions and fully expected a confrontation with his old advisory Sterling Price. He was miffed that the Department of Missouri command was less than fully cooperating or concentrating forces to corner Price. Now commanding the Army of the Border, General Curtis had an ally in Maj. Gen. Blunt who was eager to restore his reputation after his brutal handling by William Quantrill, in which Curtis had lost his son who had been under Blunt's command at Baxter Spring. Now Blunt was in command of the Army of the Border Provisional Cavalry with orders to move on Lexington, Missouri, ahead of Price's Army. Hoping to restore his badly tarnished image, General Blunt would confront the oncoming Confederates who were intent on arriving in Lexington.

Moving in three columns, the Army of Missouri moved along the dusty roads of rural Missouri, the fall colors matching the uniforms of the Confederate ramble. For Jo Shelby it was a return to his homestead at Waverly. A. J. Smith and his XVI Corps remained at a distance as General Rosecrans remembered: "The enemy apparently hesitated in the vicinity of Marshall as if uncertain whether to go west or double on his tracks between Sedalia and Jefferson."[24] Price was simply pausing for Generals Clark and Thompson to catch up and rest, and he soon sent elements to secure Waverly, Shelby's peacetime home. From this point on the campaign intensified and according to Author Shelby Foote, "at Waverly.... Shelby encountered a force of Coloradans and Kansans under Major General James Blunt ... sent forward to delay the approach of the raiders. Here were the opening shots of what turned out to be a week-long running skirmish ... with several pauses for full scale engagments."[25] Pushing on from Waverly, after a short skirmish, Shelby's force soon confronted Blunt in Lexington twenty miles away.

Major General Sterling Price had now returned to the place that provided him his greatest triumph of the war. Lexington, Missouri, stood on bluffs that were south of the easterly flowing Missouri River. Maj. Gen. Blunt, with about 4,000 troopers, had decided to delay Price and his force at Lexington for as long as possible. Price was concerned about A. J. Smith and Pleasonton's Cavalry coming upon on his rear, and wanted to move briskly on Independence. He commanded his best Lieutenant, Jo Shelby, to remove Blunt from his path. Price now found himself and his army possibly confronted between two federal armies. Shelby attacked Blunt just outside Lexington and Blunt's Provisional Cavalry made a stand that halted Jo Shelby's attack south of the town. Shelby was determined and soon sent for reinforcements. Coming to his aid was Brig. Gen. William Cabell. "General Shelby attacked Blount, who had about four thousand men, at or near Lexington, and, being hotly engaged and hard pressed, I went at once to his assistance, and in less than an hour, we had routed them and driven them off with heavy loss."[26] Moving off quickly the federals could not hold off Cabell's attack and were pursued by Shelby until nightfall when the chase was brought to a pause.

Even Price was impressed by the soldierly qualities of the Union troops: "for a time the federals fought well and resisted strenuously."[27] Ironically Generals Price, Shelby and Marmaduke knew this area of Missouri well, particularly Shelby and Marmaduke. Yet they did not pick ground or devise a plan of attack against the pursuing Union troops under Pleasonton and offer up a strategy to destroy his 7,000-odd troop command. At some time all must have known that a pitched battle of some kind would develop, yet there seems to be little record of a discussion as to how it might be implemented. There would be a battle but it would come due to the events controlling the actors instead of the other way around. Price even recorded in his report that McNeil and A. J. Smith were at Sedalia on the 19th of October, and might make link up with Blunt. Now grey and heavyset, the 55-year-old Sterling Price, "Old Pap," as he was often referred to by his troops, was finding it more difficult to sit in the saddle on these long routes and was seen more and more riding in wagons and carriages. As events would continue to show, Brig. Gen. Jo Shelby, at times, would have to take the lead in the Army of Missouri decision-making.

With Price's thoughts now more focused on securing the wagon trains, Jo Shelby had put himself and his command as the point of the spear of attack for the Army of Missouri and found himself east of Independence, Missouri, on the night of October 20, 1864. Maj. Gen. Samuel Curtis, Commanding the Border District, was in Kansas City making preparations on just how the Army of the Border would prepare to receive the Southern invaders. Union Colonel Moonlight was commanding the Union rear guard force that had held up Shelby and gave Curtis more time to plan for operations and defense against the oncoming Confederate host. "Colonel Moonlight covered his retreat, even skirmishing after dark in and west of Independence. His conduct throughout the day was exceedingly gallant."[28] It was now evident that more fighting was in the offing and Independence, Missouri, was the next target of both Union and Confederate armies.

8

Trial at Westport

Major General Samuel Curtis was increasingly frustrated as he now figured out that the Department of Missouri commander, William Rosecrans, was more concerned in keeping the Union Army's XVI Corps between him and Price's Army of Missouri. In fact XVI Corps marched to within twenty miles of Lexington on the 20th and went into camp. Blunt reported "much depends now on our prompt action and concentration with Rosecrans' forces."[1] There would be no uniting of forces; in fact, Maj. Gen. Curtis saw the Big Blue as the primary line of defense, not the Little Blue. This did not sit well with Blunt who decided to contest Price's forces at the Little Blue River crossing along the Independence and Lexington roads. "My command is in camp on the west side of the Blue, in a strong position-that I can defend this line against a largely superior force."[2] Defend was exactly what Blunt would have to do—just across the river Jo Shelby's command watched the twinkling campfires of the federals on the rise east of the Little Blue on the Lexington Road.

In Kansas City Maj. Gen. Samuel Curtis had his hands full trying to convince the Governor of Kansas to commit the state militia for his use and found that politics of the border outweighed his need for troops. Kansas Governor Carney refused to commit his troops in Missouri beyond the Big Blue River. General Curtis's hands were tied and agreed to this insolent political act on the part of the governor; he had to form much of his plan to defend at the Big Blue because of this, in spite of Blunt's belief that it would be better to face Price at the Little Blue. Curtis knew Price and read his intentions well, believing he would seek battle at the Big Blue. "The former conflicts I have had with Price's force made me familiar with his purpose, often declared to his followers, of making another effort to establish himself on the Missouri River."[3] Curtis believed that Price had the intent to seek a defining battle on the Kansas Border, take the government stores there and establish Confederate control before any effort on the part of Rosecrans could stop it.

General Curtis made it clear to all and especially to Brigadier Blunt that he would make haste to the Big Blue with most of his command, leaving only a portion to contest the Confederate crossing of the Little Blue. "I have no time to explain. Your forces must take position here ... the Big Blue must be our main line of battle."[4] Now with the Kansas Militia forces at his disposal, Maj. Gen. Curtis had a force of over 20,000 troops to engage Price's almost 15,000, though many of Price's men had seen plenty of combat whereas Curtis's forces were less seasoned. It was left to Brigade Commander Moonlight, after Blunt's departure to Independence, to confront the Confederate Army headed toward his direction. It was initially up to Moonlight's 11th Kansas Cavalry to position for the attack. Looking to deploy his artillery, Col. Moonlight saw above the Lexington Road on the north side, west of the river, a rocky promontory ideally suited to position his artillery. Setting out his pickets in the predawn hours of October 21st, the appropriately named Colonel Moonlight prepared for battle.

Samuel Curtis was probably one of the most underrated Union Generals in the American Civil War. He directed Union victory at Pea Ridge, Arkansas, and Westport, Missouri, contending with Price and Rosecrans. He wanted to finish off the Confederate force but was overruled (Library of Congress).

The Confederate plan of action was beginning to unfold. Price took a day to resupply and rest his troops at Lexington, but on the 21st he moved on Independence. In a Generals meeting it was decided by Price and endorsed by General Shelby, that the Army of Missouri would swing south once it arrived in Independence, move up the Big Blue River and at a place called Byram's Ford, crossover and swing north to take the town of Westport, flanking Curtis's force. Believing Curtis was not yet prepared Price put his plan to action. This looked good on paper and Union General Samuel Curtis did have his problems, but the Army of Price first had to move against the Little Blue River crossing. Moving west along Independence Road, Maj. Gen. Marmaduke came on the Little Blue River and found the federals behind barricaded on the other side prepared to cross, assault and flank the Union troops.

The land the Confederate forces were now entering was going to look different from the cheering crowds they had encountered at places like Boonville and Lexington. Jackson County, Missouri, was one of the four counties that fell under the Order No. 11 expulsion zone. Here the troops would find silence as they marched their way towards Independence. Empty farm homes and few livestock, including horses, would be found as the realization of the so-called pro–Southern families who had been removed from their homes in retaliation for suspicion of supporting and providing aid and assistance to Southern partisans and militia. The Army of Missouri would find that they would receive little assistance here and that the political pressure from the pro–Union state of Kansas to secure its border and stop depredation from the pro–Southern Missourians was one of the paramount reasons for the removal of so many people and a scourge on local authority.

Early on the morning of the 21st Maj. Gen. Marmaduke paused to survey the field before committing his forces. Finding the Union forces spread out below the ridge and across the road from a covered bridge, Marmaduke decided on a three-pronged assault above, at and below that feature. Immediately the Confederates drove in the Union pickets. Brigadier General John B. Clark, a young man of rank, was in the lead of Marmaduke's forces. "My brigade being in advance, Captain Stallard's escort (Marmaduke's advance guard) came upon the enemy's pickets one mile from the bridge ... on the Lexington and Independence Road. Stallard soon drove them across the bridges, which they burned to prevent rapid pursuit."[5] As Stallard's forces moved against the center, Confederate forces moved above and below the bridge. As soon as the bridge went up in flames, Major Martin Anderson, of the 11th Kansas, opened up with his artillery from the escarpment above the river. General Clark soon learned of a river ford uncovered and immediately decided to push his forces downstream below the bridge.

Colonel Robert Lawther and the 10th Missouri Confederate Cavalry sent word that the federals had no units covering a crossing downstream. He was complying with directions from his commander Brig. Gen. John B. Clark. "Under instructions from General Marmaduke I sent Burbridge's regiment (Lieutenant Colonel Preston in command) to secure the ford one mile above the bridge, and Colonel Lawther with his regiment to secure the ford one half mile below, who soon reported the lower crossing clear."[6] Not waiting for more orders Lawther immediately crossed without support and soon ran into Union forces. Col. Moonlight had moved his units back west to the Moore Farm and, finding Lawther unsupported, turned his 11th Kansas Cavalry and counter charged the 10th Missouri, driving them back. Brig. Gen. Clark sent Colonel Greene's Brigade to immediately support Lawther. "On the morning of the 21st ... my regiment was turned from the main road ... for the purpose of crossing Little Blue River below the bridge ... and had marched a short distance when it was ascertained the Lawther's regiment was routed."[7]

The Battle of the Little Blue was now turning into a major engagement for Price's Army. General Clark was incredulous at events. "Hearing quick firing to the front I hastened forward with Greene's regiment, leaving orders for the command to follow as rapidly as possible, and found that Colonel Lawther had indiscreetly attacked a very heavy force of the enemy posted behind some stone fencing ... and afforded complete protection against small arms. He was driven back and in his turn assailed by the enemy.... Colonel Greene formed his regiment in line of battle, flanked by two pieces of artillery from Pratt's battalion.... Lawther having fallen to his rear in confusion."[8] Ironically Col. Lawther does not mention this part of his participation in the battle in his later official report. It was up to Colonel Greene to stem the Union response and his force worked in military precision to drive the federals back. Colton Greene soon dismounted a number of his force across the road leading to the Moore Farm and opened fire on the oncoming Yankees.

In the morning light the federals pressed their advantage and moved to flank Greene's force and avoid the confederate gunfire from their center. Greene sprang into action and, having artillery support, moved the guns to his flanks to counter the federal move. "The moment was critical; no support arrived. Directing my wings to fire by the right and left oblique I took charge of the battery, firing Nos. 1 and 3 on my flanks, and ordered rapid volleys of blank cartridges to be fired (the position of my men prevented the use of missiles). It produced the desired effect."[9] Stunned at the site of artillery the federals reigned in their charge and were soon countercharged by the Confederates who drove them back to their original position. By 9:00 o'clock Maj. Gen. Blunt had decided to rejoin Moonlight at Salem Church after hearing the gunfire sound off near the Little Blue. Notifying General Curtis, who gave his consent, Blunt took the rest of his force to aid Colonel Moonlight.

Major General James Blunt was hoping to restore his reputation after the dismal encounter with William Quantrill one year before. Leading the 2nd Colorado, 3rd Wisconsin Cavalry and 15th Kansas Cavalry, Blunt headed toward the Little Blue and soon made contact with Colonel Moonlight. Maj. Gen. Curtis wanted Blunt to return to the defenses of the Big Blue River, but Maj. Gen. Blunt repeatedly informed General Curtis that he should make the stand at the Little Blue and that was exactly what Blunt intended to do. Early

8. Trial at Westport

on that morning Maj. Gen. Blunt reported, "I was directed to move with all the volunteer force back to the Little Blue.... The command was now pressed forward as rapidly as possible, but on arriving on the field I found that the small force under Colonel Moonlight ... had been forced backed by superior numbers.... As soon as the troops could be got into position, a gallant attempt was made to push back the enemy and retake the ground we had lost."[10]

To the surprise of the Confederates the arrival of Union reinforcements effectively pushed them back near the Little Blue. Now the Army of Missouri would have to commit even more forces in order to defeat the enemy. Brig. Gen. John B. Clark recorded, "Owing to the difficulties of crossing at the ford Greene's regiment fought at great odds unsupported, but they contested every inch of ground with the stubbornness until the arrival of Wood's battalion, when the enemy gave way, but receiving re-enforcements drove us again to our original position."[11] The focus of the battle now centered on the Moore House, which was an abandoned expulsion zone home, and the Salem Church Road; moving to reinforce his beleaguered forces, Jo Shelby, who was in nominal command of the attack, sent for Jackman's Brigade and M. Jeff Thompson commanding the Iron Brigade.

As the battle seesawed back and forth, Brig. Gen. Shelby and Colonel Jackman disagreed on where Jackman might enter the fight. Finally Jackman reluctantly agreed and took his force on a wide berth to test the Union left flank. Meanwhile Shelby brought up more of Marmaduke's and Fagan's Brigades with the intention of developing the center of his line. Shelby attacked with "one hundred and fifty of the Third Missouri Cavalry under Colonel Colton Greene and the Seventh Missouri Cavalry under Colonel S. G. Kitchen."[12] To the north, almost simultaneously with the assault of Shelby, Jackman's Brigade was surprised to find Union artillery to their front and recovering from initial contact; Jackman counterattacked and dislodged the federals. Also arriving on the field was Brig. Gen. William Cabell's Brigade in support. "Shelby's Brigade was ordered to support Marmaduke, who was heavily engaged. I was then ordered to support General Shelby, who was heavily engaged with the enemy, who was posted behind rock fences."[13] Now Shelby was positioned to strike and strike he did.

In the early afternoon of the 21st of October the air was full of the sharp fire of cannons and rifled musketry. Flashes of orange toward and from the vicinity and tranquility of Salem Church filled the air with smoke. On the Union flank, at the Moore House, the Confederates pushed the federals back. The determined assault of screaming Southerners was beginning to tell. Arriving on the field of battle just before the Confederate advance, Maj. Gen. Samuel Curtis immediately realized the threat of being flanked. "The fearlessness with which General Curtis exposed himself in the face of the enemy, while directing the action and endeavoring to hold his not over-steady militiamen to their work.... During the resistance to Marmaduke's attack here, Major Hunt opened with the two howitzers attached to Curtis' escort, from the shelter of a little group of trees, houses, and a blacksmith's shop. The Confederates promptly turned both artillery and musketry on the spot and two of the battery horses fell at their first volley."[14] This action now allowed the Confederates of Shelby's Division to rapidly move on the Union center.

With their center exposed and pressured on their flanks, General Curtis and Blunt could no longer hold and decisions had to be made. The 4th Missouri Cavalry Regiment of John B. Clark's division was moving on Jennison's Union Regiment flanking the Union right, just as M. Jeff Thompson's Brigade struck the Union center. "We were ordered to the left of Marmaduke's division, and having dismounted we soon forced the crossing to our front, and following the enemy from position to position, several of which were very strong and well defended drove him toward the town of Independence."[15] This was it for Maj. Gen. Curtis and the word went out to disengage and fall back. "Toward the close of the afternoon Curtis ordered all his hard-pressed forces to abandon the field and retire to their assigned positions in the earthworks and defences along the west bank of the Big Blue River, between Independence and Kansas City."[16] Retreating through Independence, some of the Union troops were actually fired at by local citizens loyal to the South, but maintaining discipline the army continued on their route.

It was a victory for the Army of Missouri but a bit of a pyrrhic one. The Army occupied the field but the enemy had made good his escape behind the Big Blue River near Kansas City and its defenses. Price had to bring up his long train of supply wagons that extended for miles west down dusty roads. The delay at the Little Blue River helped the Union Cavalry under General Pleasonton to gain ground on Price and he was not far off when Price entered Independence. General Curtis's Army of the Border had the luxury of now having interior lines of defense and his immediate supply needs as to Price's exposed long train of wagons. The need to move and strike Curtis was becoming paramount for success; fortunately for Price Brig. Gen. Jo Shelby's blood was up and he was itching to continue the fight, as he led the vanguard of the Army of Missouri toward Independence.

The Wallace Moore house and farm had been the focal point of action during the Battle of the Little Blue. Just like Lizzie Brannock, who lived nearby, the people who once lived there were forced to leave with expulsion Order No. 11. Did the Moore family harbor sympathy for the South and give aid? No one really knows. All that is known is they simply left everything and never did return. Empty for almost a year, the Moore house was witness to all that war could offer. The Union forces occupied it as the battle began and when forced to leave at the Confederate advance, they tried to burn it. While occupied by the Confederates, the house was targeted by both sides and was pockmarked by artillery and rifle fire. Shortly after the battle the house was used by the Confederates as a hospital, covering the wood floors with soldiers' blood. It is believed, just before Shelby's Division departed, that some officers and enlisted men were buried on the house grounds. Early the next morning, on October 22, 1864, Alfred Pleasonton's Provisional Union Cavalry rode by and over the silent grounds and fallow fields of the Moore Farm.

Now in Independence, Sterling Price was in a quandary of being between two forces. On one side he had the Army of the Border ensconced behind the well-fortified Big Blue River directly west on the Kansas City Road and now Pleasonton's Cavalry was prepared to descend on his rear guard. General Curtis had field entrenchments and abatis prepared from the Missouri River south along the Big Blue River for about fifteen miles to Hickman Mills. The main idea on the part of Curtis and his staff was to prevent a direct attack on Kansas City and Westport, believing Price and the Army of Missouri was headed for the Missouri River. General Price was headed toward Kansas City but only as a feint, having real intentions of sending his main force, under Shelby, up the Big Blue and across at Byram's Ford, then up toward Westport. His plan was to envelope Curtis's army, knowing full well that it consisted mainly of local militia.

There was a problem with the plan and although this is exactly what Jo Shelby encouraged Price to do, they must have believed that the Union Provisional Cavalry, under Pleasonton, was not a serious threat. In fact with Shelby's insistence, Price believed that he could dispose of Curtis's green militia and then turn on Pleasonton. Simultaneous events on October 22, 1864, would unmask Price's intentions and reveal just how effective Pleasonton's Cavalry would prove to be and foreshadow things to come. After the intense fighting on the Little Blue the day before, the crisp air on the morning of the 22nd broke early for the rustling Confederates. The Confederates had good reason to be restless—General Alfred Pleasonton was hard on their heels.

Early on the 22nd Brig. Gen. Jo Shelby initiated the Confederate battle plan and had Colonel Jackman's force move down the Kansas City Road. As Brig. Gen. Jo Shelby was moving to bluff toward Kansas City and then turn south up the Big Blue, the focus would soon be on a loop bend that held Byram's Ford on the Big Blue River. "The southern end of the line was formed chiefly by Colonel C. R. Jennison's First Brigade and Moonlight's Second

Brigade, the extreme southern point of the Hickman's Mills Crossing being held by Brigadier-General M. S. Grant with 100 militiamen of the Second and the Twenty-first Kansas and one brass howitzer under Captain J. T. Burnes of the Second. Such was the long line of battle which it was hoped would check Price."[17] The feint worked only for a while, but still long enough to alarm General Curtis and have him warn his lines: "look out for your positions."

All indications now led Union commanders to believe that Price was going to flank Curtis on Byram's Ford. The realization was this: Byram's Ford was going to be the key to the success of both Confederate and Union armies. By noon Shelby was moving to dislodge the Northerners on the opposite bank of the Big Blue by using the same tactics he had used in attacking those forces at the Little Blue. Finding that the approaches to the ford were heavily blocked by felled trees, Shelby unlimbered some of his artillery and began shelling the barricaded federals across the river. Concentrated at Byram's Ford, Colonel Jennison's federal force was spread thin and just below that ford the Confederates found a crossing (Hinkle's Ford) used by Slayback's command flanking the Union force.

As Slayback was searching for a crossing, Shelby and M. Jeff Thompson slugged it out across the Big Blue. Heavy rifle fire and artillery filled the air as bullets whizzed by the Confederates moving down to cross the stream. After firing for about three hours, the federals began to pull back as Jennison realized he would soon be caught between Confederates converging on his position. General Thompson reported, "A portion of the brigade were dismounted, and in the face of the enemy waded the stream and made a lodgment upon the west bank. Others soon followed, and we drove the enemy.... The brigade continued to press the enemy ... to near the town of Westport."[18] The Union retreat almost became a rout, but for the arrival of Chief of Artillery Major Hunt and Maj. T. I. McKenny, an aide-de-camp who gathered in the retreating Militia. Hunt recalled, "The general sent me out with body guard to re-enforce ... met the militia falling back in confusion; ... sent a messenger to Colonel Jennison asking him where I could render him the most service. He informed me that the enemy was flanking him ... and for me to fall back on the Westport road to keep the enemy out of town. I did so."[19]

General Shelby came within a hair's breadth of capturing Westport that evening. The Confederate rear was a different matter and was becoming more problematic. At about the same time Shelby was prosecuting his attack at Byram's Ford, General Alfred Pleasonton pressed on to Independence. Maj. Gen. John S. Marmaduke was in command of denting any pursuit by the federal cavalry, placing his troops on the streets in town and at the edge of town, between the businesses and homes mounted and dismounted. If Marmaduke's command believed that Pleasonton's force could be deterred to the federal fieldworks behind the Big Blue, the struggle in Independence would remove all doubt. In fact Pleasonton's orders were to move south and meet up with A. J. Smith's XVI Corps, but due to the fact that his cavalry were so close at hand, he modified his orders on the go and said, "I determined to push the enemy as far as possible ... to relieve Curtis."[20] As Price was moving toward Byram's Ford Maj. Gen. Pleasonton arrived at the outskirts of Independence.

Independence, Missouri, occupied an area surrounded by open prairie on all sides of the town, making it an easy approach. Deploying his command, Pleasonton moved Sanborn's Brigade to enter the town from the north side and he positioned McNeil's Brigade, the original Kansas Jay Hawkers, to the southern end, leaving Phillips's Brigade to cover the center. Driving in Confederate pickets of Fagan's command, Colonel Sanborn dismounted his brigade and began to move between the buildings on the north side of town, firing at squads of Confederates moving back and forth along the streets. Street fighting was at best a difficult task and Sanborn's forces became somewhat stalled in the process. Brig. Gen. McNeil decided not to dismount his troops and from the south side of the town, rapidly charged through the streets with guns drawn, driving the fleeing Confederates back until McNeil ran into Marmaduke's formed lines just west of the town's outskirts.

As Marmaduke stalled Pleasonton's troopers, he sent word for the need for more reinforcements. As Fagan's men were regrouping Brig. Gen. William Cabell led his brigade back toward Independence to answer Marmaduke's request; on the south and west side of town Colonel Colton Greene's regiment was just barely holding on to the Confederate right flank. "On the morning of the 22d I was notified by General Marmaduke to hold my position until relieved."[21] When Cabell arrived he helped drive the Union forces back but only briefly. Just as Cabell was preparing to extradite the Confederate forces from their positions in town, the Union forces countercharged on horseback, striking Cabell in flank and taking most by surprise, and capturing two artillery pieces before they could be limbered and moved off. Colonel Greene remembered the moment, "An hour or two after artillery and musketry firing indicated that the enemy was driving our forces and was near town, and I accordingly retired my outposts one mile, only in time to observe that the head of Rosecrans' army had penetrated the town and had driven our rear ... in confusion.... My position was extremely hazardous."[22]

With heavy smoke drifting in the streets and alleyways of Independence, flashes of gunfire defined where friend and foe might be positioned. Reining in his horse, General Cabell suddenly found himself face-to-face with mounted Union cavalry at Walnut Street. McNeil wheeled about his men and with additional troops coming up, charged again and overwhelmed the Confederates. William Cabell was now personally engaged with the bright slashes of sabers falling his way. Parrying the blows with his saber, General Cabell made off down an ally, but lost his sword as he jumped over a piece of ordnance left in the road. In Cabell's report, he related: "Just as I was coming out of the city the enemy struck me in the flank, charging down several streets, and cut off two or three hundred of my men and capturing two pieces of artillery. I escaped as they were cutting at me…. As soon as I got through the different lots…. I rode to my command, which was then in the road, faced them to the rear, checked and drove back the enemy."[23]

Witnessing the action without relief, Colonel Greene withdrew his troops slowly south, so as not to be surrounded. Most of Greene's men were wearing blue Union uniforms taken from various stores during the raid through Missouri and he now found himself separated from the main column of the Army of Missouri with Union troops between him and that force. Luckily the dusty Union troops did not recognize Greene's force because of the uniforms and Greene took full advantage of that fact as he moved to rejoin his command. "I moved on the Little Santa Fe` road…. The enemy was still ahead of me on my right, which made it impractical to join the main army, and hence I moved on for ten miles at a trot."[24] Captain West, who had been sent to relieve Greene, also found himself cut off and, joining Greene's command, made his way with him until an opportunity presented itself about ten miles up near the Big Blue; finding a Union force soon to be in their forefront turned the command to the right late that evening and made his way to Byram's Ford without incident.

The situation report for the end of the 22nd presented tactical opportunities to both Curtis and Price. Price and the Army of Missouri now controlled the river crossings of the Big Blue, particularly the crossing at Byram's Ford. General Shelby had driven the federals back from the river towards Brush Creek and Westport. Had Shelby not paused for the ammunition supply trains to catch up he may well have driven the federals even farther. Furthermore Price now had something like an interior line of defense or offense that he could now utilize to his advantage, but would he have enough troops to take advantage of just such a line? One problem glared its ugly head at the Confederates: General Marmaduke and Fagan had not dealt Union General Pleasonton enough of a blow that would prevent him from his continued pursuit. In fact Pleasonton continued the fight to near Byram's Ford well into the night of the 22nd.

For General Samuel Curtis and the Army of the Border the situation on

8. Trial at Westport

the evening of the 22nd gave him pause for thought. On the one hand Curtis actually believed that Price had more troops than he actually had and this influenced his thinking on just how to deal with Price. He had faced Price before and bested him; if he had any doubts, his doubts revolved around the fact that he had basically untried militia. Another factor was the whereabouts of General Pleasonton, the communications between the two commanders was not the best and on the 22nd Curtis's anxiety rose as to how to best utilize the cavalry command. Moving his Headquarters command post to Westport, General Curtis decided to make a stand on the ledges overlooking Brush Creek, south of Westport. If the army could make a stand there and blunt the Confederates, Curtis believed that taking the offensive would pressure Price and his army, if not destroy that army drive it from his base of operation.

Confederate General Jo Shelby was in fine spirits that early morning of October 23, 1864, after getting plenty of sleep. He had a good day on the 22nd and was planning a better one today, and believed that the Army of Missouri was on the verge of victory. The focus of the Battle on the 23rd would be the Wornall House and Byram's Ford, an area of nearly six square miles. The Wornall Farmstead covered a large area from Brush Creek to the north and the Kansas-Missouri State line directly two miles west, encompassing approximately 600 acres. On the previous day Confederate Generals Shelby and Fagan drove the federals back across the farm fields, toward Brush Creek, very near the Wornall Home to the delight of young John Wornall, who could watch the action from the second floor of his home. On the 23rd the family was anticipating even more action.

The inability to minimize Union General Alfred Pleasonton in the days prior would become problematical for Confederate John S. Marmaduke. Fought to a frazzle the day before, his men now occupied what the federals occupied the day before, the heights above Byram's Ford. It was a very tenable position. The Union forces had fortified the area with abattis and rifle pits with good field of fire for artillery on Potato Hill. It was unfortunate that the battle opened with a simultaneous assault by Union forces on the ford and Shelby's forces opposite Brush Creek. Ironically it was the federals who initiated the battle by attacking the Confederates across Brush Creek before Westport. Maj. General James Blunt, Union Division Commander, witnessed the opening. "Daylight on the morning of the 23rd revealed the enemy in force on the open prairie directly south of Westport and about two miles distant ... and at daylight my whole command was in motion, moving in column through Westport and across Brush Creek ... where Shelby's division, of Prices's army, was advancing upon my line."[25]

Simultaneously the assaults opened at Byram's Ford and at Brush Creek

(Westport), with the assault at Byram's Ford opening just a little earlier on that morning. Skirmishing at the ford began just after sunrise with rifle firing that continued to rise. General Alfred Pleasonton's Provisional Cavalry was planning an attack that was very similar to that of Jo Shelby the day before or as Paul Jenkins wrote, "a final crushing assault on Price's rear."[26] Pleasonton wanted an immediate attack on the ford at daylight and when Brig. Gen. Egbart Brown failed to implement the assault, Pleasonton rode to Brown to ask why he had not initiated an attack. Unsatisfied with Egbart Brown's explanation, Pleasonton had the man removed, relieved and then immediately placed his second, Colonel John Philips, as the brigade's new commander. By 9:00 o'clock in the morning the battle for Byram's Ford was continuing in earnest. Pleasonton's command was trying to force the crossing of the ford with the now Philips's Brigade leading the way, but was forced back by the heavy fire of the concentrated center of the Confederate line. Forced to probe north and south of the Confederate defenses, the federals were finally able to cross. Dee's Battalion of the 4th Iowa and Philips's Brigade, which sidled to the south, made crossings and flanked the Confederates on the right, helped in their movement by the heavy smoke now beginning to hang in the valley.

Fighting in an open meadow, the Confederates gave ground slowly toward a rocky ledge that fronted Potato Hill. Because of the flanking maneuver, the soldiers covering the ford had no choice but to fall back. Brig. Gen. John B. Clark watched and waited, reporting: "Greene's regiment, commanded by Captain Johnson (Greene recovering from previous wounds) and Burbridge's regiment, commanded by Lieutenant Colonel Preston, with Freeman's brigade met him first.... He contended manfully for the crossing ... but was forced back after having repulsed the enemy several times."[27] Watching the action unfolding before him below the rocky ledge, General Clark knew that the withdrawing Confederates would take up position behind Clark's men. Fighting now for three hours, the Union men came tumbling across the meadow, adjacent to Byram's Ford Road, heading straight for Potato Hill. Pressed on his flanks and now from his center Clark did what he could to stem the blue tide as Philips's Brigade, of Pleasonton's force, was moving up on Potato Hill. Now at this critical moment, around 10:30 a.m., General Clark was informed that his force was close to being out of ammunition and that they would have to be withdrawn, per Maj. Gen. Marmaduke's orders.

The failure to hold Byram's Ford and the continuing problem with ammunition arrival would be critical to the assault by Shelby three miles west. At about the same time as the action was opening at Byram's Ford, action was beginning at Westport. On the prairie very near the Wornall home, Shelby, who was nominally in command, and Fagan's divisions prepared for battle. On the Union side Maj. Gen. Blunt did not wait. Moving down and up the banks of Brush Creek, Blunt thought that a spoiling attack with his much smaller force would allow General Samuel Curtis to prepare his Kansas Militia for the larger assault. General Jo Shelby must have been annoyed by the fact that the day before he had driven the Union forces across the creek and now had to repeat the process simply because he lacked the ammunition that would have allowed him to maintain that assault. Now with replenished stores, at about 8:30 a.m., he would correct Blunt's move and drive him back.

Hearing the cannon fire off to the east, Shelby formed a line of battle and commenced his forward movement, driving in Blunt's skirmishers and sending General Blunt in slow retreat. "Inch by inch and foot by foot they gave way before my steady onset. Regiment met regiment, and opposing batteries (covering Wornall Lane) draped the scene in clouds of dense and sable smoke."[28] With General Fagan covering the right flank, connecting with Marmaduke's line, Shelby moved forward and approached the bluffs on the south bank of Brush Creek. Taking position along a rock fence overlooking Brush Creek, M. Jeff Thompson's Brigade (Iron Brigade) centered the Confederate line. The position offered Thompson a field of fire from a steep river bank and over the other side. General Shelby covered Thompson's Brigade's left flank with Colonel Jackman's Brigade on open ground away from the steep river bank, covering a considerable amount of ground near the Bent House.

Major General Samuel Curtis looked over the ground and decided that he had to launch an offensive attack against Price in order to maintain the initiative and not let the Confederates replenish and rearm. Launching a series of attacks from the other side of the creek, Curtis's forces could not dislodge the Confederates along the steep bluffs. Gaining a foothold, the three Union divisions were soon sent reeling back across the creek as Union and Confederate artillery sparred and spewed shot and shell. Colonel Jennison reported, "At this point the fighting again became severe, and a second time we were compelled to retire, a movement participated in by the entire division.... At this point a desultory fire was kept up for some time."[29] Curtis would not let up; he was determined to keep up the pressure on Price's lines. It was nearing 11:00 a.m. and events now unfolded that would undermine what seemed to be at that time a possible Confederate triumph, as originally planned by Shelby and Price.

The fighting had been going on for three hours when General Curtis was informed that an elderly gentleman named Thoman, a local farmer, believed he could guide some of Curtis's forces through a deep ravine that could conceal them from the prying eyes of Confederate skirmishers. Unbelievably, the area of the ravine would flank the Confederates on their left in an area covered by Jackman's Brigade on open and maneuverable ground. General Curtis simply stated, "I was directed by an old man, a Missouri patriot of seventy-five years, through a narrow defile to Brush Creek with Dodge's battery and other forces."[30] Holding a strong position, General Shelby was expecting to launch his own attack when word reached him that disaster had struck the Confederate right.

General Marmaduke had held his position since early morning at Byram's Ford. Now the momentum was with Pleasonton's dismounted cavalry. The veteran brigade of Brig. Gen. John B. Clark removed his command from Potato Hill in a disciplined leap frog-like withdraw covering each of his regiment in turn until reaching the reserve line Marmaduke set up to cover that force. Once Clark's men were past it was up to the reserve line to stem the oncoming blue tide. Clark could not hold; the butternut and grey uniforms soon fell back in disorder, for just behind the retreating units came the massive numbers of Union blue headed by Pleasonton himself, bearing down on that line which panicked and broke soon after their first exchange of fire. Pleasonton was ecstatic at the site and exhorted his troops, waving his riding crop, pointing at the fleeing gray, imploring them to keep up the pursuit even as his own forces ebbed. Marmaduke and Clark did what they could to restore some semblance of order and began withdrawing south, away from the action towards the roads to Little Santa Fe.

It now seemed that events had indeed conspired to undo the Confederate advance at Westport. Curtis's move onto the prairie, with the help of the local farmer, near the Bent Home dislodged Jackman's Brigade and now could infiltrate Shelby's left; simultaneously, Jennison, Deitzler and Ford advanced in unison across Brush Creek, driving all forces before them. General Price and Shelby had no reserves and even had to send some units from Fagan's Division to shore up Marmaduke. By noontime Shelby had Col. Jackman's Brigade take position behind his force, to cover him as he slowly retreated down Wornall Lane toward the Wornall House. Watching from their home, the Wornall family saw the dust and smoke of the war once again moving in their direction. Mrs. Wornall was in their garden making her way back into her home when a piece of ordnance brushed by her head, undoing her hair piece and sending her locks falling off her shoulders, startling her and giving her reason to remove the family to the root cellar.

Just a few hundred yards to the north of the house and farm, General Shelby formed a battle line to meet the oncoming federals and soon made the Wornall home a field hospital and command post. Occupying a stone fence that ran from east to west from Wornall Lane, Shelby's horsemen dismounted to try to stem the oncoming blue tide. At one point as the Confederates were withdrawing, Colonel McGhee's Arkansas Cavalry saw three artillery pieces being unlimbered some distance ahead of the supporting federal troops. The Arkansans immediately saw a chance to charge the guns in order to capture them. This brought an immediate response from the federals who countercharged on seeing the advancing McGhee and his men. Soon the combatants were fighting hand to hand amidst the dust and smoke of pistol fire; in a swirl of dust and muzzle flashes, Col. McGhee was fatally wounded. Realizing that his position at the fence was tentative, General Shelby had sent for Col. Jackman to aid General Fagan who was trying to aid Marmaduke at the onrushing federals under Pleasonton. Putting up stiff resistance, Shelby could not cover his flanks and realized that his center could now be pierced.

Major General Curtis was among the troops along with Blunt and was pleased with how events were now unfolding. Out in open ground his forces had the Confederates on their heels, Major General Deitzler of the Kansas State Militia recalled. "Both armies were now in full view each other on the open prairie.... A running fight was then kept up for about four miles, the enemy slowly retreating in a southerly direction, parallel with and about a mile from the state line ... when General Rosecrans advance, under Major-General Pleasonton, made its appearance some distance from the right of the enemy, and opened upon them with artillery."[31] It was somewhere at this moment that General Pleasonton rode up on his horse to meet with General Curtis, as their forces now acted as one in driving Price's Army. Under the circumstances, Pleasonton had acted well in seeing the intentions of Curtis's plan and acting accordingly even if the communication between the two was not always clear.

This confluence of Curtis and Pleasonton aided in Shelby's decision to move back from the Wornall Home; General Price had already moved off to help with the defense of the wagon train in the rear, east of the action. Indeed the train was under the good hands of Brig. Gen. William Cabell and Colonel Colton Greene. Union General John McNeil, architect of infamous Palmyra Massacre, was sent by Pleasonton to intercept and delay the Confederates and possibly destroy the wagon train. Cabell had kept ahead and when McNeil caught up to General Cabell's command, Cabell acted. "I moved with my brigade between the train and this column and attacked them with a heavy line of skirmishers and drove them back at least one mile.... The grass being very tall and the winds high and blowing toward the enemy, I concluded to set the grass on fire and to follow immediately behind the blaze with a line of skirmishers ... to keep up a brisk fire through the flames."[32] As he was doing this, Cabell also noticed the stream of stragglers who were coming into

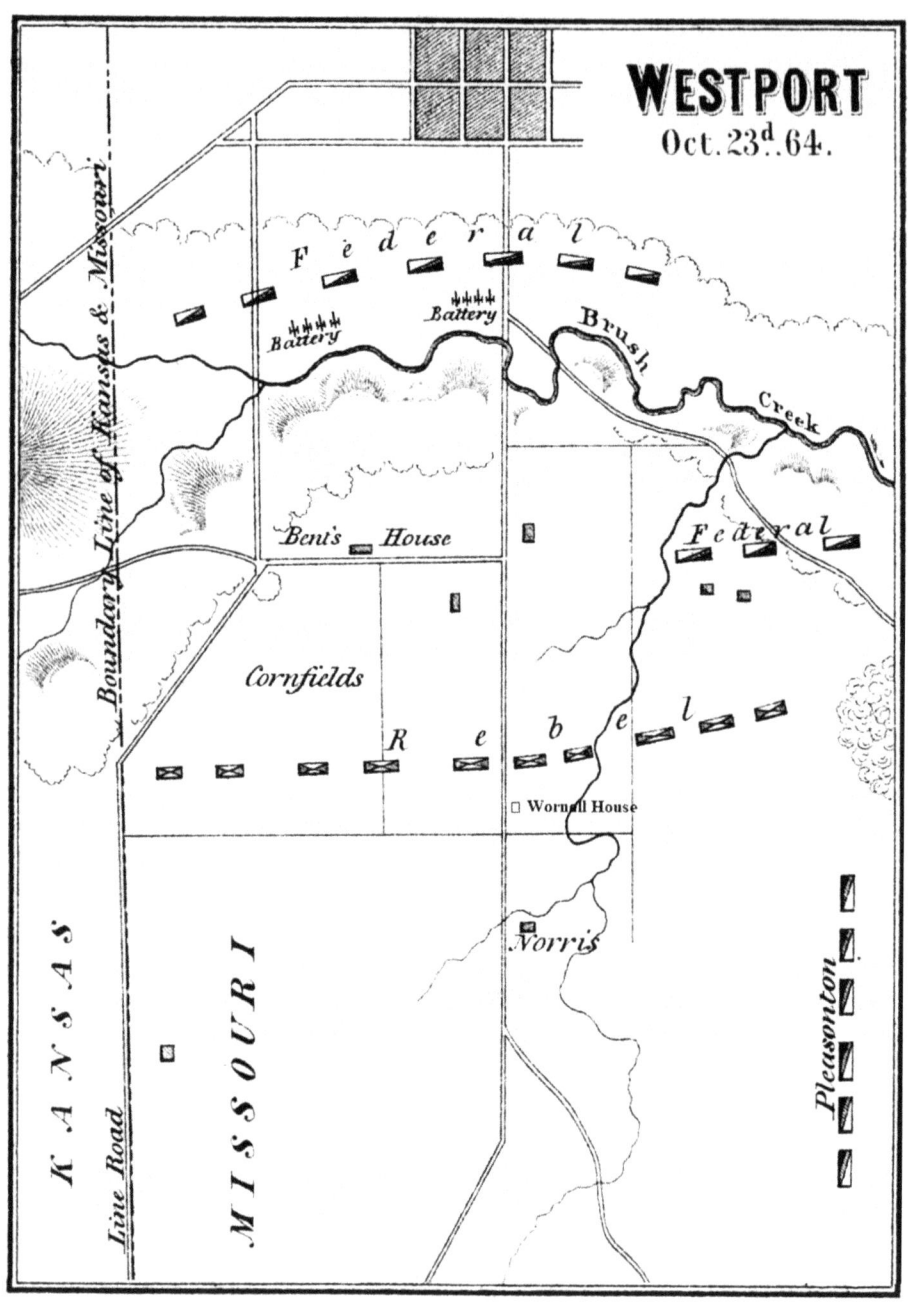

Westport, October 23, 1864 (Library of Congress).

his command. These stragglers where part of the force from the Byram's Ford debacle and the fight before Westport. Cabell had them fall into his line of march making south along the Military Road.

Looking out over the ground, one could see fallen men and horses dotting all along the prairie and stone fences. The battle had cost the combined forces of both the Confederacy and Union, with some 3,000 dead, missing and wounded, as the federals now occupied the Wornall House and tended the wounded of both sides. Shelby had moved off toward the southeast to hilly ground at a place called Forest Hill,[33] covering Price's forces and train moving south. It had turned into a disappointing afternoon according to Brig. Gen. M. Jeff Thompson as he tried to parry the Union assaults. "At this instant, while our lines where broken and our long range guns discharged, the enemy with a fresh line charged our right, and the in the first time on this campaign Shelby's brigade turned its back to the foe."[34] Fighting from horseback, the Confederates would move off a short distance and then turn and fire and repeat from their last line along the slopes of forest hills southeast from the Wornall House, joining Price's main column of the wagon trains as they moved briskly south.

It cannot be stressed enough that the appearance of Pleasonton had a demoralizing effect on the Confederates, as Union Maj. Gen. Deitzler related. "By 12:00 o'clock we have reached the open prairie four miles south of Westport, when we see on our left as far as the eye can reach long column advancing toward us. We are inspired with new and intense interest; we look and listen; we are not long in doubt; we hear the artillery of General Pleasonton … they have at last reached us and given the enemy's right a taste of their powder; we now have them; the retreat became a perfect rout; we cannot keep pace with them. The battle is over, the victory won, and nobly won."[35] The failure on the part of Price to eliminate Pleasonton early in the campaign now was plainly evident and cost him and Shelby his victory at Westport along with the continuing failure to keep his force supplied in a timely manner with the needed ammunition. The ammunition argument would have possibly given his best tactical commander, General Joseph Shelby, the instrument to keep pushing on Curtis's Kansas Militia and send them into rout. Instead it was the Confederates who lost the battle and were sent in headlong flight to save the trains.

9

Blue Grass Ridges

Major General William S. Rosecrans had made his way to Independence, Missouri, and as commander of the Missouri Military District he was having less anxiety over the situation with Price's Army of Missouri. The information coming over the telegraph wires was encouraging. General Curtis had proclaimed victory at Westport and Rosecrans had decided to relinquish command of Pleasonton's cavalry to Curtis, but he did not give up the XVI Corps and maintained nominal command of its deployment. "The enemy having been defeated at Westport ... a vigorous pursuit was necessary to prevent his taking our military posts.... The troops of General Pleasonton, the militia ... and my regular volunteers ... were now more than sufficient to pursue Price."[1] The Union Military command was now concerned that Price's intentions were focused on the U.S. Military post at Fort Scott. Originally the XVI Corps was intended to intercept Price's Army of Missouri near Hickman Mills, but they arrived much too late to take any part in the battle and Pleasonton's efforts there.

The weary XVI Corps was now no longer needed on the border and this probably set well with General Rosecrans. With Price in retreat he was no longer needed in this sector and could return to St. Louis with the XVI Corps. It was now late in October and that Corps was needed in the Trans-Mississippi sector and was eventually ordered to go to the command of Major General George Thomas at Nashville. With the fall of Atlanta, in Georgia, Confederate General John Bell Hood's Army of Tennessee was making intentions of operations in Tennessee after his failure to dent Union General Sherman in Georgia. The idea that Price could tie down a large number of Union troops in Missouri was minimal and very short lived. With the general elections of the United States very near, Rosecrans decided to return to St. Louis and had given orders for General Smith to "move his command by the most expeditious route to the Mississippi in the vicinity of Saint Louis, there to embark and proceed to Nashville."[2]

The operational situation of the Army of Missouri was difficult but not untenable; the one problem it now faced was the need for food for both men and animals. The military stores at Fort Scott were tempting, but the areas of Bates and Cass counties in Missouri were part of the Burnt Land District and had nothing to offer except burned fields and empty farms. The decision was made to move west into Kansas and there take what the Confederates needed. On the afternoon of October 24, 1864, the Confederates moved west from West Point, Missouri, and crossed into Linn County, Kansas. For the Army of the Border, at a meeting at a small farm along Indian Creek, Pleasonton and Curtis decided on operational plans to continue to pressure Price. Curtis was probably aware that Price was encumbered with a large wagon train that at times numbered some fifty wagons stretching for almost ten miles. Price and his command was now slowed in the presence of a pursing enemy. This soon would become problematic as the federals began to harass his flank and gain his rear.

General Curtis believed that the Confederate Army had been demoralized and the time was at hand for its demise; he was determined to finish Price and his command once and for all. The road to Fort Scott was essential for the Army of Missouri and it was the focus of conflict from here on. The Union cavalry of Generals Blunt, Sanborn and McNeil were now unleashed to shadow, attack and slash at Price's forces. Confederate Generals Fagan, Marmaduke and Shelby, reduced in numbers, would now have to try and prevent it. At Fort Scott, an important link on the military road, the Independent Artillery Battery was manned by the U.S. Colored Light Artillery under 1st Lieutenant William D. Matthews. Matthews was busily preparing Fort Scott's defenses for a possible assault by Price. A section of Matthews's battery had already seen action at Westport and with the help of Matthews, Fort Scott was being well prepared and equally defended.

The focus of the federal forces now centered on the Fort Scott Road through a small hamlet on the Marais des Cygnes called Trading Post. In a war council at Westport, Curtis made the decision to follow up on the Confederate rear guard. General Blunt and Pleasonton thought a westward turning movement would intercept Price but Curtis disagreed. "I ordered the march resumed.... General Sanborn, in the extreme advance, halted, sending back intelligence of his arrival near the Marais de Cygenes where the enemy was in great force."[3] The geography of this region of Kansas and Missouri was open and primarily flat prairie with few prominent features except the rivers that primarily crossed easterly in front of the Confederates' path. The one exception was where Trading Post was located. Here the old military Fort Scott Road passed between two low rising hills called the Bald Hills, rising about fifty to seventy-five feet above the surrounding terrain.

By the 24th the Confederate train made its way past the mounds and crossed to the opposite banks of the Marais des Cygnes while the Army of Missouri camped near the town. Brigadier General William Cabell offered this description: "we camped near the Marais des Cygnes, after marching over twenty-four miles. I was in the rear and the whole Brigade in line of battle at the gap of the Bald Prairie hills and on top of the hills during the night. The enemy made several attempts to drive my men from the top of the mountains and break my lines ... failing in every attempt, they retired about two o'clock."[4] The situation of the Confederate forces seemed to bristle with Napoleonic possibilities. Could the Confederate command recognize that they could use those twin hills like the Battle of Austerlitz where Napoleon broke the Russo-Austrian lines by coming down from the Pratzen Heights? The mounds seemed to be ideal to mask the Confederate force. For some reason, it was not meant to be; the Confederate command did not recognize the possibility of inflicting a defeat on the federals. At Trading Post the weather now broke with a drenching rainstorm that pelted both the Unionists and Confederates, with the Confederates maintaining their position astride the mounds.

Riding in his carriage, Major General Sterling Price's thoughts were mostly on how to keep the wagon train of plunder and supplies intact and moving, avoiding the federals who he thought would take it by his western flank on the open Kansas prairie. Ironically this is exactly what Maj. Gen. Blunt had suggested to do and General Curtis had decided against, except Blunt was not interested in the train but in destroying Price's Army. Some Confederate Officers now thought the attention that was payed to the miles-long train was folly and were perplexed as one officer remarked, "The real fighting soldiers..., scarcely disguised their apprehension that the odious train would occasion disaster for the army, and they were plainly reluctant to shed their blood to save the plunder it convey."[5] The real threat for Price was coming from his rear as the federal units began to catch up and bear down on his exhausted command. Price now decided to delay the pursuing enemy and to do it at Trading Post as he crossed his wagons at the Marais de Cygenes.

On the morning of October 25th Sterling Price gave up his unrecognized strong position at the mounds and got his wagons moving. Union Brigadier General Sanborn was not aware of this fact and prepared his force to assault the Bald Prairie Hills. Unlimbering the 2nd Missouri Light Artillery, he opened up on the heights and sent his dismounted troopers forward. Sanborn's troops soon dislodged the Confederates on his right, but found rough terrain and stiff resistance on the Confederate right. Although Confederate

General Marmaduke left only a skirmish line on the hill it delayed the federals long enough for Price and the train to move away from the Marais de Cygenes River heading to Fort Scott. Having a strong position on the hills, the Union command halted momentarily to address attacking Confederate positions astride the hills.

The Confederate skirmishers on the east hill put up stiff resistance until the west hill was taken and then withdrew down the backside through Trading Post, passing by a large number of stragglers who had decided not to rejoin the retreat. It was now evident that indeed poor morale had taken hold of a number of troops in Price's Army. Riding into Trading Post, Sanborn and McNeil were now occupied with not continuing their pursuit of Price and instead now had to occupy their time rounding up the stragglers and decide their fate. For Brig. Gen. John McNeil the decision was easy: execution. As at Palmyra in 1862, McNeil basically considered some of the enemy combatants as nothing more than criminals. Capturing about one hundred or so of the enemy, McNeil hung a number of them and then continued on with Blunt only to temporarily stall at the Marais des Cygnes because of Confederate skirmishers, positioned there by Marmaduke and abatis on the opposite bank.

By mid-morning Generals Blunt and McNeil could clearly see the wagon train of the Confederates moving off to the southwest, on the other side of the Marais de Cygenes. Union Colonel Philips was soon ordered to move on the withdrawing Confederates, particularly John Clark's Brigade, which soon outflanked him to his left. Supporting Marmaduke and his skirmishers was Brig. Gen. John B. Clark's Brigade, just a mile down the road. From here on Clark's Brigade would play a prominent role in what was to follow, a witness to disaster. In a series of movements where one Confederate brigade would relieve another, the butternut and grey removed themselves south. At a place referred to by locals as the Mary Dayson, Brig. Gen. Clark reported, "I received an order from General Marmaduke to form my brigade in line of battle, as the enemy had again appeared in our rear.... The enemy, 800 or 900 yards distant in line of battle, followed us. We were now well out on a prairie that seemed almost boundless."[6] The long line of the grey wagon train was now becoming an impediment to the operations of the Confederates and most officers realized it.

The wagons slowed to a crawl as they began to cross a remote stream called Mine Creek. With this the rear guard now had to deal with an army of Union cavalry beginning to bear down. General Clark noticed that the enemy was approaching in superior force. "We retired at a trot, the enemy in close pursuit. We continued this way, each holding about the same position, across a flat prairie some four miles, when we came suddenly upon the trains halted, the delay occasioned by a deep ravine, the enemy not more than 500 yards in our rear."⁷ Brig. Gen. John Clark soon came upon Generals Marmaduke and Fagan and it was decided to make a stand because of the Union onset. It was either abandon the wagon train, which Price would not do, or quickly turn and fight. Much of the train had crossed Mine Creek and Marmaduke decided to unlimber ten pieces of artillery and hopefully scatter the Union horsemen with his mounted lines of cavalry.

Major General Alfred Pleasonton was delighted with the way events were unfolding for his forces. The unwillingness of the Confederates to interpose their forces at the very defensible twin hills at Trading Post convinced him to aggressively pursue. "He left in great haste.... The rapidity of the march was such that the two brigades, Winslow's (then commanded by Lieutenant-Colonel Benteen) and Philips brigades, had reached the front."⁸ Pleasonton understood the time element and the need for the enemy to move on Fort Scott as quickly as they could and now had a portion of that army within striking distance. Witnessing the events from the Confederate perspective was Colonel Colton Greene, of Marmaduke's Command; he was part of the rear guard at the Marais des Cygnes and began to recognize the peril and reported his part in it. "I was ordered by General Marmaduke to move in rear.... I was ordered to quicken my gait, then a trot, and finally to join the main body at a gallop."⁹ Moving down across the prairie from Trading Post and along the Fort Scott Road some eight miles, Col. Greene drew rein at Mine Creek to act as reserve.

The setup could not have been better for the pursuing federal cavalry; moving along Fort Scott Road the Union men could not help but notice the broken down and abandoned wagons along with various personal debris strewn everywhere. The Confederate retreat was beginning to look something like Napoleon's retreat from Moscow. With the trains blocking the crossing on Mine Creek, Marmaduke and Fagan made the decision not to dismount his force because of the closing federals. Marmaduke wanted to make a stand on the south side of Mine Creek with the stream's steep banks presenting an impediment to the enemy, but the wagons and the fast-closing formation of the Yankees prevented it. Now he offered an imposing line of mounted horsemen tripled in ranks deep; Marmaduke ordered Col. Colton Greene's brigade to form in reserve. The Colonel recalled, "The main line was less then eighty yards from me, and another line covered half of my regiment.... I was notified that I was in reserve."¹⁰

It was late morning, around 11:00 o'clock, when Colonels Philips and Benteen viewed the arrayed Confederates a little distance north of Mine Creek from a low ridge above it. General Sterling Price was ahead; his designs were still on Fort Scott and he still believed the main federal army was to the west of his advance columns moving to the Little Osage. He signaled General Shelby, "I sent forward a direction to Brigadier-General Shelby to fall back to my position ... for the purpose of attacking and capturing Fort Scott."[11] Ironically Sterling Price never recognized the danger that was coming down on his rear-guard. Instead he continued to believe that the main goal was the train and eventually the military stores at Fort Scott. Up at the crossings at Mine Creek, Generals Marmaduke and Fagan now had to confront the federal columns as they deployed their lines across the Blue Grass Prairie.

The opening of the battle of Mine Creek began with the booming echoes of the contending armies' artillery. With ten pieces of the Army of Missouri's cannon, Marmaduke was hoping to hold the line with his mounted cavalry and unnerve the federals. Marmaduke formed his lines, straddling the Fort Scott Road, commanding the confederate right while General Fagan formed on the left toward the Mound City Road. The federal forces had continued their movement from Trading Post and Col. Philips reported, "The enemy withdrew on our approach. We pursued them at the gallop for three miles, pressing him so closely as to compel him to form."[12] Advancing along parallel columns, Philips and Benteen soon came into view of the arrayed Confederates along Mine Creek. Before them was a splendid view of martial mane and both Union commanders paused only momentarily to prepare their mounts and address their lines. "He took position on the open prairie with Mine Creek, a tributary of the Osage, in his immediate rear.... My ground was high and commanding. Here the whole rebel army and train were in full view ... the work before us of fearful import."[13] Benteen waited no more and to his associate's surprise lunged his cavalry forward at a charge.

General Marmaduke's flag, a white crescent on a blue background, fluttered in the air as he rode down along his mounted lines exhorting his troopers, watching the Union lines draw up north of him. Marmaduke and Fagan totaled about 6,000 troops and faced just under 3,000 federal troops, a ratio of about 2 to 1. However, the Confederate concern was with just how many more there would be coming up in support. The Union men had at that point no artillery and the Confederate batteries had already opened on the lined-up federals. Brigadier General William Cabell thought that now was the time to attack and either roll up the Union line or simply break the Union line at a charge. "I went to General Marmaduke's assistance as rapidly as I could, forming regiments into action as fast as I could I rear ... and also on his flank."[14] As General Cabell pondered the idea, a rapid-fire fight developed between the lines. This firing convinced Cabell against charging the Union men.

The Union forces were now buying time and made up the difference in numbers with the rapid-fire weapons available to them. This was not lost to the observation of Confederate officers like William Cabell. "As fast as our lines were formed, the enemy armed with Henry rifles ... forming in front of Marmaduke and Cabell's Brigades, poured a rapid and scathing fire into our commands, which far exceeded any firing we could do from our muzzle-loading Enfield rifles."[15] Held in place, the triple ranks of Confederate horsemen hardly noticed when the Union horsemen moved toward them at a charge. Brig. General John B. Clark sat uneasy in his saddle as he surveyed the battle lines ahead of him. He was on the far right ranks of Marmaduke's command as he watched the blue tide roll out on the flank of the Confederate right. "Skirmishing had already begun, the artillery in action, when the federal force ... made a furious charge on the right and left flank."[16] He watched as his men seemed to freeze in the face of a now determined enemy onslaught.

Lieutenant Colonel Benteen of the Army of the Border came on the Confederate forces lined up north of Mine Creek with Colonel Philips coming up on his right and saw what he believed was an enemy deployment error. "I immediately surmised that the rebel commander had committed a fatal blunder, and resolved to capture it. I sent an officer to the commanding officer of the brigade on my right with the information that I was going to charge, and request for him to charge with me ... formed my command in column of regiments ... and immediately sounded the charge."[17] Momentarily stalled by the initial Confederate fire, the 4th Iowa Mounted Infantry regrouped and then came on as furies, rising up against the right flank of Marmaduke's command. It was at that moment that the Southerners gave way, clashing in sabre-to-sabre and hand-to-hand combat led by Major Abiel Pierce, of the 4th. He recalled the action: "The three companies on the right of my regiment charged the line of the Tenth Missouri Volunteer-Cavalry Regiment, which was formed in their front. In that charge we crushed the enemies right completely. We pressed them so close that I cut eight rebels from their horses with my own saber."[18] Seeing Benteen's lunge at the Confederate line, Colonel Philips immediately came on the enemy's center, supporting Benteen's attack.

Lieutenant Colonel Frederick Benteen, as he was attacking the right of Marmaduke, decided to make a half right turn with his right flank and by doing so cut off a major portion of the Confederate artillery before it could limber and drive off. Beaten at Westport and demoralized by their retreat, panic soon set in on Marmaduke's troops. With rain clouds forming above the battlefield, the Confederates now began to melt away like slow burning embers in a fire. Horses now whinnied as blue and butternut banged into each other and men fell from their horses from either sabre or pistol fire or as in the case of Maj. Gen. Marmaduke, simply knocked off from his saddle in the struggle. Desperately trying to rally as many men as he could, Marmaduke soon found himself picking himself up in the face of a young and determined 4th Iowa enlisted man who, pointing his gun at the West Point trained officer, informed Marmaduke he was now his prisoner and took the general's sword before escorting him behind Union lines.

Mine Creek was now becoming an even greater disaster than Westport had a few days before. The only other West Point trained officer in Price's command, Brig. Gen. William Cabell, was in the thick of the fighting as the right of Marmaduke's forces collapsed on the right of General Fagan's Division, causing confusion and an inability to maneuver. Fagan had to withdraw in order to save what was left and Cabell moved to rally his disintegrating brigade. Men and horses did what they could to scramble over brush and up the steep creek banks one side to the other. William Cabell remembered the day, trying to rally some of Gordon's Arkansas Regiment. "The enemy seemed to know our purpose and a small squad followed.... A lieutenant of the 7th Missouri Cavalry, with three men, followed me. I attempted to jump the creek which had high banks. In jumping, my horse got his fore feet on the opposite bank and his hind feet in the creek and fell over me."[19] Cabell was taken by some Yankee Blue and sent behind the lines where he managed to escape.

That was Cabell's first time where he was captured and told to go to the enemy's rear and then would meet up with other stragglers and try to rally a force until, after the third try, he was finally physically taken by the scruff of his collar as rain began to fall on the field of battle. "I went to the front again.... I fell in a squad with Col. Gordon and went to the front as fast as we could go and ran into the 3rd Iowa Cavalry drawn up in line of battle. They turned loose a perfect volley at us.... One man came up and ordered me to surrender."[20] Realizing later who Cabell was, the guard turned him over to General Pleasonton who was now on the field. Watching on the field and held in reserve was Confederate Colonel Colton Greene's Brigade. He saw the disaster unfold and reported: "After a slight skirmish the enemy was seen to deploy from the left of his line in heavy column of attack, completely turning our right. Suddenly the first and second lines gave way.... The same wild panic seemed to seize everything. I wheeled my remaining command (B) to the right and opened on the flank of the enemy column."[21] This bought time and stunned the Yankees as Greene then made his way out of the panic covering the artillery that still remained. Greene's unit was one of the few to make their escape from the carnage at Mine Creek.

The panorama of the scene, prior to the Union assault, impressed Colonel Philips. "My ground was high and commanding. Here the whole rebel army and train were in full view. General Price on his famed white horse was plainly visible directing and urging the rapid flight of his train. The scene was grand."[22] It was grand for the Army of the Border and Generals Curtis and Pleasonton were delighted with the results, and now wanted to finish Price. Price was completely unaware of his army's misfortune and when he was informed, he made his way back to the front and immediately asked for Shelby to bring up his Brigades. What was left of Fagan's and Marmaduke's Divisions was being rallied by brigade commanders like John B. Clark, who was able to keep together Marmaduke's escort and began to gather in what soldiers they could as they removed their force to the rear.

The wagons continued to creak along the road and Brig. Gen. Jo Shelby was thinking of how he might attack Fort Scott when a rider came up alongside him with a note from General Price. It was urgent news: the Army of Missouri's rear guard was in chaos and dispersed and his division was in need of restoring the line and the day. "Day and night the retreat was continued until the evening of the 25th, when my division, marching leisurely in the front of the train, was ordered hastily to the rear to protect it, while flying rumors came up constantly that Marmaduke and Cabell were captured with all their artillery."[23] The rumors were true and Shelby peeled off the van and left Colonel Jackman in charge of the train. By the time Shelby got there the federals were in close pursuit and nearing the Little Osage River; realizing he would need more support, General Shelby sent for Colonel Jackman's Brigade to come up posthaste.

Moving out over the broad prairie lands the train soon was covered with a limited screening force as Colonel Sidney Jackman broke off and made for General Shelby's position near the Little Osage River. Between six and seven miles south of Mine Creek, the remnants of Marmaduke and Fagan's troops made their way past and through the lines of Shelby's troops as they took up position about a mile above Little Osage River. Shelby could plainly see the blue tide coming up from the north and prepared to fire volley in their upcoming ranks. Moving south from point to point and taking advantage of geographic position, Shelby's units of Gordon and Slayback of M. Jeff Thompson's Brigade performed as best they could as the Union blue pressed them rearward until Col. Jackman and his Brigade came galloping to their aid. It was a welcome site and made the difference. "Going into line at gallop, and opening ranks to let the retreating brigade through, he charged down upon the rushing enemy like a thunderbolt, driving them back and scattering their front line. The charge saved us and the day's work was done."[24]

The appearance of Shelby and Jackman was enough for Pleasonton to unlimber his artillery and fire at the Confederates as they made their way off the field and halted any further pursuit. Pleasonton had decided to now rest his force and make his way to Fort Scott to resupply and decide what action was next. It was at Fort Scott that General Pleasonton and General Curtis came to disagree on what to do next with Price and his army. Major General Samuel Curtis and the Army of the Border had no intention of letting up on the Confederates and he made this known to Generals Pleasonton and Rosecrans. Pleasonton decided to detail General McNeil and Sanborn for Curtis to use and he and Philips's Brigade would return to General Rosecrans. It was also decided to remove some of the prisoners to Pleasonton's care. Curtis was of the mind to parade some of them, particularly Cabell and Marmaduke, on a tour through Kansas towns. General Cabell got wind of the idea and was concerned that his men would be shot by Kansas militia and informed Pleasonton's Chief of Staff of his concerns, who in turn informed Rosecrans who insisted on Curtis that those prisoners, including Cabell and Marmaduke, be returned to him.[25] Curtis acquiesced to Rosecrans in order to keep McNeil and Sanborn and therefore continue his pursuit of Price, which was his ultimate goal.

For the Union command in the west something had occurred in a form of just what occurred in regards to a General's Quarrel at the time of the Second Manassas Campaign in Virginia in1862. Now it seemed to have occurred, to a lesser extent in the Union ranks in Missouri in 1864. The tension between Curtis and Rosecrans seemed to be just under the surface with regard to sharing forces in their respective commands. Curtis seemed to express his concerns with Rosecrans consistently in correspondence as to the proper assignment of his district forces. Curtis wanted more focus on the pursuit and destruction of Price whereas Rosecrans looked for just moving Price out of the district and maintaining his force at the disposal of the district commands with limited time with the Army of the Border. Even with General Pleasonton's operating effectively with Curtis, despite some moments of uncertainty, Rosecrans expected that some or all units return to their regional responsibilities, soon after Westport.

The idea that A. J. Smith's Command was really not committed to full action against Price probably angered Curtis and prevented him from squeezing Price. To his credit Rosecrans did take an active part in the campaign against Price, but seemingly always from a distance. Soon after Mine Creek, Rosecrans had Smith's XVI Corps, make his way to transports in St. Louis and then make his way to Nashville, Tennessee. The overriding interest seemed to be the destruction of Hood's Army in Tennessee rather than hounding Price as Curtis was intending to do. The difficulty in having two military districts over the Missouri area and Kansas only complicated the actions of the commanders and ultimately the responsibility of conflicting commands rested squarely on Washington, D.C., and Chief of Staff Henry Halleck who himself was very familiar with the situation in the west having initially commanded there early in the war.

10

A Newtonia Gallop

The affair at Mine Creek had cost the Army of Missouri much. Price's Army had lost over 1,000 men at Mine Creek, not to mention Generals Marmaduke and Cabell and the cost of the wagon train, which was now becoming untenable. The trail of the army was now recognizable by the increasing number of broken down and destitute wagons. The plight of Price's train was recognized by all. Moving off to the southeast General Shelby had some of the train burned by Colonel Jackman. M. Jeff Thompson, commanding Shelby's Iron Brigade, recalled, "Early in the morning of the 26th we were in the saddle, but our march delayed.... The train was burned on this morning."[1] From here on out the march of this army of Southerners was reminiscent of the Grande Armee in Russia, in 1812, as noted by the federals. "Besides the wagons captured during the day at the Marais des Cygenes, on the way to and to the Little Osage, the enemy had destroyed many, including ammunition wagons, and for twenty-five or thirty miles beyond the Osage battle-field their route was strewn with debris of burning wagons and other property."[2] A demoralizing scene presented itself as the Army of Missouri moved down the dirt roads heading south toward the Ozarks.

The route had changed for Price and the Army of Missouri. No longer would Fort Scott be in their sites for now Price had decided that the best thing the army could do was return to Arkansas through the Ozark Plateau. For the Union Federal Army officers the decision was made to layover at Fort Scott. Manned by a cadre of Kansas Colored Militia, the twenty-year-old frontier post was festooned with artillery in anticipation of Price's attack. Now it became the staging area for the renewed pursuit of the enemy. Resting his forces, General Pleasonton released Brigadier General Sanborn to resume the pursuit of the Confederates with General Curtis and Blunt commanding. Curtis was insistent on this course of action and wanted as little delay as possible. Curtis still believed he could catch up with Price's Army, bring it to battle and destroy it.

After moving south of the Little Osage River, the Confederate army angled off the Fort Scott Road back toward the Missouri state line. Making for Deerfield Church on the Nevada Road, the army would cross the Marmaton River heading to Carthage and friendlier confines. The Army of Missouri now consisted of two divisions instead of the three. The attrition of the force had much to do with the last few weeks of combat and the force now centered on Brig. Gen. Joseph Shelby's command. Heading south Shelby believed that the army could camp a night at Carthage, Missouri; unfortunately Carthage had been worn out by the war and it showed it with burned-out buildings and little to offer the Confederates in the way of sustenance for both man and beast. On October 26th, moving south, the Confederates headed toward Shoals Creek.

On the morning of October 26th, boots and saddles sounded for the men of General Blunt's forces to immediately depart in renewed pursuit of Price's Army. Major General Samuel Curtis was in fine spirits and was in the belief that the destruction of Price was at last near. He may have been routed, as stated by Pleasonton, but Price wanted more. Working out the details the night before, he had decided to send elements of his force east down the Nevada Road to pick up the Confederate trail. With General Blunt's forces in the lead, McNeil's Brigade followed and Sanborn behind him. Fanning out over the broad prairie, the units made their way to the southeast towards Shoal Creek, camping first at Shanghai, Missouri. By the time the federals reached Carthage, Price and his forces were long gone, but the debris of the train was evident. Now the blue uniforms could take in and follow that debris field as it headed south somewhere in the direction of Newtonia.

Newtonia, Missouri, sits on the edge of the prairie touching the edge of the Springfield Platform of the Ozark Physiographic Province. It was the last stop before Price and the Army of Missouri would enter back into Arkansas, making for Confederate-controlled areas. They made camp just south of the small village; Newtonia had been fought over before in 1862 where a Confederate force drove out, for a short time, a Union force. Now another small Union force occupied the town and Shelby's Brigade under the command of M. Jeff Thompson took the lead in clearing the enemy. Moving quickly, Thompson's men rode down the road, fronting the Ritchey Farmstead as they drove out their enemy. "On the morning of the 28th my brigade was given the advance, and we were directed to move on Newtonia and attack the force stationed there.... When the advance guard came in sight there was great commotion among the garrison, and they soon took to flight ... the brigade soon reached the town, but passed through to camp some two miles south."[3] Thompson also mentions in his report that the only Union casualty was the commanding officer who, attempting to rally his men, was killed.

Coming up with the train from Shoals Creek, Price, along with Shelby and Clark, joined Thompson, making camp early in the day on the fields of the Ritchey Farm. Deploying pickets outside the camp, on the Ritchey fields, the Confederates were unaware that federal forces were not that far behind. In fact Maj. Gen. James Blunt's blood was up in anticipation of gaining on the Confederate enemy. By 1:00 p.m. his men, under Colonel Ford, crested a ridge just above the Confederate camp. If the tactics at Mine Creek could be duplicated at this moment at Newtonia, Blunt and Ford probably had it in mind. Ford believed it and relates in his Official Report, "The advance soon reported that the enemy's train was in sight and but few men visible. I hurried forward at a gallop, and within two miles saw the rear of the rebel train entering the woods beyond town on the Cassville road."[4] Colonel Ford believed he had Price at a disadvantage and prepared his force to charge their line. What Ford did not know was that he was up against Jo Shelby and Shelby was a consummate fighter.

Alerted by the shots of the Confederate pickets and the sudden boom of distant artillery, Brig. Gen. Jo Shelby swung into action. Bearing down on Shelby and Price were the 15th and 16th Kansas, 2nd Colorado and 3rd Wisconsin Cavalry; Shelby thought he would correct this Union intrusion and make short work of those rude federals interrupting his rest. "On the evening of the 28th, while comfortably resting a few miles south of Newtonia, a large federal force drove in our outlying pickets quite briskly and came charging on with their usual vitality."[5] Putting on his black plumed hat, Shelby directed his lieutenants to put their men in line of battle. Not making the same mistake that Marmaduke had made at Mine Creek, Shelby had his force dismounted and deployed as regular infantry to meet the federal advance. Placing Collins's Missouri Battery in action from behind the ranks, Collins began to direct the fire of his ten-pound Parrotts on the oncoming Yankees and this he did in earnest.

Major General James Blunt was aware of the success Benteen and Philips had against Marmaduke's larger force at Mine Creek and he sent his horsemen galloping down the fields in full view of the Confederate enemy. Waiting for them was a double line of infantry with their Enfield muskets, anticipating the command to fire. In charge of Shelby's Iron Brigade, M. Jeff Thompson moved on the Union center. "The firing commenced immediately, and in a few minutes our line bravely crossed the fence and advance upon the enemy, crossing the field under hot fire of artillery and small arms, and drove the enemy into the open prairie."[6] Bullets now hissed by the advancing Confederates and Blunt's force found that they now had been outmatched. "A large force compelled me to fall back about 500 yards from my first line ... a large force of the enemy were pressing under cover of a cornfield around my left flank."[7] Blunt had not expected the resistance and did what he could to hold his line.

Driving the Yankees, General Shelby believed that he could dislodge the Union advance. With Collins's Battery making good work and having effect on the Union Batteries of Colorado Artillery, the Confederates seemed to be on the verge of victory. Moving on the Union flanks, the Confederates steadily moved through the McClain's Farm cornfield, giving the rebel yell, Shelby remembered. "The men never hesitated from the first, but drove the enemy all the time before them and advance two miles into the prairie."[8] Brig. Gen. M. Jeff Thompson and Colonel Sidney Jackman were only momentarily stalled by the Union counter-fire and addressed their lines and were moving at a quick pace as smoke began filling the late afternoon air. Fortunately for Blunt and Ford, General Samuel Curtis soon came up in support with Brig. Gen. Sanborn's Brigade.

Again Major General Sterling Price now had a decision to make. The Federal Force had caught up with his Army of Missouri once again. The decision was made to abandon the camp just made and begin again the march south toward Arkansas. Sterling Price now had to move his wagons and with Generals Fagan and Clark move what they could while leaving a number of the wagons where they were. Fortunately for Price, Shelby's troops were at the ready. As for the rest of the force, the drubbing at Mine Creek was a disappointing event and John B. Clark had managed to gather what was left of John Marmaduke's troops and kept it as an effective military unit. As the opening guns unleashed near Newtonia, Price led the rest of the Army of Missouri out of camp, heading south.

Shelby was battling and driving Blunt and his force back toward the McClain Farmstead. In fact Blunt was beginning to get concerned as his men started to falter and his ammunition ran low. Just as Blunt was to decide to remove his force from the smoke-filled field, he observed riders coming down from the northwest. The force was that of Major General Samuel Curtis with Brig. Gen. Sanborn's Brigade. Having been ordered to keep with Curtis's Army of the Border by General Rosecrans, Sanborn would be unwittingly timely on his arrival. Observing the hard-pressed Ford, Sanborn deployed immediately as the sun was getting lower in the western sky. "A battle was brought on by General Blunt, at Newtonia, Friday afternoon, in which the enemy gained advantages over him at first. I came up with my command about a half an hour after the battle opened, having left Fort Scott the morning before, and the two commands drove the enemy in confusion from the field."[9]

Shelby had been fighting for most of three hours and now recognized the Union had reinforced and calmly withdrew his men to the rear coming up to General Fagan who had been sent too late to support. It was not a rout as at Mine Creek and not the confusion that General Sanborn suggested. What may have appeared as confusion was the fact that Price had now decided to burn even more of the wagons of his train that he thought was so important to his expedition. Finally Price's Lieutenants would not have to concern themselves with the slow moving train. General Sanborn believed that Price burned approximately 50 wagons as they fled.[10] Jo Shelby remembered it this way: "Night closed the contest, and another beautiful victory had crowned Confederate arms.... That night about 12 o'clock I withdrew, leaving Lieutenant-Colonel Erwin to watch the enemy's movement until the next day."[11] Curtis also claimed victory, thereby helping support Blunt for his seeming impetuous actions that day. With casualties amounting to some few hundred men, the Union now occupied the field of action.

As the Union force regrouped at Newtonia, a bit of a controversy arose as to what the next actions would be. At times Curtis and Rosecrans could be at odds over assigning units and Pleasonton and Rosecrans believed that the respective units should return to assigned posts inside the Department of Missouri. Rosecrans believed that his responsibility was to move available units to support Sherman down in Tennessee and Georgia. Curtis was a bit incredulous. "After fighting Price at Newtonia last night he retired toward Cassville. As order from General Rosecrans withdrew his troops, and I, not being strong enough without them, came thus on my return."[12] General Sanborn wired General Rosecrans of Curtis's intention to pursue Price and had ordered him to support and Sanborn believed he did not have that authority to do so.[13] For the federals the whole matter would eventually be a moot point anyway; Curtis had picked up two days on the Federals and they would not be able to catch up.

Price's Missouri Expedition was done. Thankfully, too, for now the weather began to deteriorate. Overhead the fair-weather cumulus clouds began to darken and the air began to cool. Soon rain drops turned to snowflakes. General Shelby remarked in his official report of the condition of the army at the time of Newtonia: "The success was of eminent advantage to our army, fought as it was when some were urging the old and horrible cry of demoralization."[14] Moving on toward Cane Hill, Shelby and Price's forces had to contend with snow and ice as they made their way to the Arkansas River. In Price's report he made it sound as if the raid into Missouri was a success, referring to the number of miles marched, towns taken, recruits acquired and the proverbial number of wagons and loot. He did not talk about the eventual need for having most of that loot and wagons burned and abandoned.

It can be said that at most Price did tie down some Union forces that had been earmarked for the eastern theaters, but these too eventually made their way to those fronts in time for campaigning. What probably irritated Price more than anything on the raid was the inability to raise the banner of the local pro–Southern people to actively do more against the Yankee presence. He singles out the German Immigrants in particular in his remonstrance but also points out his fair treatment of those particular citizens and his respect for people's property. "After I passed the German settlements in Missouri my march was an ovation.... I am satisfied that could I have remained in Missouri this winter the army would have been increased 50,000 men."[15] Newtonia was the last battle between regular forces of the war in the Trans-Mississippi West and both the Union and Confederacy claimed victory. Sterling Price's Official Report of the expedition sights only what he thought the successes were (and there were some), but this report would bring an investigation by Lt. Gen. Smith as to the actual conduct of the Army of Missouri. For most, though, if victory was to be claimed, it was a pyrrhic one.

11

Afterword

Edmund Kirby Smith, who had instructed Price "to make St. Louis your objective,"[1] was skeptical of Sterling Price's Official Report of the Missouri expedition after realizing that the benefits had been minimal in spite of Price's positive take. In fact Smith convened a court of inquiry to examine Price's actions. Now, as he tried to put back together what forces he had remaining, the situation of the southern states simply started to unravel. Having made his way back to his seat of command in St. Louis, Major General William Rosecrans now concentrated on sending Maj. Gen. A. J. Smith and his XVI Corps to Tennessee. Confederate John Bell Hood and the Army of Tennessee was making for Nashville and in December 1864, with the timely arrival of Smith, the Union forces did what no other Union Army had done before—destroy, in a rout, a Confederate Army.

Depleted resources in material and manpower and the relentless pursuit of Union forces wore out what remained of the Confederacy. It was only the size of the Confederacy that slowed the inevitable end that was coming, an end that finally came in April 1865 with Lee's surrender at Appomattox to General Grant. For Kirby Smith the news was slow to arrive and Smith would not immediately react. With a large tract of territory still in Confederate hands the thought was maybe the Trans-Mississippi could go its own way. In the end it was Edmund Kirby Smith who was the last Confederate General to surrender his forces between May 26 and June 2, 1865, and with that end came the end of the court of inquiry into Price and the Expedition.

Abraham Lincoln was reelected in 1864 and his mind had been made up to bring the fractured nation together as one when the war concluded. Lincoln had always thought that North or South, the country was still made of Americans and he reinforced that sentiment in his second inaugural address. Lincoln recognized that his actions and others in his administration were at best circumventing the constitution and he tried to remedy that in his Second Inaugural summing up, as he said, "With malice toward none; with charity for all; with firmness in the right, as god gives us to see the right, let us strive on to finish the work we are in; to bind up the nation's wounds; to care for him who shall have borne the battle, and for his widow, and his orphan—to do all which may achieve and cherish a just, and a lasting peace, among ourselves, and with all nations."[2] These words were reconciliation with the nation and the people of the south who Lincoln wanted back in the Union. Lincoln did not consider them traitors.

In Missouri the man who had set the fuse to blow up the magazine at Fort Davidson at Pilot Knob, was elected Governor as the first native born Missourian in the State's History. Thomas Clement Fletcher lived in Hillsboro, Missouri, and was sworn in as Missouri's 18th governor on January 2, 1865. He dealt with amnesty for Confederate soldiers after the war and most importantly approved emancipation of Missouri slaves. The Emancipation Proclamation, by Lincoln, only covered those areas in rebellion. It did not take into account those States, like Missouri, which remained in the Union, so after elected he immediately set into motion abolishing slavery in Missouri and did so even before the 13th Amendment to the U.S. Constitution was ratified at the end of 1865.

The financial cost of such an act was a blow to the state and Fletcher recognized that fact for many now lost their property; as M. Jeff Thompson pointed out in 1861, millions of dollars in property. Along with that was the need to bring people to Missouri after the disastrous effects of actions like Order No. 11. Governor Fletcher supported the establishment of the Lincoln Institute in Jefferson City, and was instrumental in establishing the Missouri State Board of Immigration. This board helped rebuild the state's population, devastated during the Civil War years. Fletcher, like Lincoln, believed in restoring, not punishing. Many families had left Missouri during and after the war and he was encouraging people to return or resettle in the state, making it a government priority.

The idea of a Board of Immigration resulted because of many families from parts of the state who left because of their Southern leanings or support. The Burnt District was of particular despair with abandoned homes, fallow fields and dwindling towns. For families like the Brannocks at Chapel Hill, Missouri, their removal led them to return to family in Kentucky. Lizzie finally reunited with her husband after he was released from prison in St. Louis. With the war over, they settled down in Tennessee where they spent the rest of their lives. For many others, like the Masseys in St. Clair, Missouri, the only alternative was leaving the country entirely, moving to Brazil and setting up a mini-Dixie in that country that lasts to this day. The Moore House, on the Little Blue Battlefield, was never reoccupied by the family. The day they left on orders of the Federal authorities was the last day the family ever spent in the home, leaving the palatial mansion on an empty prairie.

11. Afterword

The surrender of Confederate forces became problematical for some former officers. Some men did not trust the federal authority to honor the oath of pardon that was offered and this was a deciding element for leaving the country and settling elsewhere. This is what Jo Shelby did when he led a number of his ex–Iron Brigade members into Mexico at the invitation of the then Emperor of Mexico, Maximilian, naming his settlement Carlota in honor of Maximilian's wife. Planted there by French Military forces of Emperor Napoleon III, in the early 1860s, Maximilian was looking to prop up his regime with former Confederates. This did not last as the Jauristas overthrew his regime and executed Maximilian. Benito Juarez was fond of Shelby and allowed him to stay in Mexico, but eventually Shelby simply became homesick and returned to Missouri, where he took the Oath of Allegiance and gained a pardon. At the end of the war General Pleasonton took stock of his opponents and said of Shelby that he was simply the best Cavalry Commander of the War. Jo Shelby ended up near his former field of conflict and was later buried nearby.

Captured at Mine Creek, William Cabell and John S. Marmaduke, who actually became a Major General in captivity, were released from St. Louis Gratiot Prison after the surrender of the Trans-Mississippi forces of Edmund Kirby Smith in June. William Cabell made his way back to Texas and settled near Dallas, later studying Law and becoming Mayor of Dallas multiple times. He kept in touch with his former officers and men and when he died in 1911, his marker spoke for the man: "Lover of mankind, Patriot, Statesman, Loving Husband, Devoted Father."[3] Before the Civil War broke out in Missouri, the Marmaduke name was prominent in both business and politics. Remaining in St. Louis, Marmaduke became editor of a newspaper and eventually ran for Governor, following in his father's footsteps and serving at the State House until passing away at the Mansion in 1887. He is buried in Jefferson City.

The purview of Union Authority in the State of Missouri allowed for many Union officers, during the war, to escape any type of repercussions for what could be considered war crimes. Thomas Ewing was acting on Order No. 11 backed by an order from President Abraham Lincoln to execute all violators. His actions displaced many and only feed sectional animosity that continued after the war was over. Ewing did well after the war and became a lawyer in Washington, D.C., and later in New York City, turning down an offer to be Secretary of War. John McNeil returned to civilian life after the war, settling in the city of St. Louis. The Palmyra Massacre dogged John McNeil for the rest of his life. He became clerk of county court and sheriff; the best he could do was to become superintendent of the St. Louis Branch Post Office. Ironically he is buried with a myriad number of generals, like

John Pope, William T. Sherman and Sterling Price at Bellefontaine Cemetery in St. Louis.

For Sterling Price his operation in Missouri was something of a Shakespearean tragedy. Under investigation at the wars end, Price was saved any inglorious repercussions as it was forced to cease proceedings. The end of the Confederate bid for independence probably saved Sterling Price. Price suffered in other ways, his home and livelihood now gone, and two years after the war, his life. The ravages of poor health and constant campaigning had left him somewhat of an invalid and the former Governor of Missouri died in St. Louis in 1867, the same St. Louis he had tried to make his objective in 1864. The millions upon millions of dollars that many had invested in owning another human being was wiped out in an instant at war's end with the State of Missouri outlawing slavery. The election of Thomas Fletcher made sure of that. Fletcher worked on repatriating those whom he had fought against during the war and at the same time abolished slavery in Missouri before the U.S. Congress passed the 13th Amendment to the U.S. Constitution.

If the war could be summed up it could probably be best illustrated in two towns that saw the war firsthand. Something that is not often discussed is the severe effects that the war had on the towns and communities that were caught in between the contending forces. For the towns of Athens and Danville, Missouri, the war was overwhelming and fatal for everyone living there. With both Southerners and Northerners living with one another, at the beginning of the war, the continuation of the war magnified the dividing lines that, once crossed, became permanent. The before and after of these two towns could not demonstrate the effects of a civil war any clearer.

The Boone's Lick Road makes its way from St. Charles, Missouri, through the prairie and woods of central Missouri, eventually making its way to the Missouri River at Glasgow. Originally blazed by the sons of Daniel Boone, the road was named for the salt licks mined near the Missouri River. A number of towns got their beginnings along the road and became centers of commerce along the way, where horse wagons and carriages could stop and pause for rest along the road. Danville, the County Seat of Montgomery County, was one of those towns.

Danville was a thriving town of well laid out streets of manicured grids in the mid–1800s, including a central plaza across from a Girls School of growing importance. The school consisted of an Administration Building, Classroom building and a Dormitory with Chapel, all in the then popular Greek Revival-style architecture. The town was becoming so prominent that Sylvester Baker, a state legislator, built his Federal/Greek revival style home on Boone's Lick Road just east of town. Primarily pro-Union in sentiment at the beginning of the war, there were a number of Southern families living in and around town and sending their young women to the college there.

All this changed with the war years and the ravages brought by the internecine strife. By 1864 Danville was looking different. A Union Block House now occupied a corner of the town square across from the college and Union troops occupied the town with the Block House as its headquarters. With Bloody Bill Anderson's raid in 1864, Danville was completely burned as the majority of those Union troops had been assigned elsewhere; those who remained were either killed or fled, leaving the town defenseless. Only the school was spared at the pleas of the young women. By 1865 the school was closed, and now only the chapel remains. As for the town of Danville, it simply did not rebuild and became only a shadow of what it once was before the war.

Up north, along the confluence of where the Mississippi and Des Moines Rivers meet, there were flourishing farms and plantations. Trade and commerce moved steadily on the rivers as steamboats whistled that they were approaching. One of those towns was Athens, Missouri, located on the south bank of the Des Moines River. The town was considered a prime location when the federal government decided to build a lock and dam on the Des Moines River in the 1840s. Settled by primarily Southern families, by the mid-1800 Athens was an important stop on the Des Moines River. Having a Mill and Mill Race, the town was serving the surrounding community with a number of goods and services. Laid out in an attractive grid pattern a number of stately homes gave the town a distinctly southern appearance with fifty businesses including a large hotel, two-story public school and five churches.

By 1861 the fortune of Athens would radically change with the outbreak of war. Pro-Union and pro-Southern sympathies now became magnified by the opening of the conflict and Athens on the Des Moines River became the focal point. In July 1861 Union forces entered and occupied Athens in response to its support for local Southerners, seizing and quartering soldiers in Athens homes and businesses. This set in motion the battle that occurred there in August, resulting in the repulsing of the Confederate forces and the occupation of the town throughout the war. From here on out Southern sympathizers were ostracized and bitter feelings developed as opportunists after the war drove many Southern families from the area.

The war was the death knell for Athens. The post war years brought the dismantling of the lock and dam on the river and businesses soon began to dry up in the town proper. The tensions of the citizenry never really subsided and the population of the town soon began to diminish, with many Southern families leaving the area and never returning. By the end of the next decade the town of Athens was turning into a ghost town with a number of abandoned homes and businesses. With the Mill now falling into ruin and the dam gone, Athens ceased to exist; soon only rural farms existed in and around the former commerce center. Athens and Danville are stark reminders of the Trans-Mississippi conflict in the American Civil War.

Epilogue

Across the Trans-Mississippi, graves were dug in haste in numerous battlefields and some of those soldiers, like at Helena, Arkansas, were later found and reburied in mass graves at the local cemetery. Such was the case of those who fell at Moore's Mill in Calloway County, Missouri. When the battle ended at Moore's Mill the bodies of both Confederate and federal soldiers were gathered and it was decided that they would all be buried together. At a time of the Civil War, the idea of burying both Northern and Southern dead together was simply expedient, necessary and appropriate. The site was left probably unmarked and it was soon forgotten until the 1950s when, as the centennial of the conflict approached and interest was renewed, the site was investigated. With information that the site was located just a quarter of a mile southwest of the old main store in Calwood, a sunken depression was found, indicating a possible grave. In 2013 the grave was finally located, at that spot, just off of Highway Z. The site, located on private land, now has a granite marker with the names of both Confederate and Union soldiers who gave "their last full measure" that hot July day in 1862.

Row upon row the white headstones grow as one makes their way into Jefferson Barracks National Cemetery some miles south of the City of St. Louis on the west bank of the Mississippi River. Beautiful in its settings, the cemetery sits beside the old post of Jefferson Barracks itself, which originally established it as the Post Cemetery. Now the cemetery encompasses more than 346 acres. Here thousands of Union soldiers are buried alongside more than a thousand Confederate soldiers. Established in 1826 to replace Fort Bellefontaine, which had been founded north of St. Louis, the post was founded nearby a spring which provided a water source and the base grew rapidly and eventually became the largest post prior to the outbreak of war in 1861.

The Barracks became the avenue for a number of officers who would serve the U.S. Army and for some who would end up serving both the U.S. Government and later the Confederacy. Officers like U.S. Grant and James Longstreet became friends, even suiting for the same young woman. Other officers like

Jefferson Davis served in escorting the leader of the Black Hawk War to Jefferson Barracks. Robert E. Lee, a young U.S. Army officer, was stationed at the Barracks as an engineer and worked to prevent the Mississippi River from changing its course and thereby saving St. Louis. All of them had one thing in common: They were all Americans doing something for all of us to remember. The Cemetery served as a reminder of this during and after the war.

There is a poetic silence as one moves between the headstones at Jefferson Barracks National Cemetery. You might notice that some headstones are rounded and some pointed at the top; this distinction indicates which of the buried are Union or federals (round tops) and which are Confederates (pointed). In Section 20, the remains of the six Confederate soldiers executed, by order of President Lincoln, for the deaths of Major Wilson and five other soldiers, lay one after the other in quiet solitude. Nearby these stones stands a grey granite monument that speaks to all interred here and reads, in part: "Who knows but it may be given to us after this life, to meet again in the old quarters ... and all will meet together under the two flags, all sound and well and there will be talking and laughter and cheers." Let this be your guide.

Jefferson Barracks Cemetery was located south of the city limits and became the burial ground of both Union and Confederate troops. Here in Section 20 are buried the Confederate soldiers executed in retaliation for the shooting of Major Wilson and five others. In 1866, Jefferson Barracks was designated as one of the original National Cemeteries (author photo).

Appendix I

Supreme Court Dred Scott Decision

SUPREME COURT OF THE UNITED STATES DECEMBER TERM, 1856 DRED SCOTT VERSUS JOHN F. A. SANDFORD*

(*This is an abbreviated text of Chief Justice Taney's decision.)

Dred Scott, Plaintiff in Error, v. John F. A. Sandford.

This case was brought up, by writ of error, from the Circuit Court of the United States for the district of Missouri.

It was an action of trespass *vi et armis* instituted in the Circuit Court by Scott against Sandford.

Prior to the institution of the present suit, an action was brought by Scott for his freedom in the Circuit Court of St. Louis county, (State court,) where there was a verdict and judgment in his favor. On a writ of error to the Supreme Court of the State, the judgment below was reversed, and the case remanded to the Circuit Court, where it was continued to await the decision of the case now in question.

The declaration of Scott contained three counts: one, that Sandford had assaulted the plaintiff; one, that he had assaulted Harriet Scott, his wife; and one, that he had assaulted Eliza Scott and Lizzie Scott, his children.

Sandford appeared, and filed the following plea:

Dred Scott v. John F. A. Sandford. Plea to the jurisdiction of the Court. April Term, 1854.

And the said John F. A. Sandford, in his own proper person, comes and says, that this court ought not to have or take further cognizance of the action aforesaid, because he says that said cause of action, and each and every of them, (if any such have accrued to the said Dred Scott,) accrued to the said Dred Scott out of the jurisdiction of this court, and exclusively within the jurisdiction of the courts of the State of Missouri, for that, to wit: the said plaintiff, Dred Scott, is not a citizen of the State of Missouri, as alleged in his declaration, because he is a negro of African descent; his ancestors were of pure African blood, and were brought into this country and sold as negro slaves, and this the said Sandford is ready to verify. Wherefore he prays judgment, whether this court can or will take further cognizance of the action aforesaid.

John F. A. Sandford.

To this plea there was a demurrer in the usual form, which was argued in April, 1854, when the court gave judgment that the demurrer should be sustained.

In May, 1854, the defendant, in pursuance of an agreement between counsel, and with the leave of the court, pleaded in bar of the action:

1. Not guilty.
2. That the plaintiff was a negro slave, the lawful property of the defendant, and, as such, the defendant gently laid his hands upon him, and thereby had only restrained him, as the defendant had a right to do.
3. That with respect to the wife and daughters of the plaintiff, in the second and third counts of the declaration mentioned, the defendant had, as to them, only acted in the same manner, and in virtue of the same legal right.

In the first of these pleas, the plaintiff joined issue; and to the second and third, filed replications alleging that the defendant, of his own wrong and without the cause in his second and third pleas alleged, committed the trespasses, &c.

The counsel then filed the following agreed statement of facts, viz:

In the year 1834, the plaintiff was a negro slave belonging to Dr. Emerson, who was a surgeon in the army of the United States. In that year, 1834, said Dr. Emerson took the plaintiff from the State of Missouri to the military post at Rock Island, in the State of Illinois, and held him there as a slave until the month of April or May, 1836. At the time last mentioned, said Dr. Emerson removed the plaintiff from said military post at Rock Island to the military post at Fort Snelling, situate on the west bank of the Mississippi river, in the Territory known as Upper Louisiana, acquired by the United States of France, and situate north of the latitude of thirty-six degrees thirty minutes north, and north of the State of Missouri. Said Dr. Emerson held the plaintiff in slavery at Fort Snelling, from said last mentioned date until the year 1838.

In the year 1835, Harriet, who is named in the second count of the plaintiff's declaration, was the negro slave of Major Taliaferro, who belonged to the army of the United States. In that year, 1835, said Major Taliaferro took said Harriet to said Fort Snelling, a military post, situated as hereinbefore stated, and kept her there as a slave until the year 1836, and then sold and delivered her as a slave at said Fort Snelling unto the said Dr. Emerson hereinbefore named. Said Dr. Emerson held said Harriet in slavery at said Fort Snelling until the year 1838.

In the year 1836, the plaintiff and said Harriet, at said Fort Snelling, with the consent of said Dr. Emerson, who then claimed to be their master and owner, intermarried, and took each other for husband and wife. Eliza and Lizzie, named in the third count of the plaintiff's declaration, are the fruit of that marriage. Eliza is about fourteen years old, and was born on board the steamboat Gipsey, north of the north line of the State of Missouri, and upon the river Mississippi. Lizzie is about seven years old, and was born in the State of Missouri, at the military post called Jefferson Barracks.

In the year 1838, said Dr. Emerson removed the plaintiff and said Harriet, and their said daughter Eliza, from said Fort Snelling to the State of Missouri, where they have ever since resided,

Before the commencement of this suit, said Dr. Emerson sold and conveyed the plaintiff, said Harriet, Eliza, and Lizzie, to the defendant, as slaves, and the defendant has ever since claimed to hold them, and each of them, as slaves. At the times mentioned in the plaintiff's declaration, the defendant, claiming to be owner as aforesaid, laid his hands upon said plaintiff, Harriet, Eliza, and Lizzie, and imprisoned them, doing in this respect, however, no more than what he might lawfully do, if they were of right his slaves at such times.

Further proof may be given on the trial for either party.

It is agreed that Dred Scott brought suit for his freedom in the Circuit Court of St. Louis county; that there was a verdict and judgment in his favor; that on a writ of error to the Supreme Court the judgment below was reversed, and the same remanded to the Circuit Court, where it has been continued to await the decision of this case.

In May, 1854, the cause went before a jury, who found the following verdict, viz: "As to the first issue joined in this case, we of the jury find the defendant not guilty; and as to the issue secondly above joined, we of the jury find that, before and at the time when, &c., in the first count mentioned, the said Dred Scott was a negro slave, the lawful property of the defendant; and as to the issue thirdly above joined, we, the jury, find that, before and at the time when, &c., in the second and third counts mentioned, the said Harriet, wife of said Dred Scott, and Eliza and Lizzie, the daughters of the said Dred Scott, were negro slaves, the lawful property of the defendant."

Whereupon, the court gave judgment for the defendant.

After an ineffectual motion for a new trial, the plaintiff filed the following bill of exceptions.

On the trial of this cause by the jury, the plaintiff, to maintain the issues on his part, read to the jury the following agreed statement of facts, (see agreement above.) No further testimony was given to the jury by either party. Thereupon the plaintiff moved the court to give to the jury the following instruction, viz: "That, upon the facts agreed to by the parties, they ought to find for the plaintiff. The court refused to give such instruction to the jury, and the plaintiff, to such refusal, then and there duly excepted."

The court then gave the following instruction to the jury, on motion of the defendant:

"The jury are instructed, that upon the facts in this case, the law is with the defendant." The plaintiff excepted to this instruction.

Upon these exceptions, the case came up to this court.

It was argued at December term, 1855, and ordered to be reargued at the present term.

It was now argued by Mr. Blair and Mr. G. F. Curtis for the plaintiff in error, and by Mr. Geyer and Mr. Johnson for the defendant in error.

The reporter regrets that want of room will not allow him to give the arguments of counsel; but he regrets it the less, because the subject is thoroughly examined in the opinion of the court, the opinions of the concurring judges, and the opinions of the judges who dissented from the judgment of the court.

Mr. Chief Justice TANEY delivered the opinion of the court.

This case has been twice argued. After the argument at the last term, differences of opinion were found to exist among the members of the court; and as the questions in controversy are of the highest importance, and the court was at that time much pressed by the ordinary business of the term, it was deemed advisable to continue the case, and direct a reargument on some of the points, in order that we might have an opportunity of giving to the whole subject a more deliberate consideration. It has accordingly been again argued by counsel, and considered by the court; and I now proceed to deliver its opinion.

There are two leading questions presented by the record:

1. Had the Circuit Court of the United States jurisdiction to hear and determine the case between these parties? And

2. If it had jurisdiction, is the judgment it has given erroneous or not?

The plaintiff in error, who was also the plaintiff in the court below, was, with his wife and children, held as slaves by the defendant, in the State of

Missouri; and he brought this action in the Circuit Court of the United States for that district, to assert the title of himself and his family to freedom... The defendant pleaded in abatement to the jurisdiction of the court, that the plaintiff was not a citizen of the State of Missouri, as alleged in his declaration, being a negro of African descent, whose ancestors were of pure African blood, and who were brought into this country and sold as slaves. Now, it is not necessary to inquire whether in courts of that description a party who pleads over in bar, when a plea to the jurisdiction has been ruled against him, does or does not waive his plea; nor whether upon a judgment in his favor on the pleas in bar, and a writ of error brought by the plaintiff, the question upon the plea in abatement would be open for revision in the appellate court. Cases that may have been decided in such courts, or rules that may have been laid down by common-law pleaders, can have no influence in the decision in this court. Because, under the Constitution and laws of the United States, the rules which govern the pleadings in its courts, in questions of jurisdiction, stand on different principles and are regulated by different laws.

This difference arises, as we have said, from the peculiar character of the Government of the United States. For although it is sovereign and supreme in its appropriate sphere of action, yet it does not possess all the powers which usually belong to the sovereignty of a nation. Certain specified powers, enumerated in the Constitution, have been conferred upon it; and neither the legislative, executive, nor judicial departments of the Government can lawfully exercise any authority beyond the limits marked out by the Constitution. And in regulating the judicial department, the cases in which the courts of the United States shall have jurisdiction are particularly and specifically enumerated and defined; and they are not authorized to take cognizance of any case which does not come within the description therein specified. Hence, when a plaintiff sues in a court of the United States, it is necessary that he should show, in his pleading, that the suit he brings is within the jurisdiction of the court, and that he is entitled to sue there... We proceed to examine the case as presented by the pleadings.

The words "people of the United States" and "citizens" are synonymous terms, and mean the same thing. They both describe the political body who, according to our republican institutions, form the sovereignty, and who hold the power and conduct the Government through their representatives. They are what we familiarly call the "sovereign people," and every citizen is one of this people, and a constituent member of this sovereignty. The question before us is, whether the class of persons described in the plea in abatement compose a portion of this people, and are constituent members of this sovereignty? *We think they are not*, and that they are not included, and were not intended to be included, under the word "citizens" in the Constitution, and can therefore claim none of the rights and privileges which that instrument provides for and secures to citizens of the United States. On the contrary, they were at that time considered as a subordinate and inferior class of beings, who had been subjugated by the dominant race, and, whether emancipated or not, yet remained subject to their authority, and had no rights or privileges but such as those who held the power and the Government might choose to grant them.

It is not the province of the court to decide upon the justice or injustice, the policy or impolicy, of these laws. The decision of that question belonged to the political or law-making power; to those who formed the sovereignty and framed the Constitution. The duty of the court is, to interpret the instrument they have framed, with the best lights we can obtain on the subject, and to administer it as we find it, according to its true intent and meaning when it was adopted.

Appendix II

The Palmyra Massacre

THE PALMYRA MASSACRE; UNION COLONEL JOHN MCNEIL, COMMANDER, NORTHEAST MISSOURI DISTRICT

This is the roll of the Palmyra Ten:

Captain Thomas A. Sidner, Monroe County—Letter from Captain T. A. Sidner, written to his family and friends. The letter was written in military prison in Palmyra, the day before and the day of his execution by the Union Army and referenced in text.

    Willis T. Baker, Lewis County
    Thomas Humston, Lewis County
    Morgan Bixler, Lewis County
    John Y. McPheeters, Lewis County
    Hiram T. Smith, Lewis County
    Herbert Hudson, Ralls County
    John M. Wade, Ralls County
    Marion Lair, Ralls County
    Eleazer Lake, Scotland County

Appendix III

Removal Order for Persons on Missouri Border

GENERAL ORDERS, NO. 11. HEADQUARTERS
DISTRICT OF THE BORDER, KANSAS CITY, MO.,
AUGUST 25, 1863.

I. All persons living in Jackson, Cass, and Bates counties, Mo., and in that part of Vernon included in this district, except those living within one mile of the limits of Independence, Hickman Mills, Pleasant Hill, and Harrisonville, and except those in that part of Kaw Township, Jackson County, north of Brush Creek and west of the Big Blue, are hereby ordered to remove from their present places of residence within fifteen days from the date hereof. Those who, within that time, establish their loyalty to the satisfaction of the commanding officer of the military station nearest their present places of residence will receive from him certificates stating the fact of their loyalty, and the names of the witnesses by whom it can be shown.

All who receive such certificates will be permitted to remove to any military station in this district, or to any part of the State of Kansas, except the counties on the eastern border of the State. All others shall remove out of this district. Officers commanding companies and detachments serving in the counties named will see that this paragraph is promptly obeyed.

II. All grain and hay in the field or under shelter in the district from which the inhabitants are required to remove within reach of military stations after the 9th day of September next will be taken to such stations and turned over to the proper officers there, and report of the amount so turned over made to district headquarters, specifying the names of all loyal owners and the amount of such produce taken from them. All grain and hay found in such district after the 9th day of September next not convenient to such stations will be destroyed.

* * *

By order of Brigadier-General Ewing:

H. HANNAHS, Acting Assistant Adjutant–General.

Official Records of the Union and Confederate Armies, Series I, Vol. XXII, Part II, p. 473.

Appendix IV

Special Order for Shooting Six Confederate Prisoners

SPECIAL ORDERS NO. 279.
HDQRS. DEPT. OF THE MISSOURI,
OFFICE PROVOST-MARSHAL-GENERAL,
SAINT LOUIS, MO., OCTOBER 28, 1864.

VIII. It appearing from the most conclusive evidence that Maj. James Wilson, Third Cavalry Missouri State Militia, and six men of his command, taken prisoners of war by the enemy in their late raid through the State at Pilot Knob, Mo., were turned over by some rebel officer, now unknown, to the guerrilla Tim Reves, at a place near the town of Union, in Franklin County, Mo., and that subsequently Major Wilson and his men were brutally murdered by this blood-stained outlaw; therefore, in compliance with so much of Special Orders, No. 277, paragraph 12, headquarters Department of the Missouri, dated October 6, 1864 (hereto appended), as can at this time be carried into effect, the following six of the enlisted men of the rebel army— names James W. Gates, Company H, Third Missouri Cavalry, C. S. Army; Harvey H. Blackburn, Company A, Coleman's regiment, C. S. Army; John Nichols, Second Missouri Cavalry, C. S. Army; Charles W. Minneken, Company A, Crabtree's cavalry, C. S. Army; Asa V. Ladd, Burbridge's regiment Missouri cavalry, C. S. Army; and George F. Bunch, Company B, Third Missouri Cavalry, C. S. Army will be shot to death with musketry within the limits of the city of Saint Louis, Mo., on Saturday, the 29th day of October, 1864, between the hours of 2 and 4 p.m.

Lieut. Col. Gustav Heinrichs, Forty-first Missouri infantry,
The superintendent and inspector of military prisons, is hereby charged with the execution of this order.

JOSEPH DARR JR., Acting Provost-Marshal-General

Appendix V

Battle of Fort Davidson/ Pilot Knob

BATTLE OF FORT DAVIDSON/PILOT KNOB
SEPTEMBER 27, 1864 (ORDER OF BATTLE)

Confederate Forces:

Army of Missouri: Major General Sterling Price
Fagan's Division: Brig. Gen. James F. Fagan
Cabell's Brigade
Monroe's Arkansas Cavalry
Gordon's Arkansas Cavalry
Morgan's Arkansas Cavalry
Hill's Arkansas Cavalry
Gunter's Arkansas Cavalry
Witherspoon's Cavalry
Hughey's Arkansas Battery
Dobbin's Brigade
Dobbin's Arkansas Cavalry
McGhee's Arkansas Cavalry
Witt's Arkansas Cavalry
Blocher's Arkansas Battery
Marmaduke's Division:
   Maj. General John S. Marmaduke
Clark's Brigade: Brig. Gen. John Clark
3rd Missouri Cavalry
4th Missouri Cavalry
7th Missouri Cavalry
8th Missouri Cavalry

Slemon's Brigade
2nd Arkansas Cavalry
Crawford's Arkansas Cavalry
Carlton's Arkansas Cavalry
Wright's Arkansas Cavalry

McCray's Brigade
45th Arkansas Mounted Inf.
47th Arkansas Mounted Inf.
15th Missouri Cavalry

Freeman's Brigade

Freeman's Missouri Cavalry
Fristoe's Missouri Cavalry
Ford's Arkansas Cavalry
Slayback's Missouri Cavalry

10th Missouri Cavalry
14th Missouri Cavalry
Hynson's Texas Battery
Harris' Missouri Battery
Shelby's Division
BG Joseph O. Shelby
Shelby's Iron Brigade: Brig. M. Jeff Thompson
5th Missouri Cavalry: Col. Frank B. Gordon
11th Missouri Cavalry: Col. Moses W. Smith
12th Missouri Cavalry: Ltc. William H. Erwin
Crisp's Cavalry Battalion: Ltc. John T. Crisp
Elliott's Missouri Cavalry: Col. Benjamin F. Elliott
Johnson's Cavalry Battalion: Maj. Rector Johnson
Slayback's Missouri Cavalry Battalion: Ltc. Alonzo Slayback
Collin's Missouri Battery (2 guns): Cpt. Richard A. Collins
Jackman's Brigade: Col. Sidney D. Jackman
Hunter's Missouri Cavalry: Col. DeWitt C. Hunter
Jackman's Missouri Cavalry: Ltc. C. H. Nichols
Schnable's Missouri Cavalry Battalion: Ltc. John A. Schnable
Williams' Missouri Cavalry Battalion: Ltc. D. A. Williams
Collins' Missouri Battery (2 guns): Lt. Jacob D. Connor
Tyler's Brigade: Col. Charles H. Tyler
Coffee's Missouri Cavalry: Col. J. T. Coffee
Perkin's Missouri Cavalry: Col. Caleb Perkins
Searcey's Missouri Cavalry: Col. James T. Searcey
Unattached
46th Arkansas Infantry (mounted): Col. W. O. Coleman

Union Forces at Ft. Davidson

Pilot Knob Garrison: Brig. Gen. Thomas Ewing

Infantry	Artillery
14th Iowa	Co. G 1st M.S.M.
47th Missouri: Col. Thomas Fletcher	Co. H 2nd MO Light Art.
Co. F 50th Missouri	
Cavalry	
Major James Wilson	
Co. L 2nd M.S.M. Cavalry	3rd M.S.M. Cavalry

Thomas C. Fletcher (Governor of MO, 1865–1869)
SOLDIER'S RANK IN: Colonel
FILM NUMBER: M390 ROLL 15

OVERVIEW:

Organized at Pilot Knob, MO, August 22 to September 11, 1864; attached to District of St. Louis, MO, Dept. of Missouri, to December 1864; Nashville, TN, Dept. of the Cumberland, December 1864; Pulaski, TN, Dept. of the Cumberland, to March 1865.

SERVICE:

Assigned to duty in Southeast Missouri by Companies "A," "G" and "H" in Wayne County; "B" in Jefferson County; "C" in Perry County; "K" at St. Genevieve; "I" at Fredericktown; "D" on Iron Mountain Railroad, guarding bridges; and "E" at Ironton. Companies retired before Price: Company "C" to Cape Girardeau; "A," "G" and "H" to Pilot Knob; and Company "E" to action at Ironton, September 26. Retreat to Pilot Knob, Shut In Gap and Arcadia Valley, September 26. Fort Davidson, September 26–27. Retreat to Leesburg. Companies returned to above stations: "B" at Franklin. Moved to Nashville, TN, December 12–19; assigned to guard duty at Spring Hill, Columbia, and Pulaski, TN, to March 15, 1865; mustered out March 28–30, 1865.

Regiment lost during service: 10 enlisted men killed and mortally wounded; one Officer and 82 enlisted men by disease: Total 93.

Civil War Union Brevet Brigadier General, Missouri Governor. In his profession as a lawyer, he was involved in the formation of the Republican Party and attended the 1860 Republican National Convention. His first military assignment came in 1862 as Colonel and commander of the 31st Missouri Volunteer Infantry, leading the regiment throughout the Vicksburg campaign. Two years later he became Colonel of the 47th Missouri Volunteer Infantry. After he was elected Governor of the state of Missouri, he resigned his commission. He was brevetted Brigadier General, US Volunteers, on March 13, 1865, for "gallant services at Pilot Knob, Mo.," and served as Governor of Missouri from 1865 to 1869.

Appendix VI

Vitt's Mill, Union, Missouri

VITT'S MILL, UNION, MO, OCT. 1, 1864 (ORDER OF BATTLE)

Confederate Victory:
Losses: Union: est. 10–15 killed & wounded, 65 captured
Confederate: est. 3–10 killed & wounded

Confederate Troops:
Army of Missouri, Major General Sterling Price
Marmaduke's Cavalry Division: Brigadier General John S. Marmaduke
Brigadier General John B. Clark, in overall command (2000 engaged)

BATTLE UNIT NAME: General and Staff Officers, Non-Regimental Enlisted Men, CSA
SIDE: Confederacy
COMPANY: Army of Missouri
SOLDIER'S RANK IN: Lieutenant
SOLDIER'S RANK OUT: Brigadier General
ALTERNATE NAME:
FILM NUMBER: M818 ROLL 5

John B. Clark entered the Confederate Army as a lieutenant and was promoted successively to the rank of captain and then major in the 6th Missouri Infantry. He saw action in several battles, including Carthage and Springfield. Promoted to the regiment's colonelcy, Clark commanded a brigade at the Battle of Pea Ridge. Primarily serving in Missouri and Arkansas under Thomas C. Hindman, he was rewarded with a commission as a brigadier general on March 6, 1864. He then fought in the Trans-Mississippi Theater under John S. Marmaduke and Jo Shelby, including Price's Raid. Clark fought at Ironton and Pilot Knob and at Union, MO. He was in command of assault against Union forces at Union, MO, and moved his troops against Washington, MO, and eventually all the way to Westport.

Greene's Brigade: Colonel Colton Greene, in command
3rd Missouri: Lieutenant Colonel L. A. Campbell
4th Missouri: Lieutenant Colonel William J. Preston
7th Missouri: Colonel Solomon G. Kitchen
8th Missouri: Colonel William L. Jeffers
10th Missouri: Colonel Robert R. Lawther
14th Missouri (Battalion): Ltc. Robert C. Wood
4th Field Battery, Missouri Light Artillery (Harris')
Confederate Battery: Captain S. S. Harris
Harris' Missouri Battery (1 gun): Lt T. J. Williams
Hynson's Texas Battery: Capt. H. C. Hynson
Hogan's Engineer Company: Capt. James T. Hogan
Robert R. Lawther

BATTLE UNIT NAME: 10th Regiment, Missouri Cavalry
SIDE: Confederacy
COMPANY: F&S
SOLDIER'S RANK IN: Colonel
SOLDIER'S RANK OUT: Colonel
NOTES: General Note—See also Lawthers Dismounted Cav., Mo., 1 Mo. Cav. 10th Regiment, Missouri Cavalry

OVERVIEW:

The 10th Cavalry Regiment was organized in December 1863, using M.L. Young's 11th Missouri Cavalry Battalion as its nucleus. It contained 559 officers and men and saw action in Price's Missouri Expedition. During this operation it reported 16 killed, 56 wounded, and 73 missing. The regiment was included in the surrender in June 1865. Its commanders were Colonel Robert R. Lawther, Lieutenant Colonel Merritt L. Young, and Major George W.C. Bennett.

Col. William L. Jeffers
BATTLE UNIT NAME: 8th Missouri Cavalry
SIDE: Confederacy
COMPANY: F&S
SOLDIER'S RANK IN: Colonel
SOLDIER'S RANK OUT: Colonel
PLAQUE NUMBER: 8th Regiment, Missouri Cavalry

OVERVIEW:

The 8th Cavalry Regiment was organized late in 1862 with men who had served in the Missouri State Guard. It was assigned to J.C. Porter's, C. Greene's, and J.B. Clark's Brigade, Trans-Mississippi Department. The unit was active in Marmaduke's Expedition into Missouri, fought at Helena and Bayou Fourche, skirmished in Missouri and Arkansas, and then saw action in Price's Missouri operations. It sustained six casualties with Marmaduke, one at Helena, and 29 with Price. The regiment disbanded prior to surrender in June 1865. The field officers were Colonel William L. Jeffers, Lieutenant Colonel Samuel J. Ward, and Major James Parrott.

Union Missouri Troops (300–400 engaged)

Lt. General William S. Rosecrans, H.Q. Army of the Department of Missouri

Enrolled Missouri Militia was raised in Franklin County, with duty in Franklin County. Operations against Price September and October 1864.

Colonel George Krumsick, Sep. 22, 1863; vacated Mar. 12, 1865.

Lt. Colonel John T. Vitt

Colonel Daniel Q. Gale, 54th Enrolled Missouri Militia (Franklin Co.), Co. B (in overall command)

Captain Henry Detmer, Aug. 12 to Sep. 10, 1862; vacated, Mar. 12, 1865.

1st Lt., Gerhard Hagebush, Aug. 16 to Sep. 10, 1862; vacated, Mar. 12, 1865.

2nd Lt., Henry Beincke, Aug. 16 to Sep. 10, 1862; vacated, Mar. 12, 1865.

The 54th Enrolled Missouri Militia was raised in Franklin County with duty at Union, Missouri, and operations against Price in September and October 1864.

55th Enrolled Missouri Militia (Franklin Co.), Co. E

Captain Henry Gillhause, Aug. 25 to Sep. 10, 1862; vacated by Special Order #126, 1864.

1st Lt., Austin Wilkins, Aug. 25 to Nov. 18, 1862; vacated by Special Order #126, 1864.

2nd Lt., Henry Hemper, Aug. 25 to Nov. 18, 1862; vacated by Special Order #126, 1864.

The 55th Enrolled Missouri Militia was raised in Franklin County, with duty in Union Franklin County with operations against Price in September and October 1864.

Provisional Enrolled Missouri Militia: Fink's Militia Co., independent commands Franklin Co.

Captain Andrew Fink, Sep. 16, 1864, organized under G.O. #107
1st Lt., Philip Brigleb, Sep. 16, 1864
2nd Lt., Charles Booth, Sep. 16, 1864

A number of Provisional Enrolled Missouri Militia Companies were formed in Franklin County at various times. Operations against Price, September and October 1864. At Union, Fink's Provisional Militia was better trained and disciplined than the 54th and 55th Enrolled Missouri Militia and suffered the most casualties as they stood their ground near the Mill.

Battle of Franklin (Pacific Missouri)

Union Forces:

16th Army Corps (Attached): Maj. Gen. A.J. Smith
2nd Division: Col. David Moore
Third Brigade: Col. Edward H. Wolfe
49th Illinois Infantry Regiment: Col. P. Pease
117th Illinois Infantry Regiment: Lieut. Col. J. Merriam
52nd Indiana Infantry Regiment: Capt. Eli Mattocks
178th New York Infantry Regiment: Capt. John B. Gandolfo

Confederate Forces:

1st Arkansas division (Fagan's division): Maj. Gen. James F. Fagan
1st Arkansas Brigade (Cabell's Brigade): Brig. Gen. William L. Cabell
Monroe's (1st Arkansas) Cavalry Regiment: Col. James C. Monroe
Morgan's (2nd Arkansas) Cavalry Regiment: Col. Thomas J. Morgan
Gordon's (4th Arkansas) Cavalry Regiment: Col. Anderson Gordon
Hill's (7th Arkansas) Cavalry Regiment: Col. John F. Hill
Gunter's (Arkansas) Cavalry Battalion: Lieut. Col. Thomas M. Gunter
Witherspoon's (13th Arkansas) Cavalry Battalion: Maj. J. L. Witherspoon
Hughey's (Arkansas) Battery: Capt. W. M. Hughey

Appendix VII

Battle of Westport and Byram's Ford

BATTLE OF WESTPORT & BYRAM'S FORD ORDER OF BATTLE, OCTOBER 23, 1864

Union Forces

Army of the Border: Major General Samuel Ryan Curtis

   1st Division: Major General James G. Blunt
   1st Brigade: Colonel Charles R. Jennison
   Foster's Missouri Cavalry Battalion: Capt. George S. Grover
   15th Kansas Cavalry: Ltc. George H. Hoyt
   3rd Wisconsin Cavalry (detachment): Cpt. Robert Carpenter
   Battery (5 guns), manned by 15th Kansas Cavalry: 2nd Lt. Henry L. Barker
   2nd Brigade: Colonel Thomas Moonlight
   5th Kansas Cavalry, Companies L and M: Cpt. James H. Young
   11th Kansas Cavalry: Ltc. Preston B. Plumb
   16th Kansas Cavalry, Companies A and D: Ltc. Samuel Walker
   Battery (4 guns), manned by Company E, 11th Kansas Cavalry
   3rd Brigade: Col. Charles W. Blair
   4th Kansas Militia: Col. W. D. McCain
   5th Kansas Militia: Col. G. A. Colton
   6th Kansas Militia: Col. James D. Snoddy (arrested Oct. 16); Col. James Montgomery
   10th Kansas Militia: Col. William Pennock
   19th Kansas Militia: Col. A. C. Hogan
   24th Kansas Militia Battalion: Ltc. George Eaves
   14th Kansas Cavalry, Company E: Lt. William B. Clark
   2nd Kansas State Artillery (2 guns): Lt. Daniel C. Knowles
   9th Wisconsin Battery (6 guns): Cap. James H. Dodge

4th Brigade: Col. James Hobart Ford
2nd Colorado Cavalry: Maj. Jesse L. Pritchard
16th Regiment Kansas Volunteer Cavalry (detachment): Maj. James Ketner
McLain's Independent Colorado Battery (6 guns): Cap. William D. McLain
Kansas State Militia: Major Gen. George W. Dietzler
1st Brigade: Brig. Gen. M. S. Grant (engaged at Little Blue River)
2nd Brigade: Brig. Gen. Byron Sherry (manned Kansas City defenses)
3rd Brigade: Brig. Gen. William Fishbeck
4th Brigade: Brig. Gen. J. B. Scott (not engaged)

Department of the Missouri: Major Gen. William S. Rosecrans
*Provisional Cavalry Division: Major Gen. Alfred Pleasonton
1st Brigade: Col. John F. Philips
1st Iowa Cavalry (detachment): Maj. John McDermott
1st Missouri Militia Cavalry: Col. James McFerran (arrested Oct. 23); Ltc. Bazel Lazear
4th Missouri Militia Cavalry: Maj. George W. Kelly
7th Missouri Militia Cavalry: Col. John F. Philips; Ltc. Thomas Theodore Crittenden
2nd Brigade: Brig. Gen. John McNeil
17th Illinois Cavalry: Col. John Lourie Beveridge
7th Kansas Cavalry: Maj. Francis Malone
2nd Missouri Cavalry (detachment): Cpt. George M. Houston
13th Missouri Cavalry: Col. Edwin C. Catherwood
3rd Missouri Militia Cavalry (detachment): Ltc. Henry M. Matthews
5th Missouri Militia Cavalry: Ltc. Joseph Eppstein
9th Missouri Militia Cavalry (detachment): Ltc. Daniel M. Draper
3rd Brigade: Brig. Gen. Egbert B. Brown
2nd Arkansas Cavalry: Col. John E. Phelps
6th Enrolled Missouri Militia Cavalry (detachment): Ltc. John F. McMahan
7th Enrolled Missouri Militia Cavalry (detachment): Maj. W. B. Mitchell
6th Missouri Militia Cavalry (detachment): Maj. William Plumb
8th Missouri Militia Cavalry: Col. Joseph J. Gravely
4th Brigade: Col. Edward F. Winslow
7th Indiana Cavalry (detachment): Maj. Samuel E. W. Simonson
3rd Iowa Cavalry: Maj. Benjamin S. Jones
4th Iowa Cavalry: Maj. Abial R. Pierce
4th Missouri Cavalry (detachment): Cpt. George D. Knispel

10th Missouri Cavalry: Ltc. Frederic W. Benteen; Maj. William H. Lusk
Artillery, Col. Nelson Cole
Company H, 2nd Missouri Light Artillery (4 guns): Cpt. William C. F. Montgomery (2 guns), commanded by Lt. Philip Smiley
Company L, 2nd Missouri Light Artillery (4 guns): Cpt. Charles H. Thurber
Battery (2 guns) of 5th Missouri Militia Cavalry: Lt. Adam Hillerich

XVI Corps (attached): Maj. Gen. Andrew Jackson Smith

First Division: Col. Joseph J. Woods
2nd Brigade: Col. Lucius Frederick Hubbard
47th Illinois
12th Iowa
5th Minnesota
7th Minnesota
9th Minnesota
10th Minnesota
8th Wisconsin
Battery G, 2nd Illinois Light Artillery
3rd Brigade: Col. Sylvester G. Hill
35th Iowa
33rd Missouri
Third Division: Col. David Moore
2nd Brigade: Col. James Isham Gilbert
14th Iowa
27th Iowa
32nd Iowa
24th Missouri
3rd Brigade: Col. Edward H. Wolfe
49th Illinois
117th Illinois
52nd Indiana
178th New York
3rd Indiana Battery
9th Indiana Battery

Confederate Forces

Army of Missouri: Major General Sterling Price

*Fagan's Division: Major General James F. Fagan
Cabell's Brigade: Brig. Gen. William L. Cabell (captured at Mine Creek)

Gordon's Arkansas Cavalry: Col. Anderson Gordon
Gunter's Arkansas Cavalry Battalion: Ltc. Thomas M. Gunter
Harrell's Arkansas Cavalry Battalion: Ltc. John M. Harrell
Hill's Arkansas Cavalry Battalion: Col. John F. Hill
Monroe's Arkansas Cavalry: Col. James C. Monroe
Morgan's Arkansas Cavalry: Col. Thomas J. Morgan
Witherspoon's Arkansas Cavalry Battalion: Maj. J. L. Witherspoon
Hughey's Arkansas Battery (2 guns): Cpt. William M. Hughey
Dobbin's Brigade: Col. Archibald Dobbins
Dobbin's Arkansas Cavalry: Col. Archibald S. Dobbins
McGhee's Arkansas Cavalry: Col. James H. McGee (w Oct. 23); Ltc. Jesse S. Grider
Witt's Arkansas Cavalry: Col. A. R. Witt
Blocher's Arkansas Battery (2 guns): Lt. J. V. Zimmerman
*Marmaduke's Division: Brig. Gen. John S. Marmaduke (captured at Mine Creek)
Marmaduke's Brigade: Brig. Gen. John B. Clark II
3rd Missouri Cavalry: Col. Colton Greene
4th Missouri Cavalry: Col. John Q. Burbridge
7th Missouri Cavalry: Col. Solomon G. Kitchen
8th Missouri Cavalry: Col. William L. Jeffers
10th Missouri Cavalry: Col. Robert R. Lawther
14th Missouri Cavalry Battalion: Ltc. J. F. Davies
Hogan's Engineer Company: Cpt. James T. Hogan
Freeman's Brigade: Col. Thomas Freeman
Ford's Arkansas Cavalry Battalion: Ltc. Barney Ford
Freeman's Missouri Cavalry: Ltc. Joseph R. Love
Fristoe's Missouri Cavalry: Col. Edward T. Fristoe
Artillery: Maj. Joseph H. Pratt
Harris' Missouri Battery (1 gun): Lt. T. J. Williams
Hynson's Texas Battery (4 guns): Cpt. Henry C. Hynson
*Shelby's Division: Brig. Gen. Joseph O. Shelby
Iron Brigade: Brig. Gen. M. Jeff Thompson
5th Missouri Cavalry: Col. Frank B. Gordon
11th Missouri Cavalry: Col. Moses W. Smith
12th Missouri Cavalry: Ltc. William H. Erwin
Crisp's Cavalry Battalion: Ltc. John T. Crisp
Elliott's Missouri Cavalry: Col. Benjamin F. Elliott
Johnson's Cavalry Battalion: Maj. Rector Johnson
Slayback's Missouri Cavalry Battalion: Ltc. Alonzo Slayback

Collin's Missouri Battery (2 guns): Cpt. Richard A. Collins
Jackman's Brigade: Col. Sidney D. Jackman
Hunter's Missouri Cavalry: Col. DeWitt C. Hunter
Jackman's Missouri Cavalry: Ltc. C. H. Nichols
Schnable's Missouri Cavalry Battalion: Ltc. John A. Schnable
Williams' Missouri Cavalry Battalion: Ltc. D. A. Williams
Collins' Missouri Battery (2 guns): Lt. Jacob D. Connor
Tyler's Brigade: Col. Charles H. Tyler
Coffee's Missouri Cavalry: Col. J. T. Coffee
Perkin's Missouri Cavalry: Col. Caleb Perkins
Searcey's Missouri Cavalry: Col. James T. Searcey

Battle of Newtonia (Order of Battle), October 28, 1864
Union Forces

1st Division: Major Gen. James G. Blunt
1st Brigade: Col. Charles R. Jennison
Foster's Missouri Cavalry Battalion: Cpt. George S. Grover
15th Kansas Cavalry: Ltc. George H. Hoyt
3rd Wisconsin Cavalry (detachment): Cpt. Robert Carpenter
Battery (5 guns), manned by 15th Kansas Cavalry: 2nd Lt. Henry L. Barker
2nd Brigade: Col. Thomas Moonlight
5th Kansas Cavalry, Companies L and M: Cpt. James H. Young
11th Kansas Cavalry: Ltc. Preston B. Plumb
16th Kansas Cavalry, Companies A and D: Ltc. Samuel Walker
McClain's Colorado Battery

Confederate Forces

Shelby's Division: Brig. Gen. Joseph O. Shelby
Iron Brigade: Brig. Gen. M. Jeff Thompson
5th Missouri Cavalry: Col. Frank B. Gordon
11th Missouri Cavalry: Col. Moses W. Smith
12th Missouri Cavalry: Ltc. William H. Erwin
Crisp's Cavalry Battalion: Ltc. John T. Crisp
Elliott's Missouri Cavalry: Col. Benjamin F. Elliott
Johnson's Cavalry Battalion: Maj. Rector Johnson
Slayback's Missouri Cavalry Battalion: Ltc. Alonzo Slayback
Collin's Missouri Battery (2 guns): Cpt. Richard A. Collins
Jackman's Brigade: Col. Sidney D. Jackman
Hunter's Missouri Cavalry: Col. DeWitt C. Hunter

Jackman's Missouri Cavalry: Ltc. C. H. Nichols
Schnable's Missouri Cavalry Battalion: Ltc. John A. Schnable
Williams' Missouri Cavalry Battalion: Ltc. D. A. Williams
Collins' Missouri Battery (2 guns): Lt. Jacob D. Connor
Tyler's Brigade: Col. Charles H. Tyler
Coffee's Missouri Cavalry: Col. J. T. Coffee
Perkin's Missouri Cavalry: Col. Caleb Perkins
Searcey's Missouri Cavalry: Col. James T. Searcey

Appendix VIII

Missouri State Guard and Confederate Troops

Missouri State Guard Organizations Cooperating with Confederate Troops Record and Pension Office, War Department, Washington, DC: Government Printing Office, 1902.

Cavalry

First Regiment, First Division. First Battalion, First Division. Became Third Cavalry Regiment, First Division, First Battalion, Independent Rangers (Second Cavalry Battalion, First Division). First Regiment, Fourth Division. First Regiment, Fifth Division. First Regiment, Sixth Division. First Battalion, Seventh Division. First Regiment, Eighth Division.

Second Regiment, First Division. Second Battalion, First Division. Also known as First Cavalry Battalion, Independent Rangers. Second Regiment, Sixth Division. Second Regiment, Eighth Division. Third Regiment, First Division. See First Cavalry Battalion, First Division.

Third Regiment, Eighth Division. Fourth Regiment, Eighth Division.

Fifth Regiment, Eighth Division. Sixth Regiment, Eighth Division. Seventh Regiment, Eighth Division. See below, Vernon County Cavalry Battalion.

Eighth Regiment, Eighth Division. Ninth Regiment, Eighth Division.

Tenth Regiment, Eighth Division. Eleventh Regiment, Eighth Division. Twelfth Regiment, Eighth Division.

Thirteenth Regiment, Eighth Division. Fourteenth Regiment, Eighth Division. Bruce's Regiment, Second Division.

Burbridge's Regiment, Second Division. Callaway Guards (Capt. D. H. McIntyre's company, Second Division. Probably cavalry, but not positively ascertained). Extra Battalion, Fourth Division, attached to First Infantry Regiment.

Missouri State Guard and Confederate Troops

This list is made up from such official data as has been discovered on the files of the War Department; however, the rolls of the State Guard organizations are not on file, and other records are meager. The list, although probably not complete, is as nearly complete as it can be made from the records of the Department.

MISSOURI TROOPS CONFEDERATE

*Franklin's Regiment, Second Division. *Green's Regiment, Second Division. Hawkins's Regiment, Second Division. Kennett Rovers (Company B, First Cavalry Regiment, First Division). Major's Regiment, Third Division. Missouri Rangers (Company A, First Cavalry Regiment, First Division). Plattin Rangers (Capt. White Kennett's company. Probably cavalry, 7" ascertained). Vernon County Battalion. Became Seventh Cavalry, Eighth Division.

ARTILLERY

First Battalion, Fifth Division. Probably composed of O'Reirdon's, Richardson's, and McDonald's batteries, Companies A, B, and C. Bledsoe's Battery, commanded by Capt. H. M. Bledsoe (reorganized for Confederate service Clark's Battery).

Reorganized for Confederate service Gorham's Battery. Reorganized for Confederate service Guibor's Battery. Reorganized for Confederate service Kelly's Battery or Kneisley's Battery. McDonald's Battery C commanded by Capt. Robert McDonald. Reorganized for Confederate service (see First Artillery Battalion). O'Reirdon's Battery A and Richardson's Battery B (see First Artillery Battalion). Wade's Battery, Reorganized for Confederate service.

Chapter Notes

Prelude

1. Patricia L. Faust., ed., *The Historical Times Encyclopedia of the Civil War*.
2. Dred Scott v. Sandford 19 How. 393; 15 L. ed. 691 (1857.)
3. "War of the Rebellion," U.S. War Department Official Record, Ch. X, Vol. III, Government Printing Office, Washington, D.C., 1880, Vol. 3, Ch. 10, 4–5.
4. *Ibid.*
5. *Ibid.*, 61.
6. *Ibid.*, 61–62.
7. *Ibid.*, 100–102.
8. *Ibid.*, 268.
9. *Ibid.*, 261.
10. *Ibid.*, 270.
11. Grant, *Personal Memoirs*, 161.
12. Alfred T. Mahan., *The Gulf and Inland Waters* (New York Charles Scribner's Sons), 1883, 19.
13. *Ibid.*, 19–20.
14. "War of the Rebellion," Vol. 8, Ch. 13, 196.
15. *Ibid.*, 198–199.
16. *Ibid.*, 202.
17. Shelby Foote, *The Civil War* (New York: Random House, 1958), 187–188.

Chapter 1

1. Jeremy Neely, "'A Most Cruel and Unjust War': The Guerrilla Struggle along the Missouri-Kansas Border," *Civil War on the Western Border: The Missouri-Kansas Conflict, 1854–1865*, http://www.civilwaronthewesternborder.org/essay/"-most-cruel-and-unjust-war"-guerrilla-struggle-along-missouri-kansas-border.
2. Lizzie E. Brannock, Letter, 1864 (C0224), Civil War Manuscripts wcic0224p0001, The State Historical Society of Missouri, Columbia, MO.
3. *Ibid.*

4. *Ibid.*
5. *Ibid.*
6. *A State Divided: Missouri and the Civil War*, Missouri Department of Natural Resources Division of Parks and Historic Preservation.
7. Nathan Bedford Forrest p. 160
8. "Official Records: The Battle of New Madrid and Island No. 10," Shotgun's Home of the American Civil War, http://civilwarhome.com/island10.htm
9. Ibid
10. *Ibid.*
11. *Ibid.*
12. Lynn N. Bock, "The Island No. 10 Campaign," New Madrid Historical Museum, New Madrid, MO.
13. "The Battle of New Madrid and Island No. 10."
14. *Ibid.*
15. *Ibid.*
16. Shelby Foote, *The Civil War*, Random House, New York, p. 306.
17. *Ibid.*
18. "The Battle of New Madrid and Island No. 10."
19. "The Island No. 10 Campaign."
20. "The Battle of New Madrid and Island No. 10."
21. *The Civil War*, p. 308.
22. *The Gulf and Inland Waters.*

Chapter 2

1. "Porter's 1862 Raid," U.S. Grant Trail, Northeast Segment, www.mocivilwar.org.
2. "Col. Joe Porter's Raid," *History of Monroe and Shelby Counties, Missouri*, Ch. VIII, Vol. II, National Historical Co., St. Louis, 1884, 741.
3. *Organization and Status of Missouri Troops in Service During the Civil War*, Government Printing Office, Washington, D.C., 1902, 48.

4. *Ibid.*
5. *Ibid.*
6. Charles D. Collins., *Battlefield Atlas of Price's Missouri Expedition of 1864* (Fort Leavenworth, KS Combat Studies Institute Press, 2016), 15.
7. "Col. Joe Porter's Raid," 743.
8. *Ibid.*
9. *Ibid.*, 745.
10. "A Confederate Soldier's Account of the Battle of Moore's Mill," *The Mid-Missouri Civil War Project*, http://law.missouri.edu/bowman/moores_mill/confederate_account_moores.html, 171.
11. *Ibid.*
12. *Ibid.*, 176.
13. *Ibid.*
14. *Ibid.*
15. *Ibid.*
16. *Ibid.*, 178.
17. *Ibid.*
18. "Col. Joe Porter's Raid," 747.
19. A.A.G., Dept. of Kansas, Fort Leavenworth, Kans. Reports, Number 1. Colonel John McNeil, Second Missouri Cavalry (Militia).
20. *Ibid.*
21. "Col. Joe Porter's Raid," 757.

Chapter 3

1. "Col. Joe Porter's Raid," p. 757.
2. *Ibid.*, p. 759.
3. *Ibid.*, p. 761.
4. Missouri State Library, Missouri State Archives, Palmyra Massacre Collection.
5. *Battlefield Atlas of Price's Missouri Expedition of 1864*, p. 19.
6. *Ibid.*, p. 16.
7. *The Civil War*, Vol. II, p. 142.
8. *Ibid.*, p. 140.
9. *Ibid.*, p. 601.
10. "War of the Rebellion," Ch. 34, Vol. 22, p. 196.
11. *Ibid.*, p. 197.
12. *Ibid.*
13. *Ibid.*
14. *Ibid.*, p. 204.
15. *Ibid.*, p. 198.
16. *Ibid.*, p. 790.
17. *Ibid.*, p. 286.
18. *Ibid.*
19. *Ibid.*, p. 287.
20. 1st Nebraska Battle Marker Fort D, Cape Girardeau, Missouri Department of Natural Resources Division of Parks and Historic Preservation.
21. "War of the Rebellion," Ch. 34, Vol. 22, 290.
22. *Ibid.*, p. 287.
23. *Ibid.*, p. 292
24. *Ibid.*, p. 259.
25. *Ibid.*, p. 292
26. *Ibid.*, p. 259.
27. *Ibid.*

Chapter 4

1. Shelby Foote, *The Civil War* (New York: Random House), Vol. II, 601.
2. Quiner, E. B., *The Military History of Wisconsin* (St. Croix Valley, WI: Civil War Roundtable, 1886), 984.
3. *Ibid.*, 770.
4. *The Civil War*, Vol. II, 605.
5. Excavations in 2002 around the site of Battery D revealed six Confederate soldiers buried in shallow graves. The Fagan Six, as they are called, were reinterred at Maple Hill Cemetery in Helena.
6. *The Civil War*, Vol. II, 776.
7. Jeffery S. Prushankin., "To This Fatal Blunder," *North & South* Magazine, Vol. 5, No. 6, September 2002, 78.
8. James R. Furqueron., "Point Blank Business," *North & South* Magazine, Vol. 5, No., 6, September 2002, 24.
9. *The Civil War*, Vol. II, 776.
10. Phillip W. Steele., and Steve Cottrell, *Civil War in the Ozarks* (Gretna, LA Pelican Publishing, 2009), 96.
11. *Ibid.*
12. "War of the Rebellion," Ch. 34, Vol. 22, 670, 678.
13. *The Military History of Wisconsin*, 915.

Chapter 5

1. Brannock, Letter, 1864 (C0224).
2. "To This Fatal Blunder," 78.
3. Shelby Foote, *The Civil War* (New York: Random House), Vol. II, 74.
4. Ulysses S. Grant., *The Personnel Memoirs of Ulysses S. Grant* (Old Saybrook, CT: Konecky & Konecky Press 1886, reprint 1992), 411.
5. *Organization and Status of Missouri Troops*, 78.
6. *Ibid.*
7. *Ibid.*
8. *Ibid.*, 79.
9. "To This Fatal Blunder," 78.
10. "War of the Rebellion," Vol. 41, 729.
11. *Ibid.*, 135.

12. "War of the Rebellion," Vol. 41, 307.
13. *Ibid.*, 143.
14. *Ibid.*, 187.
15. *Ibid.*
16. *Ibid.*, 307.
17. *Ibid.*, 446.
18. "Prices Raid into Missouri and Kansas in the fall of 1864," Official Report William Cabell, The State Historical Society of Wisconsin 1900 Battle of Pilot Knob State Park Library and Staff, Missouri Department of Natural Resources, 4–5.
19. "War of the Rebellion," Vol. 41, 308.
20. *Ibid.*, 447.
21. *Ibid.*, 308.
22. *Ibid.*, 447.
23. *Ibid.*
24. *Ibid.*, 448.
25. "Prices Raid into Missouri and Kansas in the Fall of 1864," 6.
26. *Ibid.*
27. David Agnew, "Personal Recollections of the Battle of Pilot Knob, 6 June 1906," box 8, folder 8, Missouri History Museum Library, St. Louis, MO.
28. "War of the Rebellion," 448.
29. Agnew, "Personal Recollections of the Battle of Pilot Knob, 6 June 1906," box 8, folder 8, Missouri History Museum Library St. Louis.
30. "Prices Raid into Missouri and Kansas in the Fall of 1864," 5.
31. *Ibid.* p. 5.
32. "War of the Rebellion," 449.
33. "Personal Recollections."
34. *Ibid.*
35. "Prices Raid into Missouri and Kansas in the Fall of 1864," 6.
36. "War of the Rebellion," 449.

Chapter 6

1. *Organization and Status of Missouri Troops*, 187.
2. "Centralia Massacre and Battle: An Account of the Civil War Events in and Near Centralia Missouri on the 130th Anniversary," Centralia Area Chamber of Commerce Brochure.
3. *Ibid.*
4. *Ibid.*
5. *Organization and Status of Missouri Troops*, 189.
6. "War of the Rebellion," Vol. 41, 309.
7. *Ibid.*, 652–653.
8. *Ibid.*, 653.
9. *Ibid.*, 309.
10. *Ibid.*, 653.

11. *Ibid.*
12. *Ibid.*, 680.
13. *Ibid.*, 310.
14. Gregory, Ralph, *Price's Raid in Franklin County, Missouri,* Missourian Publishing Co., Washington, MO, 1964, 5.
15. *Ibid.*, 6.
16. "War of the Rebellion," Vol. 41, 680.
17. *Price's Raid in Franklin County*, 7–8.
18. *Ibid.*, 6.
19. "War of the Rebellion," Vol. 41, 698.
20. *Ibid.*, 688.
21. *Price's Raid in Franklin County*, 8.
22. "Prices Raid into Missouri and Kansas in the Fall of 1864," 6.
23. "War of the Rebellion," Vol. 41, 310.

Chapter 7

1. "Official Records Headquarters Department of the Missouri Office Provost Marshal-General," October 29, 1864, The State Historical Society of Missouri, St. Louis, MO.
2. *Ibid.*
3. *Ibid.*
4. *Ibid.*
5. "War of the Rebellion," Vol. 41, 653.
6. *Ibid.*, 311.
7. "War of the Rebellion," Vol. 42, 375.
8. *Ibid.*, 654.
9. *Ibid.*, 632.
10. "Prices Raid into Missouri and Kansas in the Fall of 1864," 7.
11. *North & South* Magazine, 20.
12. "Prices Raid into Missouri and Kansas in the Fall of 1864," 8.
13. *Ibid.*
14. *Ibid.*
15. "War of the Rebellion," Vol. 41, 311.
16. *Ibid.*, 681.
17. *Ibid.*, 655.
18. *Ibid.*, 664.
19. *Ibid.*, 665.
20. *Ibid.*, 681.
21. *Ibid.*, 689.
22. *Ibid.*, 437–438.
23. *Ibid.*, 699.
24. *Ibid.*, 312.
25. *The Civil War*, Vol. III, 580.
26. "Price's Raid into Missouri and Kansas in the Fall of 1864," 9.
27. Charles D. Collins. *Battlefield Atlas of Price's Missouri Expedition of 1864.* Ft. Leavenworth, 67.
28. "War of the Rebellion," Vol. 41, 478.

Chapter 8

1. "War of the Rebellion," Vol. 41, 144–145.
2. *Ibid.*, 145–146.
3. *Ibid.*, 464.
4. *Ibid.*, 144.
5. *Ibid.*, 682.
6. *Ibid.*
7. *Ibid.*, 690.
8. *Ibid.*, 682.
9. *Ibid.*, 690.
10. *Ibid.*, 574.
11. *Ibid.*, 683.
12. Jenkins, Paul, *The Battle of Westport*, Franklin Hudson Publishing Co., Kansas City, MO, 1906, The State Historical Society of Missouri, Civil War eBook Collection, 57, http://cdm.sos.mo.gov/cdm/compoundobject/collection/shscivilwar/id/367/rec/4.
13. "Prices Raid into Missouri and Kansas in the fall of 1864," 9.
14. *The Battle of Westport*, 58.
15. "War of the Rebellion," Vol. 41, 666.
16. *The Battle of Westport*, 61.
17. *Ibid.*, 65.
18. "War of the Rebellion," Vol. 41, 666.
19. *Ibid.*, 483.
20. *Ibid.*, 340.
21. *Ibid.*, 690.
22. *Ibid.*
23. "Prices Raid into Missouri and Kansas in the fall of 1864," 10.
24. "War of the Rebellion," Vol. 41, 690.
25. *Ibid.*, 486–487.
26. Jenkins, Paul, The Battle of Westport State Historical Society of Missouri, Civil War eBook Collection, 57–58.
27. *Ibid.*, 684.
28. *Ibid.*, 658.
29. *Ibid.*, 488.
30. *Ibid.*, 486.
31. *Ibid.*, 487.
32. "Prices Raid into Missouri and Kansas in the Fall of 1864," 10.
33. Forest Hill later became a cemetery and the resting place of General Jo Shelby and many of his men.
34. "War of the Rebellion," Vol. 41, 667–668.
35. Ibid p. 487.

Chapter 9

1. "War of the Rebellion," Vol. 41, 49.1.
2. *Ibid.*, 315.
3. *Ibid.*, 493.
4. "Prices Raid into Missouri and Kansas in the Fall of 1864," 11.
5. Edwards, Shelby and his men p. 471.
6. "War of the Rebellion," Vol. 41, 684.
7. *Ibid.*
8. *Ibid.*, 341.
9. *Ibid.*, 691.
10. *Ibid.*
11. *Ibid.*, 636–637.
12. *Ibid.*, 351–352.
13. *Ibid.*, 353.
14. "Prices Raid into Missouri and Kansas in the Fall of 1864," 11.
15. *Ibid.*
16. "War of the Rebellion," Vol. 41, 684.
17. *Ibid.*, 332.
18. *Ibid.*, 336.
19. "Prices Raid into Missouri and Kansas in the Fall of 1864," 12.
20. *Ibid.*
21. "War of the Rebellion," Vol. 41, 691.
22. *Ibid.*, 352.
23. *Ibid.*, 659.
24. *Ibid.*, 660.
25. "Prices Raid into Missouri and Kansas in the Fall of 1864," 14–15.

Chapter 10

1. "War of the Rebellion," Vol. 41, 669.
2. *Ibid.*, 314.
3. *Ibid.*, 669.
4. *Ibid.*, 609–610.
5. *Ibid.*, 661.
6. *Ibid.*, 669.
7. *Ibid.*, 577–578.
8. *Ibid.*, 661.
9. *Ibid.*, 333–334.
10. *Ibid.*, 334.
11. *Ibid.*, 661.
12. *Ibid.*, 332.
13. *Ibid.*, 334.
14. *Ibid.*, 661.
15. *Ibid.*, 640.

Chapter 11

1. O.R. Vol 41, 729.
2. Lincoln's Second Inaugural Address.
3. Missouri State Library, Thomas Clement Fletcher, 1865–1869; Office of Governor, Record Group 3.18; Missouri State Archives, Jefferson City.

Bibliography

Books, Letters and Articles

Agnew, David, "Personal Recollections of the Battle of Pilot Knob 6 June 1906," box 8, folder 8, Missouri History Museum Library, St. Louis, MO.

Bock, Lynn N., "The Island No. 10 Campaign," New Madrid Historical Museum, New Madrid, MO.

Brannock, Lizzie E., Letter, 1864 (C0224), Civil War Manuscripts wcic0224p0001, The State Historical Society of Missouri, Columbia, MO.

Brennan, Patrick, "Thunder on the Plains of Brandy," *North & South* Magazine, Vol. 5, No. 3, April 2002.

Cape Girardeau Convention and Visitor Bureau Brochure, Civil War sites of Cape Girardeau, Missouri's Civil War, 1861–1865.

"Centralia Massacre and Battle, An Account of the Civil War events in and near Centralia Missouri on the 130th Anniversary," Centralia Area Chamber of Commerce Brochure.

Collins, Charles D., *Battlefield Atlas of Price's Missouri Expedition of 1864*, Combat Studies Institute Press, Fort Leavenworth, KS, 2016.

Engel, Brent, "Louisiana Historical Museum Preserving Civil War Flag," *Courier-Post*, May 2016.

Foote, Shelby, *The Civil War*, Vol. 1, Random House, New York, 1958.

Foote, Shelby, *The Civil War*, Vol. 2, Random House, New York, 1963.

Foote, Shelby, *The Civil War*, Vol. 3, Random House, New York, 1972.

Furqueron, James R., "Point Blank Business," *North & South* Magazine, Vol. 5, No. 6, September 2002.

Grant, Ulysses S., *The Personal Memoirs of Ulysses S. Grant*, Konecky & Konecky Press, Old Saybrook, CT, reprint 1886, 1992.

Gregory, Ralph, *Price's Raid in Franklin County, Missouri*, Missourian Publishing Co., Washington, MO, 1964.

"Col. Joe Porter's Raid," *History of Monroe and Shelby Counties, Missouri*, Chapter VIII, Vol. 2, National Historical Co., St. Louis, 1884.

"Index to the Civil War in Franklin County, Missouri," The Missouri Commandery of MOLLUS,, Union, MO.

Lyman Gibson Bennett Collection, Rolla Research Center, The State Historical Society of Missouri, Rolla, MO.

Mahan, Alfred T., *The Gulf and Inland Waters*, Charles Scribner's Sons, New York, 1883. Miscellaneous manuscripts, Battle of Lexington State Historic Park Library and Staff, Missouri Department of Natural Resources, Jefferson City, MO.

Miscellaneous manuscripts, Fort Davidson State Historic Park Library and Staff, Missouri Department of Natural Resources, Jefferson City, MO.

Monnett Battle of Westport Self-Guided Walking and Auto Tour brochures, Kansas City Parks and Recreation.

Morison, Samuel Eliot, *Oxford History of the American People*, Oxford University Press, New York, 1965.

"OFFICIAL RECORDS HEADQUARTERS DEPARTMENT OF THE MISSOURI OFFICE PROVOST MARSHAL-GENERAL," October 29, 1864, The State Historical Society of Missouri, St. Louis, MO.

"Prices Raid into Missouri and Kansas in the fall of 1864," Official Report William Cabell, The State Historical Society of Wisconsin 1900 Battle of Pilot Knob State Park Library and Staff, Missouri Department of Natural Resources.

Prushankin, Jeffery S., "To This Fatal Blunder," *North & South* Magazine, Vol. 5, No. 6, September 2002.

Quiner, E. B., *The Military History of Wisconsin*,

Civil War Roundtable, St. Croix Valley, WI, 1866.
Shapiro, Martin, and Rocco Tresolini, *American Constitutional Law*, 5th ed., Macmillan Publishing Co., New York, 1979.
Shelby, Joseph Orville, "Letter from a Confederate brigadier general to a friend, giving his reasons for the Civil War," Letter, 1885 (C0521), folder 1, The State Historical Society of Missouri, Columbia, MO.
Steele, Phillip W., and Steve Cottrell, *Civil War in the Ozarks*, Pelican Publishing, Gretna, LA, 2009.
Thompson, Meriwether Jeff, Papers, 1854–1935, 1030 C .25 linear feet; also on 1 roll of microfilm, The State Historical Society of Missouri, Columbia, MO.
Thurmond, Nicholas, Letter, The State Historical Society of Missouri, Columbia, MO.
"War of the Rebellion," U.S. War Department Official Record, Government Printing Office, Washington, D.C., 1880.
Wornall/Majors House Museums Library, Kansas City, MO.

Internet Sources

"Civil War," Library of Congress. http://www.loc.gov/pictures/collection/civwar
"Civil War," National Park Service. www.nps.gov/civilwar/soldiers-and-sailors-database.
"Civil War Resources," Missouri Digital Heritage, Missouri Office of the Secretary of State, Missouri State Library, Missouri State Archives. https://www.sos.mo.gov/mdh/CivilWar/Resources
"A Confederate Soldier's account of the Battle of Moore's Mill," *The Mid-Missouri Civil War Project*. http://law.missouri.edu/bowman/moores_mill/confederate_account_moores.html.
Ike Skelton Combined Arms Research Center. http://usacac.army.mil/organizations/cace/carl.
Jenkins, Paul, *The Battle of Westport*, Franklin Hudson Publishing Co., Kansas City, MO, 1906, The State Historical Society of Missouri, Civil War eBook Collection. http://cdm.sos.mo.gov/cdm/compoundobject/collection/shscivilwar/id/367/rec/4.
"Missouri Confederate Unit Rosters," *Sons of Confederate Veterans*, Missouri Division. http://www.missouridivision-scv.org.
Neely, Jeremy, "'A Most Cruel and Unjust War': The Guerrilla Struggle along the Missouri-Kansas Border," *Civil War on the Western Border: The Missouri-Kansas Conflict, 1854–1865*. http://www.civilwaronthewesternborder.org/essay/"-most-cruel-and-unjust-war"-guerrilla-struggle-along-missouri-kansas-border.
"Official Records: The Battle of New Madrid and Island No. 10," *Shotgun's Home of the American Civil War*. http://civilwarhome.com/island10.htm.
Organization and Status of Missouri Troops in Service During the Civil War, Government Printing Office, Washington, D.C., 1902. http://digital.shsmo.org/cdm/ref/collection/amcw/id/20584.
"Porter's 1862 Raid," U.S. Grant Trail, Northeast Segment. www.mocivilwar.org.
Price's Last Missouri Raid, No. 145, *Sons of Confederate Veterans*. http://pricecamp.org/lastraid.html.

Index

abolitionist 5-6
Allsmen, Andrew 42-43
Anderson, Bloody Bill 82-84, 102
Arcadia 62, 70-73, 75, 163
Arkansas 3, 13-14, 46, 48, 51-53, 56-57
Army of Arkansas 67
Army of Liberation 24
Army of Mississippi 23
Army of Missouri 101-103, 110-111, 113-115, 118-119, 126-128, 137-138, 140, 164
Army of Northern Virginia 54, 57
Army of Tennessee 21, 57, 126, 143
Army of the Border 106, 108, 114-115, 127, 132, 134-135, 168
Army of the Cumberland 57
Army of the Potomac 100
Army of the Southwest 12-13, 21
Army of the West 8, 13-15, 21
Arrow Rock 105
Athens, MO 146-148; battle at 30
Atlanta, GA 66, 68
Auxvasse River 34-35, 37

Bates County 40, 127; in Order No. 11 168
Batesville, AR 48, 68
Beauregard, Maj. Gen. P.G.T. 14, 21, 26-28
Belmont, battle at 10-11
Benteen, Col. Frederic 130-132, 139
Benton Barracks 68, 86, 102
Big Blue River 109-100, 115-118; Expulsion Order No. 11 158
Blunt, Maj. Gen. James 60-61, 107, 109-110, 172
Boonville 6, 8, 59, 111
Boston Mountains 12-14, 45-46, 48
Brannock, Lizzie 18, 62, 104
Brown, John: Potawatomie Massacre 5
Brush Creek 118-119; Expulsion Order No 11 158
Burnt District 17, 71, 127
Bushwhackers 19, 97
Byram's Ford, battle at 110, 115-120, 122, 125, 168

Cabell, Brig. Gen. William (CSA) 71, 75; attack on Fort Davidson 77-78, 84; captured at Mine Creek 133-135, 145, 161, 167, 170; at Franklin 88-89, 91-93 100, 103-104; at Independence 117-118, 131
Cairo, IL 9-10, 25
Callaway County 34
Camp Jackson 6-7
Camp Johnston 10-11
Cape Girardeau, battle at 9, 49-51, 53-56
USS *Carondelet* 27-28
Carthage 12, 59, 138
Centralia, battle at 82-84
Chalk Bluff, AR, battle at 51-53
Chattanooga, TN 57, 60
Cheltenham Post 85
Clark, Brig. Gen. John B. 69, 92-93, 104-105, 111, 113-114, 120, 122, 129-130 132, 134, 140, 161, 164, 171
Cleburne, Maj. Gen. Patrick 29
Clopper, Capt. John 32-34
Cobb, Capt. Alvin 34-36
Collins Battery 50, 52, 139, 162, 172-173
Colorado Artillery 140, 172
Colored Units 39-40, 60, 127
Columbus, KY 10-12, 22, 50
Curtis, Maj. Gen. Samuel R. 12-14, 45, 101, 106, 108, 109-110, 112-116, 118-119, 121-123, 126-128, 134-135, 137-138, 140-141, 154, 168

Danville 103, 146-148
Davis, Pres. Jefferson 21, 44, 150
Deitzler, Maj. Gen. George 122-123
Des Moines River 30, 147
Detmer, Capt. Henry 93, 166

Ewing, Brig. Gen. Thomas 17, 19, 71-80, 86-88, 97, 99, 145, 159, 162
Expulsion Order No. 11 17-19, 40, 72, 77, 111, 114, 144-145, 158

Fabius River 33, 41
Fagan, Maj. Gen. James 55, 113, 117, 121, 123, 127: at Mine Creek 130-131, 133-134, 140-141, 161, 167, 170
Fink, Capt. Andrew/Fink's Militia 92-93, 166-167

Fletcher, Col. Thomas 72, 74, 79; abolished slavery 146, 162; governor 144
Florida, MO 34, 41
Forest Hill and cemetery 51, 125
Forrest, Maj. Gen. Nathan B. 56, 64–65
Fort Bankhead 22–23, 25–26
Fort Blair 60
Fort Curtis 56
Fort Davidson, battle at 70–73, 78–80, 161, 163
Fort Scott 60, 127, 134–135, 137–138; Fort Scott Road 130–131
Fort Smith 60
Fort Snelling 4, 153
Fort Thompson 22–26
Franklin (Pacific), battle at 48, 88–96, 163, 166–167
Franklin County 68, 88–96, 160
Freeman, Col. Thomas 76, 120, 161, 171
Frémont, Maj. Gen. John C. 9, 12

General Order No. 19 31
General Order No. 176 69, 82
Georgia 64, 66, 126, 141
Glasgow 104–106; battle at 105–106
Grant, Brig. Gen. M.S. 116, 169
Grant, Lt. Gen. Ulysses S. 1, 9–12, 14, 27–28, 49, 64, 66–67, 84, 143
Gratiot Street Prison 62, 145
Greene, Col. Colton 49, 51, 92–93, 106, 112–113, 117–118, 120, 123, 130, 165–166, 171
Guitar, Col. Oden 34–37

Halleck, Maj. Gen. Henry 18, 44, 136
Hannibal 41
Harris Missouri Battery 92, 165, 171
Hartville, battle at 47–48
Helena, AR, battle at 54–56
Hickman Mills 115–116, 126, 158
Holmes, Maj. Gen. Theophilus 48–49, 54–56, 58, 62, 66
Hughey, Capt. W.M. 90–91, 161, 171

Illinois 9–10, 21, 23, 25, 41, 167, 160–170
Independence 100, 107–111, 114–115, 117, 146, 158
Independence 100, 107–111, 114–117, 126; in Order No. 11 158
Iowa 2, 10, 35, 132–133, 169–170
Iron Brigade (Shelby's Brigade) 20, 69, 80, 84–85, 99, 104, 113, 121, 137, 139, 145, 172
Island Mound, battle at 39–40
Island No. 10: battle at 22–23, 26–28

Jackman, Col. Sidney 105, 113, 115, 121–123, 134, 162, 172–173
Jackson, Governor Claiborne Fox 5–6, 20
Jackson, Stonewall 69
Jackson County: Order No. 11 111, 158
Jackson Road 50
Jayhawker 19, 39

Jefferies, Sally, and family 92–93
Jeffers, Col. William 92, 165–166
Jefferson Barracks 6, 86, 149–150, 153
Jefferson City 35, 58, 99–101
Jennison, Col. Charles 18–19, 116, 121, 168, 172
Johnston, Lt. Gen. Albert Sidney 13, 15, 21, 26–27
Johnston Maj. A.V.E. 83–84

Kansas 19, 39–40, 45, 56, 60–61, 100, 106, 108–111, 116, 119, 123, 127, 128–169; General Order No. 11 158–159
Kansas City 108–109, 114–115
Kansas Colored Infantry 39–40, 137
Kansas-Nebraska Act 4–5, 17
Kentucky 21–22, 50, 144
Kirksville, battle at 38–39, 41–42
Kitchen, Col. Solomon 105, 165, 171

Lane, James, Kansas Jayhawk 39
Lawrence, KS 5, 19, 46
Lawther, Col. Robert 92–93, 106, 111–112, 165, 171
Lee, Lt. Gen. Robert E. 1, 150
Lexington, battle at 46, 95, 100, 106–107, 109–111
Lexington, MO 12, 29, 45, 71, 95, 100, 106–107, 109–111
Lincoln, President Abraham 5, 20–21, 45, 57, 65, 143–145, 150
Little Blue, battle at 109–110, 112–116, 144
Louisiana 13, 63, 66
Louisiana Purchase 3–4
Lyon, Maj. Gen. Nathanial 5–6, 9

Marais des Cygnes 5, 40, 129–130
Marion County 30, 37, 39
Marmaduke, Maj. Gen. John S. 6, 45–56, 58, 63, 69, 71–72, 75–76, 78, 80, 86–88, 91–94, 104, 107, 111, 113–114, 161, 164, 171; at Byram's Ford 117–123, 127; capture at Mine Creek 129–135, 137–140, 145
Marshall 59, 62, 104, 106
Martial Law 21, 31, 43–44
Massey Family 1, 144
Matthews, Lt. William D. 39, 127, 169
Maximilian 145
McCown, Gen. John 12; at New Madrid 23–27
McCoy, Capt. Arthur 85–86
McCulloch, Maj. Ge.n Benjamin: at Pea Ridge 12–14; at Wilson Creek 6–8
McNeil, Brig. Gen. John 32–34, 83, 99, 101, 117–118, 123, 127, 129, 135, 138, 157, 169; at Cape Girardeau 49–53; at Kirksville 37–39; Palmyra Massacre 41–43, 45
Merrill, Col. Samuel 47, 89
Merrill's Horse 32–33, 35, 38, 89
Mine Creek, KS, battle at 129–134, 137, 139–141, 145, 171
Missouri 1–6, 9–24, 26, 29–53, 56–60, 63–75, 79–80, 82–86, 88–115, 117–119, 126–128, 131–

147, 149, 151–153, 155; General Order No 11 157–175
Missouri Compromise 3–4
Missouri Home Guard 30, 32–33
Missouri Military District 9, 12, 15, 35, 45, 101, 135–136, 151; St. Louis District 65, 67–70; Southeast Missouri District 9, 80
Moonlight, Col. Thomas 108, 110–113, 168, 172
Moore, Col. David 30
Moore Family expulsion 111–115
Moore's Mill, battle at 33–35, 149

Napoleon 7, 128; retreat in Russia 130
N.E. Missouri Cavalry 34, 41, 43
Nebraska 4–5, 17; 1st Nebraska Inf. 50–52
New Madrid 12, 21–27
Newtonia, battle at 137–142, 172
Northeast Missouri 29–30, 32, 34, 37–39, 41–43, 45–46, 157

Osage River 99
Ozarks and Ozark Plateau 70, 88, 138

Palmyra Massacre 32, 41–43, 83, 99, 129; Palmyra Ten 157
Pea Ridge, AR, battle at 13–16, 21, 29, 45, 164
Philips, Col. John 120, 129–132, 169; at Mine Creek 134–135, 139
Pilot Knob 9, 70–75, 78–80, 82, 85–86, 95, 98, 160–164
Pleasonton, Maj. Gen. Alfred 56, 100–102, 107, 114–120, 141, 145, 169; at Byram's Ford 122–123, 127, 130; at Fort Scott 133–135, 137–138
Polk, Maj. Gen. Leonidas 10–12
Porter, Col. Joseph 21; at Kirksville 37–38, 41–42; at Moore's Mill 29–34; wounded at Hartville 45–48, 50
Potato Hill (Bloody Hill) 120, 122
Price, Maj. Gen. Sterling 6–9, 14, 18, 21, 29, 40; at Helena 55–57, 63, 66–67, 71, 75, 78–80; investigations into the conduct of the Army of Missouri 137–143, 146, 161, 164, 166; Missouri Raid 82–86, 88, 91, 95, 98–103, 106–107, 109–110; at Westport 114–119, 123, 125–131, 135
Provisional Enrolled Missouri Militia 15, 31, 41, 65, 67–69, 166–167, 169

Quantrill, William 85–88 115, 144, 151

Reves, Tim 70, 72, 96–98, 160
Reynolds, Governor Thomas C. 56, 66, 93, 99
Rosecrans, Maj. Gen. William 17–18, 57; Missouri command 64–69, 71–73, 82, 84, 86, 88, 91, 95, 97–101, 109, 123, 126, 135, 141, 143, 169

St. Clair 1, 88, 91–92
St. Louis 4–6, 9, 12, 15, 17–18, 21, 24, 26, 45, 49, 53, 62, 64–69, 71, 80–82, 84–88, 91, 93–95, 97, 99–103, 126, 143–146, 149–151, 153
St. Louis Arsenal 1, 5–6, 86
St. Louis Rock Road 91–93
Saint Patrick Rock Road Church 88
Sandford, John F.A.: Supreme Court Decision 151–152
Schofield, Maj. Gen. John 7, 30–31, 37, 45, 64–68, 91
Scotland County 30, 32–33, 37
Scott, Dred 4, 151–153
Scott, Harriet 151–153
Sedalia 104–107
Shelby, Brig. Gen. Joseph O. 20; at Cape Girardeau 48–52; at Little Blue River 113–116; in Mexico 145, 171–172, 162, 164; Missouri Raid 56–63, 69, 71–73, 80; at Newtonia 137–141; Price's Raid 84–88, 93, 98–99, 104–110; at Westport 118–123, 125, 134
Sherman, Maj. Gen. William T. 2, 66, 68, 72, 126, 141
Shiloh, TN, battle at 27–28
Sidner, Captain Thomas 43, 157
Sigel, Brig. Gen. Franz: at Wilson' Creek 7–8, 13–14
slavery in Missouri 3–5, 144; abolished in Missouri 146, 152–153
Smith, Maj. Gen. A.J. 68, 71–72, 89, 95, 101, 107, 117, 135, 143, 170; XVI Corps diverted 84–86
Smith, Lt. Gen. Edmund K. 43–44, 49, 62, 64–66, 88, 100, 143, 145
Special Order No. 101 30
Special Order No. 279 97–98, 160
Special Order No. 277 97–98, 160
Springfield, battle at 46–47, 49, 164
Stewart, Brig. Gen. Alexander 24, 26

Taney, Roger 21; *Scott vs. Sandford* 151, 154
Taylor, Maj. Gen. Richard 62–63
Tennessee 3, 14–15, 21–22, 27–29, 47, 56–57, 64–66, 126, 141, 143
Thompson, Brig. Gen. M. Jeff 9–10, 12, 19–20, 23–25, 80, 84; Command of Iron Brigade 104–105, 113–114, 116, 121, 125, 137–140, 144, 162, 171
Thompson Col. G.W. 49–53
Totten's Battery at Wilson's Creek 7–8
Trading Post, KS, battle at 127–131
Trans-Mississippi 2, 12, 43–44, 49, 54, 56–57, 88, 126, 142–143, 148–149, 164

USS *Tyler* 55
Union 59, 91–93, 164, 166
Union XVI Corps 68, 106, 109, 126, 143, 170

Van Dorn, Maj. Gen. Earl 13–15
Vassar Hill, battle at 33–36, 37
Virginia 3, 44, 47, 64–66, 69, 101, 135
Vitt s Mill, battle at 91–92, 164, 167

Wagon Train 94, 123, 125, 127–130, 137
Washington, George 20
Washington, AR 59, 65–66, 123, 133, 137, 161–162, 164, 167, 169, 171
Washington, D.C. 17, 48, 57, 67–68, 101, 136, 145, 174
Washington, MO 93–94, 96
Waverly 56, 106–107
Westport, battle at 57, 109, 115–116, 118–120, 122, 125–127, 133, 165, 168
Whaley's Mill 41–42
Wilson, Maj. James 70, 72, 91, 160; death of 96–97
Wilson's Creek, battle at 6–9, 12–13
Wolfe, Col. Edward 89–90, 167, 170
Wornall House 119, 125
Wornall Lane 121–122